*f*Empowerment®
A Guide to Unleashing Your Inner Bond Girl

Sandy Shepard

MOLLYDOOKER PRESS
San Diego, CA

Copyright © July 7th, 2007 (007/007/007) Sandra J. Shepard. Because we just had to.
All Rights Reserved.

Published by Mollydooker Press

No part of this book may be reproduced, scanned, or distributed in any printed, mechanical or electronic form (including recording or photocopying) without written permission, except in the case of brief quotations embodied in critical articles or reviews. Please do not participate in or encourage piracy of copyrighted materials in violation of the author's rights. Please only purchase authorized editions.

This publication has not been prepared, approved, sponsored or licensed by any entity that created or produced the ever-popular James Bond books or films, including but not limited to Metro Goldwyn Mayer Studios, Inc., its wholly owned subsidiary United Artists Corporation, Danjac, LLC, Eon Productions Limited, or any other owners, producers, and distributors of the James Bond franchise.

Every effort has been made to ensure that the information contained in this book is complete and accurate. However, neither the publisher nor the author is rendering professional advice or services to the individual reader. The ideas, procedures, and suggestions contained in this book are not intended as a substitute for consulting your own personal professionals. All matters regarding your health require medical supervision. Neither the author nor the publisher shall be liable or responsible for any loss or damage allegedly arising from any information or suggestion in this book. The author does not have any control over and does not assume any responsibility for third party websites, books, or their content.

ƒEmpowerment® and ƒEmpower® are registered trademarks of Double Oh! Productions.
Bond Girl Graphics by Scion Creative Syndicate; Silhouette by the ever-Bond-Grrlish Domino.

Helen Keller quote on page 171 courtesy of the American Foundation for the Blind, Helen Keller Archives. Used with Permission.

Library of Congress Cataloging-in-Publication Data

Shepard, Sandra J.
ƒEmpowerment: A Guide to Unleashing Your Inner Bond Girl / by Sandra J. Shepard.
p. cm.

ISBN: 978-0-6151-5979-9

1. Bond, James (Fictitious character). 2. Intentionalism. 3. Success. 4. Self-actualization (Psychology)
I. Shepard, Sandra J.
II. Title.

All typographical and grammatical errors are here on purpose, because some people look for them and we want to please as many people as possible.

For information contact:
Mollydooker Press
11835 Carmel Mountain Road, Suite 1304-412
San Diego, California 92128-4609
415-532-2298
ISBN: 978-0-6151-5979-9

DEDICATION

This book is dedicated to your Inner Bond Grrl.
She is savvy, sensual, calm and alluring. I can't wait to meet her.

A Guide to

Unleashing Your Inner Bond Girl

Do you long to discover your authentic self and explore your inner Bond Girl?

Yes — you do have one! This book utilizes the Bond Girl as a paradigm to help women uncover and unleash their authentic selves and coax their inner beauty out. The mission is to build a better world, one Bond Girl at a time.

Sandy Shepard, B.A., M.A., J.D. is passionate about helping women weave sensual femininity into their daily lives. A successful businesswoman and lawyer for well over a decade, she has first-hand experience with the personal/professional balancing act required of every woman, every day. Sandy believes that women can be confident, empowered guides by developing their authentic selves, mastering internal and external congruence, and taking charge of their own sensuality. Sandy is the 'go to grrlfriend' every woman should have in her grrls-only Little Black Book. Sandy leads Æmpowerment seminars and workshops; her students rave that learning from Sandy is 'like having a knowledgeable, fun big sister' with answers to all the questions they have been dying to ask!

To balance her left-brained business and attorney activities, Sandy is also a certified massage therapist. Moreover, she uses feng shui principles to help people feel comfortable and healthy in their home and work environments. She has incorporated some of these principles into this book. Sandy's life experiences include Marine Corps boot camp; organic farming and draft horse training with the Amish in Sugar Creek, Ohio; flying biplanes at the Flying Circus Barnstorming Airshow (flyingcircusairshow.com); driving cattle through Australia's Snowy Mountains; and hiking the length of the French Alps with her 'James' and making sure he had a cold cocktail at the end of every trail! She has an Associate degree in Sex Education and is completing her degree in Clinical Sexology at The Institute for Advanced Study of Human Sexuality, and holds certificates in authentic movement study and practice from the Authentic Movement Institute and in advanced bartending from the San Francisco School of Bartending (a member of the World Bartender Training Association). Sandy is a member of the National Speakers Association, and also of the Association for Coaching, a non-profit dedicated to promoting excellence and ethics in coaching.

Acknowledgements

∞

My warmest thanks to:

Allison "Domino" Fortini, without whom none of this would have ever happened. Who would have thunk it that two grrls secretly addicted to Bond Movies would fess up to one another — and birth an enterprise?

Shendl Diamond and Sallie Goetsch, without whom this book would still be scribbled notes on crumpled paper napkins.

Clancy, Sumo, Reuben, and Eliot, for your keen feline input, and Jake, for your border collie sensibilities — without you, the bed, and the laptop, editing just would not have been the same. And to all my grrl editors, especially including Sue Bird, Sherry Prescott-Willis and Jessica Garidel. Thank you for your patience and perspective.

Maria Alexander, Laurinda Allen, Elizabeth McNeill-Leicester, and Andrea Nelson-Novak, my Bond Grrl mentors, as well as Nina, Jan, Randy, Lynn, Sandy O., Kelli, Colleen Q., Heather and Nancy; you all make supporting your "Jameses" look effortless as you each also run your little corner of the known Universe.

Nancy Mimms, best personal trainer ever, and brave voyager from Poser Bond Grrl to Advanced Bond Grrl Divine. And to Gold Rush, Sophia, Ruby Skye, Snipah, Ginger, Bubbles, Vixen and the rest who poked me in the flesh, and Mica, who poked me over cyberspace, to share my thoughts and seminars more widely. With a special further shout-out to Mica, for helping me learn how to coach through the written, rather than the spoken, word (look Ma, no body language, silent stares or waving hands!).

Michael Solinger, for the most awesome films ever, of course, and also for our entrée to Bond for the Cure — I can never repay you; you rock.

Oprah Winfrey, Paul Kyriazi, Sheila Kelley, Jerry & Esther Hicks/Abraham, John Gray, Mehmet Oz, Wayne Dyer, Barbara Sher, SARK, Susan Bremer, Neala Haze, Tina Stromsted, Michael Beckwith, and others far too numerous to state, who have contributed to my rollicking journey on the path to Bond Grrl soul synthesis and spiritual enrichment, while reminding me to stay Present and have Fun! Thank you for leading the way.

Derek Daly Racing Academy, Sheri's Ranch, and in particular Steve Krystek of Progressive F.O.R.C.E. Concepts — Vegas 101, soon!

Ian Fleming, for the concept — and Danjac, Eon Productions, Harry Saltzman and especially Cubby Broccoli for bringing it to life. And to Barbara Broccoli and Michael G. Wilson for continuing the adventures and making each one more exciting than the last.

To Mom, my first and forever Bond Grrl Model, and Dad, my first and her forever James. And finally but most importantly to Herbert, my Forever and Always. Before you start reading this... can I shake you a Negroni?

*f*Empowerment®
A Guide to Unleashing Your Inner Bond Girl

Sandy Shepard

MOLLYDOOKER PRESS
San Diego, California

ƒEmpowerment®

A Guide to Unleashing Your Inner Bond Girl

TABLE OF CONTENTS

OVERVIEW 1
    What Is ƒEmpowerment®? 1
    What's This About 'Being Number One At Being Number Two'? ... 1
    The Bond Girl Metaphor 4
    What Skills Does A Bond Girl Need? 11
    The ƒEmpowered Lifestyle 14
    Two Types of Women: Which Are You? 15
    Bond Grrl Qualities 17
    How to Get There 22
    Make A Promise Now 24

1: CLEANING OUT 27
    Clutter = Death 27
    First Week/First Steps 28
    The Bond Grrl Look 35
    Clearing Your Closets 36
    Linens and Things 50
    Week Two: Peeling Off 63
    Travel Light 67
    Passport To Success 67

2: CLEARING OUT 75
    Inner Appearance 76
    Set Aside Space 78
    Blocking Out Time 81

    Accomplishing Your Mission 95

    Banishing Negative Thoughts 110

    Letting Friends Go 116

3: CREATING YOURSELF 121

    Mission Possible: You 125

    Walk The Walk… 131

    …And Talk The Talk 137

    Love To Laugh 140

4. BOND GRRL TRAINING 145

    Get Ready for Action 145

    Preparing for Paris 152

    Making Impressions 155

    Laugh at the Villains 168

5: TAKING ACTION 173

    Financial Congruency 175

    Bond Grrls in Business 191

6: JAMES 207

    R-E-S-P-E-C-T 207

    Etiquette: Take Two 209

    Men Are Dogs 212

    Reliance = Respect 217

    Bond and Marriage 219

    Reclaim Your Sensual Spark 220

    Sex 223

    What Men Really Want 236

THE END — OR A NEW BEGINNING? 240

OVERVIEW

What Is ƒEmpowerment®?

ƒEmpowerment stands for Feminine + Empowerment. Being ƒEmpowered is about being congruent with and empowered by your femininity. It's not about being feminine to manipulate a man and "catch" him. And it's not about being a doormat, either. ƒEmpowerment is about being a Best Supporting Actress. It's about feeling the empowerment of being Number One at being Number Two.

What's This About 'Being Number One At Being Number Two'?

It's about being the best (#1) at being supportive (#2, to someone else's #1). At some point in life, everyone takes a supporting role. But some women have lost track of how indispensable the Number Two role can make them. In my experience, women (and in particular, working or executive women) push to be Number One all the time, even at home, while expecting their men to be Number Two. Or even, once kids enter the picture, Number 3, 4, 5... sometimes, the man completely loses his rank!

Do you always want to be Right? Do you believe that every supportive action that you give your "James" should be met by an equal (or greater) submissive action on his part? Do you laugh all day with your grrlfriends about how Men Are Dogs? Why is this acceptable?

I have met a lot of successful, fast-paced, high-powered "C-level" (*e.g.*, CEO, CFO) and executive-type women through my years of leading ƒEmpowerment training seminars. These women consider themselves Number One — at everything. They are looking for an ROI (Return on Investment) in their jobs — and in their relationships. (They put money/energy in? They'd better get ten times that out of this "investment"!) I have also met women at the other extreme of the spectrum, and some of these women do let themselves be walked on; these are women who need to be a little more empowered and a little less subservient. Yes, I said "let themselves," because no one is a Victim unless they allow it. However, most women that I meet, either personally or through my seminars, are the fast paced, high-powered, executive-type women. Beautiful, accomplished women who can't get a date, have orgasm issues, and take anti-depression meds to get through the day. Women whose husbands have an affair with someone not half as accomplished as they are — or even 1/4 as beautiful. "How could this happen to kick-*ss me?" they ask. It seems that by becoming a highly-paid, hard-charging part of what's generally a Man's World, these women have often lost touch with true, relaxed happiness; they've lost touch with the ability, and more importantly the desire, to be "of service." Which is what a Bond Girl is, in relation to James Bond.

Being of service is one of the main components of being Desirable. Somehow, however, being of service has become synonymous with being subservient. In a Man's World, it's generally "push, push, grab, testosterone, get out of my way." From what I've observed, this is not how women work. In large part, women are the harmonizers. The ones with "groupthink." But there has been a breakdown. Somehow, being feminine and supportive has become equated with being weak and a servant.

ƒEmpowerment® isn't about wearing little dresses with bows, and it's not about dressing in a black catsuit and being Lara Croft. It's about striking your own balance; about being empowered and feminine. Or to put a finer point on it, empowered by your femininity.

It's about not trying to lead when it's your turn to follow, and being a good follower. And ƒEmpowerment definitely is not about man-bashing, or being a victim. Because if you're not taking responsibility for your life, if you're blaming anyone or anything for where your life is right now, you're getting something out of/enjoying Victim status. ƒEmpowerment gives you some tools to get a grip on your life, and move forward into your future in a congruent and empowered way. This book is a toolbox, containing the most potent and useful tools I have designed in my coaching business, to jumpstart your ƒEmpowerment and help coax your inner Bond Grrl out.

 ### *Lance Armstrong… "Domestique"*

I recently went to a lecture on teamwork. The speaker talked a lot about Lance Armstrong. Lance Armstrong is hailed as the best long distance bicycle rider ever. However, Lance needs a whole team supporting him, in order to do what he does.

These folks are referred to in the bicycle world as *domestiques* (maids). If the main rider needs a drink, they get it for him. Some trail mix — they get it. He crashes his bike — they give up theirs.

You know that main rider's name; you don't know the names of his domestiques. But he could not be who he is or do what he does without them.

Interestingly, the speaker mentioned a recent tour that Lance Armstrong did in California. In this race, Lance Armstrong rode as a domestique. Whining and moaning about being subjugated? Nope. He did all he could to make the main rider succeed in that race.

Isn't this the perfect Bond Grrl analogy? In the Tour de France, Lance Armstrong is Bond. And the domestiques do what it takes to help him succeed. They're #1 at being #2. And when he succeeds, they succeed.

Like Armstrong in the Tour de France, when a Bond Girl is doing what *she* does, whether it's being a nuclear physicist or a deep-sea fisher, she is #1. And while she's doing it, Bond is her domestique. He hands her the water bottle, so to speak.

The Bond/Bond Girl teams in the movies last as long as they are productive and the team is moving forward. It's just like the bicycle teams: for the duration of the race, everyone works to get the main rider over the finish line. Everyone has the ability to leave, to change teams. So it is with you and your James. There is no reason to stay on a team if it's not productive, but the first thing to ask is this: What are you doing to support the team's success? Are you being the best domestique that you can, or do you say to your James, "Yeah, you ride all day, but get your own dang Gatorade, what do you think I am, your maid?"

Remember, this isn't a sexist thing. I am not saying: "Women, be subservient to men." Yes, James Bond happens to be a man. And the Bond Girls all happen to be women. But the domestique role is not exclusive to women. If a star like Lance Armstrong can do it, you can too, grrlfriend.

Why This Book?

In my ƒEmpowerment business (BeABondGirl.com), I use how-to tips and a "best girlfriend" style to coach and coax women out of the Blame Game and into realizing their authentic selves, using the Bond Girl from the James Bond movies as a metaphor. My students, in return, coached and coaxed me into writing this book, so that a wider audience could be exposed to the idea of living a ƒEmpowered lifestyle. So here I am — hopefully providing you with a new take on the standard self-help material. I hope that you will be committed to coaxing your inner authentic self out, because once you are committed, there are some fairly easy changes you can make that can have long-lasting effects on your life and the lives of your loved ones.

 A Bond Girl On Bond Girls

"The Bond Girls say to women, 'Embrace your sexuality, experiment, explore, break free of the bounds of society.' To men, the Bond women say, 'Do not fear that a strong, confident, sexually assured woman will make you weaker. No, she will be the best thing ever to happen to you.'"

— *Bond Girls Are Forever,* M. d'Abo

The Bond Girl Metaphor

In all of popular mythology, I can't think of a better example of ƒEmpowerment than the Bond Girls found in the James Bond books by Ian Fleming and the ever-popular James Bond movies. I'm not talking about the throw-away Bond girlies that are on screen for about 30 seconds, sigh "Oh James!" and become a notch on Bond's bedpost. No, I mean the lead Bond girls — Pussy Galore, Octopussy, Dr. Christmas Jones, and the like. Even the villain Bond girls like Xenia Onatopp and May Day. These Bond girls run their own businesses. They know who they are, and they are experts in their fields. They are passionate. But, they also take a supporting role, without arguing, when the situation demands it.

My use of the Bond Girl metaphor has raised some hackles (isn't that a great word?). These detractors think that Bond Girls are empty-headed bimbos whom James Bond has sex with, then discards. They feel that I am advocating a second-class citizen status for women, when my seminars help women to understand the power of being Number One at being Number Two.

Some women who have taken my ƒEmpowerment® seminars have even fallen into this category before taking a class. They are generally women running their own businesses, executives climbing or having reached the top of the corporate ladder, heads of the PTA, outspoken soccer moms, or otherwise powerful, fun, stand-out women. But on the path to becoming who they are now, they have often forgotten (or discarded as Weak) the power of being Number Two. How to want to be and feel sexy. How to listen and be curious in a conversation, instead of spilling forth about themselves at every opportunity. They are often unwilling to be supportive of their partners, and look for a *quid pro quo* (in Latin, 'something for something') for any supportive action. They badger their husbands, boyfriends, and partners to be more "supportive" of them, and then when the men ask for the same, the women shout, "You're trying to oppress me!," then, they go dish with their girlfriends. In fact, they love to get together with their girlfriends and dish the dirt, and to dog men in general, which they think is hilarious. They are forever sending all the women they know the man-bashing emails and lists that are so prevalent on the Internet. By becoming Æmpowered, these same women have told me time and again that they have reclaimed a power that they didn't know that they had lost; that they feel both feminine and grounded in their newly re-discovered, non-bashing, authentic selves. I believe that one sure way to change the world for the better is not by heading the largest corporation or kicking the most butt, but by taking just ten minutes out of your day to soothe your partner, or to give up being "right" all the time. I bet it'll be harder than you think, but it can change your world forever.

I advocate balance — which is what the Bond Girls exemplify. Bond Girls run businesses they are passionate about, but in an easy, successful, graceful way. They are not braggarts or blowhards. In reading this book, you will find some specific suggestions that my students implement to change their lives, but first, you must commit yourself to being centered. You must be committed to getting out there and running your business or volunteering or taking care of your kids (whatever you're passionate about), but to be feminine, yin, supportive, and, well, needed and desirable, too.

I'm not suggesting subservience. Bond Girls are anything but subservient. In a way, Bond is really the subservient one. He is seldom in the situation where the Girl is a hindrance to him — even in the beginning. The Bond Girl might get in trouble, but she's usually able to take care of herself and he helps her, if necessary, like he would a partner. Often, she is helping him. Sex is always a key ingredient — but on her terms.

Bond Girls as Role Models?

Even decades ago, Bond Girls were ahead of their time. The jobs they did and the respect accorded to them was far higher than that found in the viewing audience. Pussy Galore, for example, is a pilot with her own flying circus, and Octopussy owns and runs a regular circus (and smuggling ring). Dr. Christmas Jones is a physicist, and what she says goes when she's acting as one.

Bond women have their own very full and rich lives without Bond. And to James Bond, the Bond Girls are far from being throw-away sex toys. Usually, a Bond Girl has a depth of knowledge in a specific area, and Bond utilizes and needs that specific knowledge to reach his goal. The Bond Girl takes a supporting role in relation to Bond; it's his Mission, not hers. But while she might not be the one out fighting the bad guys in the water outside the submarine, she is the one controlling the hatch switch to let Bond back in, once *he* fights the bad guys. She's the Sixth Man.

 The Sixth Man

Basketball uses a five-man team. The "sixth man" usually refers to the fans, who are considered by some to be integral to the team's success without actually touching the ball. My Uncle Walter used to tell a story about the Sixth Man, and the analogy fits my view of Bond Girls:

A guy wanders into a Navy SEAL bar and sits down next to a man who is obviously One Of Them. After a bit of small talk, he finally gets up the nerve to ask this man what he does for the SEALs. The SEAL says, "I'm the 6th Man." The first guy is puzzled by this response and says "What's that mean?"

The SEAL says, "Well, we have Dan, he's the crack sharpshooter of the outfit. He can shoot anything from so far away that you can't even see it. Then we have Jimmy, who is our bomb expert. He can smell a bomb from 500 yards, and is so fast that he can diffuse it before you even know what's going on. Then, we have Joe, who's our ciphers expert. He can crack any code the enemy can throw at us. And Bob, he's our strategy expert. He can figure out what the enemy is thinking, before the enemy even thinks it. Lastly is Alan, our 'black ops' guy. He does what needs to be done. We don't ask too many questions, but when Alan is done, it's done, say no more." The SEAL takes a sip of beer. The other guy says to him, "Well, if you're the 6th man, what do you do?"

"Oh," says the SEAL, "I drive the boat that gets them there, and pick them up when they're done."

The guy in the boat doesn't have a sexy-sounding job. He might not even be considered an Operative. But who is really the most important?

Bond Girls Are Ordinary Women in Extraordinary Circumstances

Bond Girls are regular women who rise to meet extraordinary circumstances. Bond needs them to get a job done, and he appreciates and counts on them in his own way. Without the Bond Girls, in many of the movies, Bond would have had a much harder time getting his mission accomplished, if he could have done it at all.

An author I heard interviewed recently said that the characters in her books are not heroes, but wind up being heroic nonetheless. She said something like,

"They are terrified the whole time, but they do it." In other words, they have a choice to sink or swim and they swim (maybe after sinking a little).

To me, this epitomizes a Bond Girl. If you look at Lara Croft, James Bond, Wonder Woman, Charlie's Angels, etc., they are all straightforwardly heroic. (Though you might not think of an Angel as a hero, she is being paid to get a job done and to do it without fear.) A Bond Girl is often dropped into a situation where she is required to do heroic things — and she succeeds. She is required to rise to the occasion, to help get Bond out of trouble. In the movie *Goldeneye*, computer programmer Natalya Simonova's courage comes from inside, not out of her interactions with Bond or because it's her job to be courageous. She rises from her desk job to become an integral asset to Bond.

Bond Girls rise to the occasion. And, though often referred to as one-dimensional, to me they are less one-dimensional than a James Bond or Lara Croft. Bond Girls are afraid, guilty — sometimes they panic. They don't come in with guns blazing. Usually, they don't even know how to fire a gun! They are just like you and me — or at least, how I hope I would be in a similar situation. They are brave, they make the best of it, they hold their breath, and help get the job done.

 ### *The Bond Girl's World*

When Bond finds the Bond Girl, he has invariably stepped into her world. His mission has brought him into a gorgeous, exotic locale, and this is where the Bond Girl lives. These women aren't trudging to jobs that they hate, gossiping about their co-workers, and returning to their dingy apartments by way of a shopping mall, putting more unnecessary purchases on their maxed-out credit cards to make themselves feel less empty. Bond Girls are serenely present and at home in a world we'd all like to live in. Sure, Bond has a job to do there, but don't forget, he's in and out. He doesn't live there. The Bond Girls do.

Freedom through Femininity

The defining characteristic of a Bond Girl is that she is completely in charge of her life, without being either an alpha or what some might call "butch" female. Even though she can play as rough as the boys, she is not an androgynous action/adventure female character. A Bond Girl is feminine, sensual and alluring, while also being empowered. Bond Girls represent personal freedom without being bitchy, self-centered, biting, whiny, or controlling. They don't use their femininity in a calculating way. They might use the power of sex and sensuality, but without abusing that power. Even in the very first Bond films, decades ago, Bond Girls made sexuality fun. By being feminine, self-assured, and aware, they seem confident that ultimately, somehow, things will go their way.

Baseball Scores and Bond

Let me tell you a short story. I have a client, a high-powered business woman, who was recently divorced. When she started out on the dating circuit, men would ask her what she did — and she would tell them. They would then ask more questions, and she would tell them more about her high-powered life. The men would then often offer stories about their own high-powered lives in sympathy — if indeed they could match hers! But after these great conversations, laughing and sharing war stories, she could never understand why she didn't get a second date.

Or there is another client, who doesn't seem to have a lot of male companionship romantically. She is quite knowledgeable about wine and spirits — and everyone knows it. Perhaps it's just nerves that bring out this show-off personality. Again, she has spirited conversations about wine and cocktails with men, she has a lot of male friends, and often she hears that the guy really learned something from what she had to say. But these guys aren't clamoring to get in her bed on a cold winter night.

All "Jameses" like to show their prowess in the minutiae or statistics of life. If it's not baseball scores or how an engine works, then it's the precise vintage of the precise brand of champagne. Jameses like to be appreciated by their audience; they like to have the good stories and facts. A Bond Grrl doesn't give the impression that she will second-guess her James' choices or one-up his stories. (How deflating is that to the male ego, which we all know is intricately linked to the male libido?) She doesn't monopolize the conversation. She doesn't blunt her femininity and allure by talking about her latest negotiation conquest or other alpha characteristics. This does not mean that a Bond Grrl doesn't have these attributes — she just understands that they are not who she *is*. They are what she *does*. And she lets a man find out about these attributes slowly. She doesn't throw her trophies out on the table in those first dates, to show how much she knows or how great she is. Though I believe this often stems from nerves (and the fear of seeming uninteresting or shallow), this can overwhelm the guy or make him competitive; make him wonder whether he has any subject that isn't going to be matched or topped. If he feels this way, his brain kicks into competition mode, which doesn't jibe with seduction mode. After that great war story swap, off he'll go, to a woman who will listen to him, where he doesn't feel his life must be totally under control at all moments; where he won't feel competitive or potentially judged as unworthy.

In short, Bond women have elegance, intelligence, style and taste — but they are nonchalant about it. They don't strut their stuff. They are strong, exotic, and sexually aware. When it comes to words that contain "self," a Bond woman is self-possessed, self-assured, and self-aware. Not self-centered.

When I think of talking, it is of course with a woman. For talking at its best being an inspiration, it wants a corresponding divine quality of receptiveness, and where will you find this but in a woman?

— *Oliver Wendell Holmes*

 *Being A Mystery Can Be An Asset*

In the most recent Bond films, the bad guys figure out who Bond is quite quickly, because he makes no secret about who he is through disguises or the like. (How exactly this is a great trait for a spy eludes me, but that's the way it is.) The Bond Girl, however, hasn't bragged about who she is and what she can do — which often allows her to quietly help get Bond out of trouble. The Bond Girls are something else first (cellist, pilot, deep sea fisherwoman, chemist) and an ally to Bond by accident. So they can lay low. It's hard to do that if you've already spilled the beans about exactly who you are and where you're going! The mystery created by reticence can be a good thing. Or as one of my male friends said the other day after another frustrating dating experience, "She was interesting but after a while I just wanted her to shut up, maybe ask me a few questions about myself, smile at me, let me let my guard down. How hard can that be?"

A Specific Character

Each Bond Girl has a very specific character and history — and a specific attitude towards life. But even inside her own area of expertise, she does not act like a know-it-all. And she doesn't "need" a man. Bond walks into the Bond Girl's life, she didn't seek him out. In fact, she gets along very happily without him. Afterwards, Bond is off on another Mission, at the request of the government; a mission very much like the one before. But the Bond Girls continue doing what they are doing in their deep and three-dimensional lives; Bond remains the one-dimensional, suave action hero without a rooted place or life.

fEmpowerment in Action

I am learning pole dancing through Sheila Kelley's S Factor (SFactor.com). If you have an S Factor near you, give it a try! It's a wonderful way to explore your sensuality and get in shape! If you don't have one near you, check out Sheila Kelley's books and DVDs.

As founder of S Factor, Sheila Kelley sends e-newsletters full of thoughts and inspirational stories to students. I have a copy of the August 2006 newsletter tacked to my bulletin board, and I read it to my classes frequently. She has been kind enough to allow me to republish it for you. And it goes like this...

Sheila set a friend of hers up on a blind date. She describes her friend Rebecca as thirty-two, nice looking, a "lawyer who went into the stock market, got out good, and is set for life," who, "like most people, wants a great love in her life." Sheila and her husband went on a bowling double date with this friend and Sam, also a buddy.

As related by Sheila,

"...I look across the lane at Rebecca and Sam. He's sitting at the score table, smiling. She's standing there, prepping to roll a ball, and I can see yet another strike written all over her face. He's admiring her form. She's driven to conquer. I look up at the scoreboard. She's got 125, he's at about 110. He checks her butt out. She rolls. It's a strike. She raises a fist up to the ceiling like a Masai Warrior. He tries to catch her eye for a congratulatory smile but she's already set on the next set of 10 pins.

He stiffens a bit around the shoulders, looks up at the score board, and nods his head a little. I pull her away from the lane, look her in the eye and ask, "You like him?" "Yeah, he's cute," she says with a smile, "I really like him!" I get real somber. "Then it's time to roll a gutter ball." Her face is blank. "What?" "Roll a gutter ball, Rebecca." "Are you serious?" I gaze steadily into her eyes, "Never been more." "I don't get it," she says. "Why would I do that?" "Well, do you want to totally emasculate the guy or do you want to titillate him, flirt with him?" I ask. Rebecca smiles, shrugs off my request and rolls yet another strike, and wip-dee-shit wins the game by a long shot.

Therein lies everything I've ever observed about women and men and the all-around game of missing each other over and over again. You are on a date with a man you like. You think he's hot. You go bowling with him. You want to 'hook up' so to speak. So you kick his ass because you are such a great bowler. For some reason, this means more to you than finding a true love, warm arms and a symbiotic connection.

Why the hell do women do this? I would, by the way, say the same thing to a guy friend in the same situation. I would tell him to roll a gutter ball, wake up and see that he's alienating this woman that he wants to impress. I'm not saying lose the game but make it close, for God's sake. Tease him with the game, flirt with him through the game, make the game about connecting with him, not winning and losing.

...I'm not endorsing that anyone should make any less of themselves, but I did want Rebecca to see that the guy she was with wanted to make a connection to her but she was so busy playing a hard game that she wasn't looking at the signs. She didn't see him looking at her, checking her out. Instead, she was overwhelmed by her mission to win.

... If you want to take it even further, are you here in this life to win at all costs or are you there to connect to another human being while having a great time? In that game, there are no losers.

... I take it as part of my job in life to make my man feel powerful, virile, utterly male and adored. He makes it his journey in life to make me feel feminine, adored — no, no, no — more like worshiped, powerful and divine.

Two weeks after the bowling date, I see Rebecca and she asks about Sam. She wants to know if he has said anything about her? Yeah, actually, he did. He said he liked her but... (I bet it's something many a man has said about her)... she was a little "hard." "Yeah, she's cute but didn't seem interested." "Yeah, I like her but she's a little, boring." Even, "Yeah, she's hot but a little tough — not someone I would want to cuddle up with in a storm." I soften his actual comment a little with, "Yeah, he liked you but he's not sure you're a match." She smiles tightly, wants to move on from the conversation but forces herself to ask, "What was that thing you said about rolling a gutter ball?"

What Skills Does A Bond Girl Need?

A Bond Girl doesn't run the Mission. She's usually part of it by happenstance. But she is not an Eek Girl either. Whatever is thrown her way, she takes a deep breath and does it. By "it" I mean actions that I believe everyone should know how to do. Swim. Drive a stickshift. Climb a ladder. Hold on. So that's part of the training I offer in my seminars. At the very least, a Bond Girl is prepared with some basic skills, because she is likely to need them before her adventure with Bond is over; she'll die and Bond will die too trying to save her, if she can't swim, or if "Eek," she's afraid of heights and refuses to climb. But she's not Bond, Lara Croft, or a Charlie's Angel, either (to use other popular mythology figures). She isn't the one navigating the minefield, but she can take over and steer if Bond needs to shoot.

Imagine if in *The World Is Not Enough*, when Bond tells Dr. Christmas Jones that he will swim out of the submarine to take care of the bad guy and she is to "stay here and push this button" to let him back in, she had said, "Oh NO. I want to be Number One. I want to swim and get the bad guy. You stay back here and push the button." In the time it would take to argue the point, they both would have drowned.

In sum, Bond Grrls know when to lead, and when to follow. If you want to be literal about it, though he's the Star of the Show, Bond is just a government employee — and there are at least a handful of others just like him (as he's "007" in the current lineup of "Double Os"). In contrast, each Bond Girl is unique and holds her own when she's suddenly drawn into Bond's drama. Seven different actors have played Bond, but no Bond Girl's character repeats with a new actress playing her. Remember that when someone says that Bond Girls are just interchangeable bimbos.

 ## Why "G-R-R-L"?

When I refer to Bond Girls from the Bond books or movies, I use the regular spelling of G-I-R-L. However, in my fEmpowerment® seminars and training, and so in this book as well, I help women uncover and unleash their Inner Bond Grrl (with two Rs). Why?

I adopted the Double-R-Grrl spelling because, every time I read Bond Girl, I thought "girlie-girl." And since I didn't come up with the phrase Bond Girl, I can't change it without losing the mental link to the metaphor.

Hence - Grrrrrrrrrl. A "girl" with "Grrrr"... with a tiger in her tank, to quote the old gasoline ad campaign. This spelling makes me happier with the term, and I hope helps to eliminate the "girlie-girl," weak, "Oh, James!" images that could pop into your mind.

This is not to say that some of the Bond Girls are not "girlie-girls." A couple of them in the movies from the '70s were even "Eeek Girls"! But I hope that in reading G-R-R-L, you won't mentally see that girlie-girl, less-than-a-woman image that the word G-I-R-L used to bring out in me.

 Don't Be an Eeek Girl

A friend recently told me a story. She was invited out on a skeet shooting party (yes, really). She was interested in one of the guys that had invited her along. Like many if not most women, she has never shot a gun, and is in fact anti-gun. (Anti-gun, but she went along on a shooting party, remember.)

So, the guy that she's interested in asks her whether she'd like to have a try. What's her reaction?

Eeeeeek! No! I don't touch guns! Eeeek! Eeeek! Eeeek!

I'm not sure why she went on this skeet shoot to begin with. Maybe she was staying over at their place for a weekend, and it would have been a social faux pas not to go. Or maybe she just followed this hottie out to the skeet range. Whatever. But she does the Eeek thing, doesn't even have a go — and wonders why the guy never calls. And then tells me the story, because she thinks it's hilarious, but also that there is "something wrong with" the guy.

Though you might say she was trying to be attractive in an "Oh Rhett! Save me from that scary gun!" sort of way, I don't think so. I actually think that she didn't want to look stupid. She likes to be an expert in what she does, which would have been impossible in this situation. So instead of having him teach her about shooting, and cuddling into his arms and chest as he tries to steady the gun — she did the Eek Girl routine.

A Bond Grrl generally doesn't know how to do things outside her area of expertise, but she is infinitely curious and willing to learn. Even if it's something she might not like, she is game to try — and can usually find a way to turn it into a sexy situation!

If you are in a position where whatever you're offered isn't actually going to kill you ("Would you like to join me in this pit of poisonous snakes, hon?"), then give it a go. Come on. Quit the "helpless" bit. Of course, if you're a crack shot, don't shoot his pants off, either — just be competent and quiet about it.

What might have been a better Bond Grrl reaction? Well, if you really are anti-gun, then decline the invitation to go out on the shoot. Say something like, "I'm actually not a big gun person, but ya'll have a great time. I'll have some martinis ready when you Big Game Hunters come back with your brace of prize skeets!" Don't try to change them with your gun rhetoric — what a buzzkill. And if you *do* go, then *have* a go. Let them be instructors. Listen, learn, don't be an Eek Girl, give it a try, don't close your eyes, be serious in learning this new trick, but not too serious that you lose track of the fact that you're there to have fun (and there's that cuddling into his arms bit!) If you're terrible at it — laugh! If you're great at it — don't brag.

Everything that you can learn might actually get you out of a jam. Let's face it: we hear about crazy things going on out there every day. I hope you never face a situation where shooting a gun or escaping on a motorcycle is really important. But if someone wants to teach you to do these things — come on, how bad can it be to learn a few new tricks? Allow yourself to be bad at stuff. Let yourself be taught. And have fun. Don't take yourself so seriously all the time.

I personally can fly a biplane, ride a motorcycle, fire a few weapons, crew a hot air balloon, crochet, drive a team of horses, tell a joke, mix a martini (using a pasta jar)... and some of these not at all well!! But any time I'm presented with something new to learn, I try to jump right on it. OK unless it involves that heights thing. Or knitting. Man, I really suck at knitting.

Does all this make for interesting conversation? Sure. But I don't bring these things up myself, and I try not to one-up someone in conversation either. A lot of women listeners share their experiences right back at the speaker, perhaps to show that they appreciate the story, or to forge an experiential bond. These folks hear a story, then say "Oh my! That's just like when I..."

This *used* to be me. All it does is make the speaker feel you really weren't listening to their story; that their great experience was just a launching point for your own. Instead, try this: Next social occasion, make a game out of saying as little about yourself as possible. Gather as much as you can about others. If you go out with your James or a grrlfriend, see who gleans the most interesting tidbit from the crowd. Maybe put a wager on it: A double dip Baskin-Robbins for the winner? Or pretend you're a reporter, and need to come back with a great "scoop"!

It's not particularly attractive to be an Eek Girl — or to act like a know-it-all. Be game, have fun, listen, laugh, and be a student of life. And let someone else be the expert as often as you can. They will think you're awesome for it.

What Are Bond Girls Made Of?

Whether a Bond Girl is fighting beside Bond or trying to kill him, she is naturally, unconsciously alluring (though the bad ones preen more). Adjectives that describe Bond Girls include unique, strong-willed, elegant, engaging, resilient, gorgeous, smart — dangerous. Mysterious. Autonomous. Timeless. Intelligent and sexually independent. A Bond Girl knows how to ride a horse, how to drink, how to dress, and how to behave at a black tie affair. She has a confident self-awareness. She unconsciously walks into a room in a manner that turns eyes naturally towards her.

While Bond Girls often have double-entendre names: Plenty O'Toole, Xenia Onatopp, Holly Goodhead (and of course the infamous Pussy Galore), they state these names matter-of-factly, daring you to be as confident as they are.

Bond Girls are of service, but anything but subservient. They are a reminder of what most men have realized all along: feeling comfortable with yourself is an incredibly attractive attribute. And due to her quiet confidence, a Bond Girl can (and does) do anything she wants. Her attraction to Bond makes him attractive; otherwise, he's just a government employee, or an assassin.

A large part of a Bond Girl's desirability is her sexual confidence. It's important to note that Bond's seductions are never rape. These women are strong and independent — Bond takes them on their own terms and vice versa.

You can still be a Bond Grrl if...

Are you making excuses for yourself as you read this? Are you saying, "I can't be a Bond Grrl because I'm [in a wheelchair/200 pounds overweight/too far in debt/80 years old]?"

Stop it right now. It's not riding motorcycles or scuba diving that makes a Bond Grrl. It's not being young and skinny either. If you think something or someone is holding you back, you're right — that person is You. Are you whining? Stop it. Are you talk-talk-talking about how you would get on with your life, if some obstacle was magically removed? Stop it. Are you schlepping around in your wheelchair in a stained shirt and mismatched shoes? Stop it. Project "out" instead of concentrating "in" on your Failings. Listen. Flirt. Be sexy. Be chic. Be magical. Believe.

fEmpowerment is about Attitude, and about finding your Path To Passion™. Let your inner Bond Grrl out, within whatever boundaries you have. And don't give those boundaries more power by complaining about them. They only stop you because you think they do. If you don't think that, no one else will, either.

Although in some of the films the Bond Girl might be trapped, she is never weak — and usually Bond doesn't rescue her so much as help her see her way out. Although she might be a victim of circumstance, she does not have a Victim mentality. Bond Girls don't blame others for their circumstances — even pretty bad circumstances. Since they take responsibility for their own lives, they are able to seize a chance when they see one, and don't look back.

The ÆEmpowered Lifestyle

The main attractions of living the life of a Bond Grrl are that (a) you live a life of passion and (b) you are indispensable to someone. One of the keys to the ÆEmpowered lifestyle is that a Bond Grrl needs to be prepared to be spontaneous — she needs to keep time free, to say "No," and to have time for herself.

If her James comes home one day and says "Let's go to Paris!," she is prepared to be spontaneous; her answer is not "Oh my, no, I have to take the kids to soccer, I have to (dot dot dot)." In this book, I hope to give you some tricks and tools to help.

By living the ÆEmpowered lifestyle, a Bond Grrl is indispensable, because she is her James' support. She doesn't argue that she is somehow in a secondary or "one down" position. She is not part of the vile female gossip machine that belittles and disrespects men. If you don't respect someone, it shows. And why should that man respect You, if you don't respect Him?

Not Just Indispensable — Treasured

The only way to be treasured, in my opinion, is to be in a supportive role. Though I know that there are women who are dominated by their husbands, the women I coach are usually the dominant and successful ones. When we discuss being supportive in class, I often hear that "That's not why we had the Women's Revolution."

But are women happier now? I think women today have taken on (or are expected to take on) way too much, then complain about being overwhelmed. They also seem to have been convinced that the moment they offer support, they are a submissive doormat. And in fact, they often throw this in the face of their Jameses. I have a male friend who told me that any time he looks for just a little nurturing at home, his wife of 30 years states that she is "not going to be a doormat." He's considering an affair, "not for sex, but just for a little support. Though gee, sex more than once a year would be a nice change, too." His wife expects his support, then cries out if he asks for some back.

I look at my own family for examples. My mother still runs her own high-powered business, but makes dinner every day, does the dishes, listens to what went on in my father's day, etc. This doesn't make her a doormat. This makes her treasured by her man, my dad.

I try to do the same. I do my best to make my "James's" life a little easier — while I also run my businesses. It's a matter of priorities. I drop my competitive attitude on the doormat when I come home, and my home is a better place for it. I am treasured at home, because I make it my business to be loving and supportive of my James. And in turn, because he feels that support, he can be comfortable in showing me his softer, supportive side. Our society has always made that difficult for men; now it's even difficult for women to feel that being supportive is all right. He has to Go First. And I'm here to tell you, Bond Grrl, that you need to be the one to make that first move, and make it safe enough for your James to reflect it back to you.

Remember, a Man is not a Woman. That may seem obvious, but women seem to have lost sight of this. Don't share all your troubles with him. That's what you have your Grrlfriends for.

Bond Grrls treat their men like men. They aren't doormats, but they do a few nice things for their Jameses consistently, that are worth the minimal effort it takes. Do you take a second to look nice when you get home? Do you leave your troubles on the doorstep? If you're a harried or overwhelmed mother/wife/etc., how'd you get into that position? You made choices. You still have choices. Suck it up and stop being a victim.

Two Types of Women: Which Are You?

Very generally, two types of students come to me to help set their inner Bond Grrls free.

The first are the women who might be described as shy, or retiring, or self-effacing. They don't believe that they have a Pussy Galore or Honey Rider or Xenia Onatopp in them. Being liked is immensely important to them — sometimes to the extent that they have changed, melded or shaped their own personalities to match or complement that of their James or their best grrlfriends. If you have seen the movie *Runaway Bride*, remember the scene near the end of the movie where Julia Roberts is testing different types of egg dishes to see what she *really* likes to eat? Because with each successive fiancé, she had ordered her eggs, her food, and her life to be Just Like Him?

This was me, before my current relationship and my determination to discover, then unleash, my inner authentic self. I would allow situations to choose me, instead of choosing them. I didn't understand what a little choice could do for my confidence, and a little control could do for my sense of security. Through trial and error, I learned that Independence doesn't mean that you have to *be* on your own — just that you know that you *could* be.

So if this sounds like you, unleashing your inner Bond Grrl is going to involve finding out what you're really passionate about, and then pursuing it. It's having real commitment to yourself; uncovering what you stand for when no one is looking. And not feeling guilty about that choice. This often means that you will need to sort through, examine, and discard some things currently in your life, because you can't truly have all things at once. Think about it — can you have a Soloflex body and enjoy all the food you want? Not likely. If you love food, think of yourself as luscious and don't guilt out every calorie. We don't apply adjectives like Juicy, Luscious, and the like to runway models. If, instead, you passionately want to look like a fashion model, great, knock yourself out. But then no complaining when you can't chow down pizza. Choose. Complaining is just being a victim, and Bond Grrls are not victims.

The tools and tricks in this book will help you figure out what you're passionate about — then help you be committed to bringing that passion into your life. Don't have a fractured consciousness about this; by wanting the 6-pack abs and 6-course meals, it's nearly impossible to enjoy either thing. When you're doing one, you're thinking about the other. Do what is good, and what works, for you. Don't live that *Runaway Bride* life. Remember what I've said before about Bond Girls — they are the ones with the interesting, very specific lives, that Bond drops in on. Once you've figured out what floats your boat then go with it, and your zest for life will show through. What makes you attractive to another is not that you do what that person loves, but that you do what *you* love. It's not about being a Size 2, unless that rocks your world. How you Feel is what we're after. And being of service, especially to your James, will be part of that. Once you're balanced and doing what you love, and you're out of Victim mode, there will be a lot more time to be of service and to help others by supporting their passions, too. There is nothing more empowering.

I heard this put another way in a speech recently by San Francisco District Attorney Kamala Harris. She said that each of us seems to understand that we are here for a reason. But some women downplay this, saying that if they don't accomplish or find it, they will perhaps be less fulfilled, but so what? Ms. Harris explained that there is much, much more to it than that: We are each put here for a unique Purpose. And if we do not pursue it, if we do not fulfill it, then it will never, ever, enter this world. The way that you will accomplish this Purpose and follow your Passion will be unique to the world, and if you do not live up to your highest Passion and potential, then the world will never, ever have that chance again and will be worse off for it. Forever. If you do not do it, the world will never experience it. Ever. Powerful, huh? So, I'm here to help you figure it out — then, go for it!

So what's the second sort of woman that approaches me about becoming ƒEmpowered? I've talked about her before. She is the hard-charger who will have it all, and her way. While the first woman is like a huge tuning fork resonating everyone else's energy back to them without resonating much of her own music, the second doesn't have a tuning bone in her body! There has to be a balance, a yin and yang to this. And part of your Bond Grrl journey will be finding that balance in a way that's comfortable for you. And realizing that being supportive can be a lot more fun, and a lot more rewarding, than you might think.

Bond Grrl Qualities

Unleashing your inner Bond Grrl doesn't mean putting on an act. It means becoming authentic and congruent. Once you get over yourself, it can be easier than you think. We will discuss these qualities in this book, but what are a couple of guidelines?

Don't Be a Hard-*ss

I'm not saying that if, for example, you're an avid martial artist, you shouldn't continue on that path. Just don't brag about it. I have wonderful women friends who teach in the martial arts arena or in other areas that are often thought to be macho bastions (race car driving, high-risk SCUBA diving, judo, etc.). After protesting about how it Shouldn't Be That Way, they usually agree that when faced with male students, there is nearly always pushback about them being women and good at what they do. They say that even women often don't listen to women instructors as well as they do male instructors. I know that's not how it should be. It just is. So if you're a black belt — great. But that's just not what you're going to be talking about with a potential James in cocktail conversation. You should be listening and gathering information at that cocktail party, anyway!

Definitely Don't Be a Bimbo

Why do people take the Bond Girl and turn her into a bimbo? I mean, really, how exciting, after a while, would it be to live with a bimbo, anyway? Bond Girls are nonchalant experts in an area that Bond needs. So have something that you love and do well; something special that a guy can respect. In the long run, if there's nothing to respect, then no matter how much a man thinks he might love this, after a while it'd just be boring. But a man might originally pick a so-called bimbo because she listens to his stories, appreciates what he does for her, and is supportive of him. The balance is to do these things, while being your awesome, passionate, Bond Grrl self.

Ginger Rogers did everything Fred Astaire did, except backwards and in high heels.

— Bob Thaves

Learning to Dance

Ballroom dancing is a good metaphor for fEmpowerment. In any dance couple, there is a leader and a follower. If you want to be the leader — go ahead. Just make sure you're the one facing forward. I'll tell you a little secret, though: the follower is the one who makes the couple look great. But she has to follow. It's not her job to know what lies ahead (for goodness sake, she's going backwards). Her job is to feel each nuance of every movement from her partner's body, and to effortlessly flow in that direction. His job is to keep her out of harm's way. And both of them need to do their part, to make the team flow towards perfection.

If the follower is trying to "back lead," there's a power struggle. If you trust your leader (that's the key here, grrls: you must trust), then following is the ultimate high. When it really works, your leader makes you look great, and you can just let go.

The whole point of following is that you don't know where you're going. You trust that your leader will watch out for you, and you concentrate completely on staying congruent with where you are being led. This is much harder than being the leader! Take it from me: if you have a lousy leader, all you want to do is "back-lead." But a leader can't learn how to give you the right cues if you're always back-leading. If you are dancing to choreography, you also can't just do the choreography; you need to let him lead you into a move, not do the move yourself because you know what comes next. By back-leading or doing the choreography without him leading you into it, you do the leader a disservice. He never learns how to lead. And you do yourself a disservice too, because you will never be able to let go, and be in the flow.

The leader is always worried and concentrating on what's around him: who might bump you, where to go next, what move goes with what follow-through move. If you're the follower, and you're with a good leader, you get to just float and fly. You have to be totally present and congruent, sure. You are always vigilant, because you have to be ready if he has to twist you in a new direction to avoid some clod who isn't watching where he's going. So that's your job: to be ready, vigilant, on your toes, and indispensable to making the team look amazing. By letting him lead, you stand out as the beautiful one — the effortless one.

Give

Let's face it: in every interaction, there really is, subtly or not, a #1 and a #2. I don't believe it when people tell me that they have a "totally equal" partnership. Particularly in a man/woman relationship.

When it comes to interfacing with others, in some aspect(s) of your life, you need to embrace the role of Best Supporting Actress. In the Oscars®, the Best Supporting Actress/Actor receives that same golden trophy, for being the best in a role that supports the "main" actor/actress in that movie. So, for example, if you're the head of your division at work (#1), you still report to your boss (there, you're #2). And, even if you are the CEO, you still are supporting the shareholders, the Board of Directors, and the like. Or if you're a sole proprietor, you are #2 to the desires of your customers.

By being of service to another/others, you become indispensable. Bond really needs the Bond women. I'm not so sure that I would say the same back. And the trick is that Bond believes it's all his movie: it's all him, all the time. Is that so bad? That's something you want to keep in mind when you look at your James. He wants to be considered to be the leader. Why is it so important that you beat this out of him?

Bond leads. The Bond Girls help him to lead, without complaining or arguing. And the team succeeds. But outside the Bond movies, men seem to get the short end of the stick. Most women are working, trying to take care of the kids, and exhausted all the time. They don't feel that they should be "required" to take care of their James, too. So these men wind up fending for themselves — or finding some other woman who would be perfectly happy to be #2 to their #1.

Remember, a businesswoman Bond Girl still knows how to care for (or seduce, or even have her way with) Bond. You don't see her asking James to take out the garbage, or, as she comes home in a huff, to fix her a martini because she sure had a bad day. No. Bond Girls show that their responsibility is to take care of themselves, while also taking care of Bond. Because if he's mollified, she's a lot more likely to get what she wants anyway.

A Bond Grrl feels and is "in" her power. By doing a bit of soothing to her James, she remains in her power. In being fully supportive, she is going to get what she wants — unless what she wants is to manipulate her James or turn him into a girlfriend who will listen to her every complaint and want more. Men are, by and large, just not hardwired in this way.

I recently saw Dr. Wayne Dyer speak. Dr. Dyer stated that everyone should go through life with the question "How may I serve?" topmost in their minds. To paraphrase, he stated that it's time for everyone to take their sights off what's in it for them, and instead concentrate on what they can do to help others. He explained that giving begets giving: when you shift from "What can I have?" to "How can I serve?," the Universe concentrates on giving to you. It's not about being a servant, it's about being of service.

If you take this seriously, you become like the head butler, housekeeper and cook in the movie *Gosford Park*. You are a professional, and you are quietly indispensable. The Master thinks that he's in control — but who really runs things? Things literally can't run without the Staff — but they don't point this out every chance they get. They take pleasure from the smoothly-oiled machine and from knowing that their part is important, perhaps even more important than that of the estate owner or whoever is #1. Because while owners come and go, the Staff's indispensable role remains.

 Too Many Chiefs, Not Enough Indians

At one of my Big Corporate jobs, they gave a New Age test to all the high-level executives (ah, the late 90s). When the expert came to interpret the results, she singled me out particularly. (How embarrassing!) The executive team was made up of dot.com rock stars; people who envisioned themselves on the front of *Newsweek* and, if the company had been started a wee bit earlier, might have gotten there. OK, and me. The expert brought in personality-related charts and graphs, based on the Very Expensive tests that she had administered to us. And this is what she said.

I was the only Indian in the group. (Her metaphor.) What she told the whole gang of executives (the management team) was that every single one of them had a Chief personality — except me. I was the only one who would pick up the balls that they juggled when they dropped them; I was the only one who wanted to make sure their wishes and ideas were carried out. She told them that they all had Grand Ideas, but no way of putting them into action without people to carry the ball. To mash in another metaphor, they were all Quarterbacks — and I was trying to play all the other positions on the team. The problem was, the way that they had structured the goals, strategies, and rewards for the company, I was being forced to be like them and lead my team in that manner, as well as do what came naturally (following and supporting the Chiefs).

My father, in first hearing the Bond Grrl analogy, said that it reminded him of this time in my life. He reminded me that at that time, I had told him that one of the most important things that I did in that job was not preparing the company to go public, negotiating multi-million dollar contracts, or acquiring three other companies in less than a year. I was great at that, as General Counsel. But my worth to the company really revolved around making sure that the Chiefs had a cup of tea… had support… had Legal when they needed it… and that they had someone to listen to their dreams and aspirations and help make them a reality. My talent was not being another alpha/Chief/Bond, going out to kill the bad guy. I was there to open the submarine door when they needed it, and dry them off.

Reclaim Your Femininity

Women often say that they feel they have lost touch with their sensual Spark. I believe that part of this comes from trying to one-up their men and thereby winding up on the short end of the stick with respect to gender identification. Women are now expected, or taught, to earn their own way, be powerful, take charge, be in control, kick down doors. They are almost never taught how to feel empowered by their femininity, sensuality, and sexuality. Bond women know how to run their businesses, and how to shut it off and Be A Woman. And, as you will learn, while you don't want to have secrets from your James, you still want to remain mysterious. Letting it all hang out is just taking the lazy, easy way. Not getting dressed or made up for your James to come home... whining and complaining... sound familiar? What's up with that? By taking a tiny effort to make your James feel special, he almost always will turn around and make you feel special. And if not — if he's an honest-to-goodness beer-guzzling couch potato — time to plan your exit.

Get fEmpowered

Yes, you say, but what if my guy gets used to me being there waiting at the door, martini in hand, when he gets home? What if he gets used to me paying ten good minutes making him comfortable, listening to his day, and helping him relax?

Well, what if he does? If you're worried about this, as some of my students have been, it means that you're looking for a big fanfare each time you do something that's not just selfishly all about you. What about thinking about your partnership with your James? A wise man once told me that partnership is where each person is prepared to give 100%. You want to be appreciated, sure. But maybe you need to look for your appreciation inside, rather than in having him fall all over you when you do something just a little civilized for him.

In the Bond films, the Bond Girls usually bring home their own bacon. They meet James on their own terms. He has his job to do, but they have their own whole and complete lives without him in the picture. And when he is in the picture — which is a miniscule amount of their day, really — they make sure that they are memorable to him. And for that moment, he only has eyes (and other things!) for them.

I hate hearing my Grrlfriends complain about their husbands and lovers. It's time to understand where our Jameses are coming from — and to let them. In exploring your inner Bond Grrl, it's time to take a critical look at yourself and your relationships, and to see whether or not you're concentrating on making your life easier for you and for your James. And if not, to figure out how you can.

I'm not saying you need to have dinner on the table every night at 6:00 for an ungrateful beast. A Bond Girl would walk. (Remember, she's a powerful being.) If you're in any work/love relationship where you're not appreciated, or your James is jealous (because he doesn't trust you, regardless of what he says), maybe that's not the right James. Remember, Bond takes for granted that the Bond Girls are going to stand up for themselves and lead their own lives, and he takes care of them, or dies trying. You need to be empowered in your choice, and know that it's really not that difficult to keep your James happy, either, while remaining ÆEmpowered yourself.

Jameses aren't that difficult to figure out. What does a James want? A goal. To feel appreciated. Yeah, I know, you do too, but don't you realize that you're probably the only one that your James has to turn to? You have your Grrlfriends. In general, men don't have this same network. They might have poker nights with the guys or tennis matches, but that's not going to feed a guy's soul or make him feel appreciated. That's what you're about. So come on. Don't emasculate him by ordering the wine and discussing things with the waiter. Or making him change the diapers when he's returning from a business trip worn to the bone, so you can go to a Girls' Night Out.

Moreover, by schlepping around the house in a T-shirt and sweats, what are you telling him? That he's not important enough to rate for you to clean up for him. Not only that, you're telling yourself you don't rate either. If you set things up right (I'll help), he'll be very happy to come home to you, and you'll be happier in the process. What about a little meditation before getting together with him, such as listening to wonderful, soul-refreshing music on your way home from work instead of the news, where you only hear about how scary and bad life is? How about some candles to light when you get home? If you set a tone in your house or apartment, when you return, you can effortlessly slough off the outside buzz instead of dragging it into your home. Try to keep the rush rush rush out on the doorstep — does it feel like Bond Grrl energy? Think about it — an unrushed life is one of the hallmarks of the Rich. And in reality, you don't need money to do it, you just need some forethought, attitude, and commitment. This book will help you see your way.

How to Get There

So do you get the Bond Grrl Attitude? By changing your behavior, you can change how you feel — and by changing how you feel, you can change everything. Sometimes it's just a matter of getting started with one small step. Paul Kyriazi, in his book *The Complete James Bond Lifestyle Seminar*, starts out his nascent 007s with the purchase of a money clip and a new watch. We will take similar steps both literally — by changing the way you walk — and figuratively — by taking steps that could change your life forever. And have faith. As Dr. Martin Luther King said, "Faith is taking the first step, even when you don't see the whole staircase."

 ### The Bond Grrl Lifestyle

"Beginning with Ursula, who braved Dr. No's dangerous Crab Key Island to collect shells and sell them for a profit, Bond girls have been intelligent, resourceful, self-reliant, articulate and usually professional businesswomen. To think of them or any women in terms of only physical beauty is to miss the best points of what Bond women have to offer."

— Paul Kyriazi

Acting As If

What's the first step? To be committed to get out in front of your life. To act As If you are already the luscious Bond Grrl that is inside. This does not mean acting As If you have a million dollars by spending it — that's a great way to get beaten up on the Suze Orman Show! No, what I mean here is more along the lines of the phrase "Fake it 'til you make it." I am not advocating that you become a fake. Instead, I'm advocating that you act As If you have the attributes that you desire, by exuding the personality characteristics that you will, ultimately, embody. I will give you some tricks and tools in the next few chapters.

If right now as you read this you feel out of sync with Life, the first learning is also to understand that it's not anyone else's Fault. It's that You are not resonating at the energetic level that will attract whatever it is that you are looking for and all that you can be. You are the Master of this, 100%. No excuses. Where your life is now is the product of all the concentration, all the energy and all the resonations you have made in the past. Don't dwell on it, and make it continue into your future. (Unless of course it's fabulous!) I'll help you learn how.

Choosing Your Life

Part of being positive and attractive to this resonance is choosing your life because it makes you happy — not because it makes your mother happy, or your husband happy, or anyone else happy. Though you want to nurture those who mean something to you, you want to look and pick carefully. Avoid the energy vampires out there!

Being ÆEmpowered starts, not with changing yourself, but in understanding yourself. In creating from the inside out. Letting your feelings inspire you to behave differently, not using your behavior to feel better. ÆEmpowerment means getting the feeling right first, then the actions will come to you. You will set aside time and space to resonate with whatever feelings you passionately desire (abundance, joy, calm, etc.) and to create a little virtual reality where you can feel yourself in this state. Then wait for the Universe to deliver it to you. Your responsibility is to stay present, feel, and resonate your gorgeous Bond Grrl self. Stay In the Now, Get Out of the How. (Wouldn't that make a great bumper sticker?) In other words, don't get caught up in "how" what you are resonating and concentrating on will happen. Just feel it, and trust. Don't dwell on the past, or obsess about the future. Stay in the Now. If you don't restrict the path with "I can'ts" or litter it with obstacles, then the Universe gets free rein on how to deliver your optimum life to you.

Make A Promise Now

All self-help books say the same thing. (Believe me, I feel like I've read them all.) Set a goal, and the time you're giving yourself to reach that goal, or you'll never get anywhere. One of my clients put it another way. She said that *goals* are a male-oriented thing; what a woman needs to do is make a *promise* to herself. Because if a woman really makes a promise (and means it), she will keep it. No fingers crossed behind your back! This book will help you make promises to yourself; promises that might seem unattainable right now. There are going to be some things to do along the way (for example, cleaning out your closet and your purse!), to help you along. Is there a promise you could write down right now, that could come from your inner Bond Grrl? Planning a fabulous party, where you are the effortless hostess? Flying to Paris? Paying all your debts? Losing some weight, and getting some exercise so that you can fit into an awesome Bond Grrl outfit? Going back to school? Whatever it is, it's time to write it down, and make a contract with yourself. Because whereas a promise is powerful, a binding contract is even more powerful.

Contracts can help you facilitate the process for making things happen in your life. Imagine how powerful a contract is with your signature on the dotted line, containing your approval to carry out the terms in the contract! This not only makes a statement, it making a binding agreement to yourself. There are contract templates out there on the Internet that are easy to download and easy to fill out. But if you go to www.likemindspress.com/bgcontract, you will find a free template that this awesome company has set up, just for readers of this book. Fill out this contract, or just write one down in paper. If you're writing your own, put at the top that you (put your full name) promise that by X date, you will accomplish the following things — and then list them. If you are committed to paying all your debt off and saving for a trip to Disneyland with your family, well then, you are not going to be partying as much, or picking up new shoes or purses on the spur of the moment. You are going to open all your credit card bills, and really write down where you stand. You are going to feel some pain — but that's secondary to the accomplishment you will feel when you do what you set out to do. Whatever that thing is, you have to be passionate about it. You have to resonate happiness around it, not guilt or fear. It has to be a positive, passionate, heartfelt contract within the bounds of realism. Don't write that you'll retire by the end of the year, if you're $50,000 in debt and getting kicked out of your apartment! Stretch, definitely. But if you need to lose 100 pounds, it's not coming off in a month. Keep the action and the time congruent, or you will feel like a failure when you don't keep this impossible promise to yourself.

After you have written your contract, or printed it out if you used the website, sign and date it. Pin it up somewhere where you can see it, like on your fridge. Now you're committed. If something gets in your way, remember: you are the only one who can move forward and make your promise your reality. You are not a Victim of circumstances. You make your own Luck. You make your own Reality. It's really only you who is getting in your own way, so vow not to. Now go and write down that promise! If you feel stuck, don't worry — there are exercises in Chapter 2 to help you uncover your passions. But either way — the first step is uncluttering your life — so let's get started!

A verbal contract isn't worth the paper it's written on.

— Attributed to Samuel Goldwyn

Chapter 1

Cleaning Out

We buy our way out of jail but we can't buy freedom,
We buy a lot of clothes when we don't really need them,
Things we buy to cover up what's inside.

— *Kanye West*

Clutter = Death

Under the ancient principles of Feng Shui, there are nine sectors in any locale — for example, your house, your office, or your cubicle. The sectors make up a 3x3 square called a bagua. The quadrants, starting at the top left, are Wealth/Abundance, Fame/Reputation, Relationships/Love, Family/Ancestors, Health/Balance, Creativity/Children, Knowledge/Learning, Career, and Travel/Helpful Friends (bottom right). If you have clutter in your house, under Feng Shui principles, you superimpose that 3x3 square/grid bagua onto your floor plan, and anywhere containing that clutter is dead energy in that sector of your life.

To me, Feng Shui is not magical, it's a system. By having nine sectors in a certain order, Feng Shui gives your brain a way to order your life. Since these nine sectors are in a specific order if, for example, you are looking for something that will inspire you in Abundance, you look to that "top left" sector, whether it's on your desk, in a room, or even in your car. There, you see something you have specifically placed in that sector, that reminds you of how Abundant your life is. Or if you're having trouble with your Relationship, you look to that "top right" quadrant, and see a photo or a shell from a walk with your honey on the beach, or the like, to energize you in that respect and remind you not to do or say something (in the heat of the moment) that you might regret!

This is not a Feng Shui treatise. For that, I'd suggest you start with Terah Kathryn Collins' *The Western Guide to Feng Shui* (see also: wsfs.com). It can give you a way to order things, on small to large surfaces. And it's always good to have a system!

The bedrock idea here in starting your fEmpowered life is a commitment to No Clutter. If you are cluttering up an area, you have items and dead energy that are not working for you. One of the main tenets of Feng Shui is that if you haven't used something for a few months or it doesn't tug on your emotions every time you see it, you shouldn't have it out on a shelf. It's just a dust magnet. Now mind you, this is not easy for me: I have a lot of interests, and clutter seems to follow me like a tail follows a dog!

The essence of being a Bond Grrl is to be surrounded — 100% — by things that you love and adore. Nothing gathers dust, and neither do you! When a Bond Grrl is tired of something or it doesn't warm her heart any more, she lets that thing go to its next "best use" elsewhere. Think about it: if your cup is totally full of beer, how are you going to get the champagne in there? Get rid of the beer, get rid of the clutter. And then concentrate on the champagne. You might even be able to make use of a smaller glass — and think of the benefits! Or pour your beer into someone's glass, which was only filled with water before. So here we go. Ready?

First Week/First Steps

Unless you have a mansion, your first goal is to go through every single drawer, cabinet, nook and cranny of your house this week. (OH NO, says you. OH YES, says me!) It's important to touch EVERY SINGLE THING in your house — and make sure you love All Of It. If you have a mansion or you could be a candidate for one of Oprah's Clutter Episodes, I give you a week and a half.

That's your goal, period. If you didn't know what to write on your Contract, here's a great promise to document. "I, [Suzy Q], promise to myself that I will touch and clean every item in my house by [date 7 days from today]. Signed, [Suzy Q]." And you know, if you put some thumpin' tunes on your MP3 player, it's not that bad. It's easier for me to do cleaning and de-cluttering with music, because my emotions don't kick in so much when I hit an item I know I need to get rid of, but still feel tied to. Like something that I bought because it was cute, but I have never worn. Or something someone gave me that is just gathering dust, that I keep because I don't want to upset the giver. Or an item that's tied to an emotional event, that doesn't give me that Zing any more. For some reason, having tunes on helps to silence that part of my brain that wants to keep it all.

If you have kids, have them help you out, and make it Fun. The goal here, remember, is to touch everything. Anything that you haven't used or loved in the last season goes in a pile on the floor. If you're really organized and have bags or boxes, that's easier, but get everything out of your drawers and closets — then clean in there! If you're working with kids, this is a great way to teach them about Charity — reminding them about how Wealthy they are, and how Wealth has nothing to do with what they have in their closets. Materialism in children is taught, or at the very least allowed or encouraged, by parents. It's better to have one truly loved teddy bear than a bunch of beautiful but dust-gathering dolls, games and, as they grow up, T-shirts, shoes, and the like. (Did they learn that from you...?) Sure, materialism is all over the TV, movies, and magazines. But if you teach your kids that their Wealth is their awesome selves, then maybe the house will be a little less cluttered, and your bank account a little less strapped. And the way to start is by you taking on this reality first, then expanding it to those you love.

Consignment Day

A friend's son's school sponsors a Consignment Day. Everyone brings in old toys, books, clothes, etc. and each item is tagged with the kids' names. At the end of the day, that child gets the money from their stuff that has sold. Everything that doesn't sell goes to a charity that the kids have learned about in school and picked.

My friend said that this has been the biggest lesson for her two kids. They love getting that money, and often they give away items that she bought for them, but they've never used. This has taught her as well!

Start with the Kitchen

It's usually easiest to start in the kitchen. There is always a ton of stuff in your kitchen cabinets that you bought and didn't eat. And you know you bought it more than three months ago. Grrrrrl, what do you want to put that in your body for?

You want it out of the cabinets. Anything that's not open, you're going to take to the local shelter. They're going to love you. And you never know — separate out the opened and unopened stuff, and take the opened stuff down as well. Shelters are so desperate these days for help, they might have some use for the opened stuff too. I mean everything: herbs and spices, boxed stuff, the whole kitchen.

When I did this most recently, it was amazing how much stuff I had. Tea was a big culprit. The essential oils in tea just don't taste the same after a few months — get rid of it. What about the tub of Vitamin E pills from Costco/Sam's Club? I would have had to have literally made a bath out of the stuff (pricking open each little golden pill at a time...) to use it all before the expiration date. (I suppose I could have used the tub *as* a bath to get some use out of the darned thing.) Or flour! Why did I buy that whole big bag, to make one batch of cookies? I now purchase just enough flour in the bulk bins at the store, and store it in the freezer until I use it, to keep it fresh. Go on — go through it all. Scary how much stuff we have, isn't it?

Now, sure, someone out there is going to say "But, we need to have 20 days' worth of canned goods in case there is an earthquake/tornado/what-have-you." If that's really why you have that pile of soup gathering dust in the back of your closet, I still ask you — when did you buy it? Do you really want to be eating something out of a can that you bought a year ago (and was probably canned way before that)? Eee-yew. So start eating it now and replace it out fresh, or take it to the church/homeless shelter. Don't forget to get a receipt: it's a tax-deductible charitable contribution!

Going through your drawers really does mean *all* of them. Do you need all those dish towels? Gadgets? Magnets on the fridge? If Bond were to walk in right now and open a drawer, would you cringe? Is it all necessary? Is anything soiled or just, well, ugly? One great thing to do is to get all the gadgets out of all your drawers, and put them in baskets. If you use an item, put it back in the drawer. If you haven't used an item by the end of a date that you put on your fridge (such as three months after your clean-up), then those items go to charity. You'd be surprised (as I was) how few utensils you really need and use. I had a ton of spatulas (spatulae?), and I discovered I only really use two of them. If you don't have room to put everything out in a basket, at least transfer it into a drawer you've cleaned out (I know you will have at least one drawer's worth of space), and then add it back into the utensil drawer as you go. And what about your Junk drawer? Yes, I have one as well — but I go through it every three months. What do you need all those rubber bands, half-used, dry tubes of Superglue, and such for? How about your towel drawer? Can't you just imagine the thankful looks on the faces of your local Humane Society volunteers, when you bring some down to them? (And sheets too — we'll get to that, later.)

Remember, you are a Bond Grrl. You are Prepared and Cool. Touch every single thing in your house, and either (1) have a use for it now or very soon, or (2) cherish it emotionally every time you see it. If not — it's gotta go to someone who can use it now, and/or love it.

I said everything, right? Right.

Still Stalled?

So what if you can't stand the idea of cleaning your whole house/desk/purse? What will make you start? Like I said, I usually start in the kitchen. But if you're having trouble, start with the least awful room (or least awful drawer in the least awful room). It might be a bathroom, it might even be your dining room or your patio! Touch everything, and make a conscious decision to keep each item because it has energy for you, or an immediate use. Put all the mementos and knick-knacks that don't either have a use or give you an energetic feeling in a box or on the floor. You don't have to get rid of them right now, but you do have to have them out of the room/drawer/etc. that you're working on. We will do them last.

Often, my students get to one of these "energy poor" items, stall out, then quit. Some rooms/drawers/closets have a lot more of these items in them than others. So schedule time in your daybook, and write down specifically what you're going to do, and when. Then do it! Don't put it off. If you're starting with a room, you're also going to clean everything that's left in it — and baseboards and ceilings and behind and under things, too. Allow enough time so you're not rushed. And if you're like me, put on the tunes! I divorce myself from the emotions tied to objects (or dust bunnies behind the couch) by rockin'. If you are lucky enough to have a housekeeper or someone who helps you do the house, you can go faster — just keep everything pulled away from walls so that they can do that deeper cleaning.

Please don't say, as you read this, that you will Try. When students say they will Try, they're not really committed. (Remember what Yoda said: "Do, or do not. There is no Try.") If you say you will do it — you will. Did you sign that contract with yourself? If not, put this book down and do it — or just write and sign the promise to yourself right here in the margin! Be truly committed to the process, and to the end result. You're worth it.

Part of the clutter problem comes from expanding to fit your space. A friend told me that a snake will grow to the size of the cage it's kept in. It doesn't matter how often you feed it, the cage determines the size. She laughingly mentioned that our possessions seem to be rather snakelike in this respect, and I definitely agree!

In fact, I recently heard Sarah Susanka speak. She wrote a book called *The Not So Big House*. The book deals with decorating, storage, and the like for small homes. A member of the audience asked her, "How big is Not So Big?" She answered, "It's 30% less than what you currently have."

This is a great definition. Her book has to do with downsizing to a degree — but she also believes, as I do, that everyone has at least 30% too much Stuff, regardless if they live in a mansion or in a cabin. Like the snake, they expand — or overexpand! — to fit their cage.

Solitaire Cleans House

Before I married and moved in with my James, I processed through my house. I knew I would be moving in with him, which meant I would have a lot less space to myself. How did I do it? I laughingly told my James I was off limits, then I just did it. I took three full days, and sorted through every drawer and closet, my yard, my car, my purse, my desk... You name it, I did it. WOW! There was a lot of stuff that went into a Don't-Quite-Want-To-Get-Rid-Of-It-But-Don't-Want-To-Have-It-Out Box — even more went into the trash, and a lot was given to charity!

I threw out more spoiled and soiled things than I care to admit. Then, I kept some items, gave others to friends, and brought the rest to various charities that could use them. For example, a Baptist Church that feeds the homeless got the food, tea and so on, Image for Success got the good clothes, and Freecycle.org got the rest. (Freecycle.org is an email board where you post what you have and folks just come and get it... check to see if there's one in your area.)

Personal photos and mementos that didn't give me an emotional hit any more went from my walls to a scrapbook. I can pull the scrapbook off the shelf any time I want — but you know what? I don't. I have a few photos still out that inspire me and make me grin when I look at them, but these are living memories. If I don't pull those scrapbooks out every week, why did I have all those framed pictures out where I had to spend energy dusting them? These are the things you need to think (and be ruthless!) about.

For the stuff in the Box — which actually turned out to be a bunch of boxes — I had a big potluck party and invited all my local Grrlfriends. I told them that my party gifts to them were all the things in those Boxes; things that I didn't particularly want to part with. I told them that I hoped that they would like some of those items, so I could go visit them, but at *their* houses. My Grrls were all over that! I had put some clothes in the Boxes, lots of knickknacks like candles, candleholders and picture frames, hair stuff, some jewelry I'm never going to wear, pillows, books — you name it. It was nearly all gone by the end of the party — and what wasn't gone, I Freecycled.

After that, I moved in with my James. His house was 100% full — as mine had been, though my house was half the size. So I had to go back through everything (after I felt I had cut down to the bare minimum!), and get rid of half of it again! That was really enlightening. Because if you had asked me after I did the first purge, I would have told you that I couldn't part with anything I'd kept. But I wound up parting with more again, as my James and I touched everything in Our house, and figured out what truly should stay.

Memorabilia

I have a friend who has a ton of photos in her house. Lots of them are of her kids — who are grown and have their own families now. She mainly dusts them. I know she doesn't really see them. So... why? I had a student in this situation; when she got her house painted, she really thought about each photo before she put it back on the wall. The freshly-painted wall looked so good, she didn't want to put holes in it!

A lot of us get into what I call Grandma's House Syndrome as we age. But the reality is that energy has to Flow, and mementos and art you don't really see, books you don't read, and the like are dead energy. If you have a lot of photos, old medals, trophies, and such on your mantels and walls, put them in a scrapbook or, for trophies, take a picture of them, and put that in the scrapbook. Think about whether you really need that trophy any more. Is it more than three years old? Are you still doing what you got the trophy for? If not, all they are doing is subtly reminding you that your Glory Days are in your Past... and I am here to tell you that your Glory Days are Now.

This goes for kids' stuff too. Are you teaching your kids to be attached to material items so much that they won't relinquish stained/non-fitting/threadbare favorites? Why? I'm not a child psychologist, but to me, if a kid imbues a shirt or a blanket with Special Powers, then s/he doesn't feel those Special Powers are in him/herself. Does your James have a ratty-but-favorite/lucky poker shirt? Same deal here. Again, more than I want to deal with right now, but everyone has to know that clothes don't hold the luck — the wearer does! If these items are ugly, dirty, ratty, or the like, then it's time to talk to the wearer (is it you?) about why they feel those Special Powers don't live inside them. Remember Disney's Dumbo: It wasn't until he lost the "magic" feather that he held in his trunk that he realized that he could really fly without it.

You Should Be So Proud Of Yourself

I once heard that when we're talking to kids, we should be aware of our phraseology. One phrase that was constantly harped upon was "I am so proud of you!" This phrase, perhaps like that lucky blanket, can make the recipient feel that the power of approval is outside themselves. It leads them to look for approval outwardly, sometimes acting up to get it. Instead, the suggested phrase is "You should be so proud of yourself!" This leads the person who accomplished the goal to look for inner reward, instead of looking outward for appreciation.

Example: Buenos Aires or Bust

Let's pretend that your James came to you and said, "Hey gorgeous, I have the greatest idea. I want to pack up all our stuff, and move to Buenos Aires for 6 months. I am going to pay for everything to get us there — and we're going to have a fully furnished apartment that is to die for. We just need to bring our essentials, then pack up what we want to get back into when we come home." Take a breath, and imagine this. And while you're at it, listen to any excuses that your inner Eek Grrl comes up with and shoot them down: it's going to be fine with your kids' soccer coach, with your boss, with whomever your inner Eek Grrl is using as an excuse not to go. (By the way, we will deal with some of that in a later Chapter.)

The point of this exercise? Storage is expensive — as is shipping your stuff to Argentina. (Or Paris. Or Rio. Or Miami. Or California. Or...) So you have to divide up all your things in your mind. First, pack the stuff that you literally Can't Live Without for six months. Remember, though, you have a fully furnished house down there. Next, pack up everything you're going to put into storage because you won't need it for six months, but you'll definitely not be able to live without when you get back. Then, get rid of the rest.

Okie dokie, so now imagine you're in Argentina doing the tango with your James, and you find out that the storage unit was hit by a hurricane, and only half of your stuff survived. What are you super hopeful made it?

You see what I'm getting at. If you envision this exercise, and start going through your house this way, you'll find stuff that wouldn't have even made it to the storage unit (clothes that aren't fashionable, are stained, or don't fit; pictures you never look at; books you have read). This stuff, you're ready to let go. After that comes stuff you want to keep, so it goes to the storage unit — but it really isn't irreplaceable or necessary (books you loved and wanted to re-read some day; DVDs, furniture, old toys, pots and pans, kids' report cards). This is the stuff that you hope the hurricane took, when it smashed the storage unit. You really don't want to relinquish it, but in the end, it's OK that it's gone (though a little painful). Next, there is stuff that actually *is* irreplaceable — the stuff you hope the hurricane left in the storage unit (scrapbooks; your grandmother's silver; a particular drawing by your child; a favorite sculpture).

Finally, there is the stuff you'd bring with you, that you believe is Necessary. This includes your grandma's antique brooch and her recipe for butterbeans, clothes you love, toys your kids really love and play with every day, a pair of comfy shoes, a pair of dressy shoes — you get the picture. (We'll talk more about clothes in a second.)

You know what I'm going to say now, right? You gotta get rid of everything but the last two categories — the irreplaceable, and the necessary/loved. I know it's painful. But in moving in with my James, that's what I did (and am still in the process of doing, in fact, as I write this book). I hated it, but in the end, it's so freeing. Because, if you think about it, how much of all this really just represents silent bragging ("Look at my trophy!"), or extra dusting?

The Bond Grrl Look

In your clothes avoid too much gaudiness; do not value yourself upon an embroidered gown; and remember that a reasonable word, or an obliging look, will gain you more respect than all your fine trappings.
— Sir George Savile, 'Advice to a Daughter,' 1688

Now that you've cleaned your house, it's time to venture into your closet. Remember, being a Bond Grrl is a state of mind. It's not a state of your clothes, purses, or shoes. Although in my seminars and in this book I address clothing, the walk, the talk, and the rest, it is merely to help coax your Inner Bond Grrl out; to help you be congruent on the outside with your awesome Bond Grrl inside.

Not everyone looks alike — far from it. So what's your Bond Grrl Look? The idea is to realize who you are on the Inside, then be congruent in the look and attitude you present the world Outside. By portraying something else, you are, in effect, lying. The key to being a Bond Grrl is that a Bond Grrl is who she is (unlike Bond, who might take on disguises since he's a spy). What You See Is What You Get (WYSIWYG). If you are putting on an act, that's not being a Bond Grrl. That's being a faker, more concerned with putting out energy to please your audience than relaxing into your own Self. Think about this, and make a decision to let your Inner gorgeous awesome self shine Out.

Dress for the Mission

Going through your wardrobe is one of the first and potentially easiest things that you can do to start getting your Outside congruent with your Inside. Set aside the time and the mental energy to do this. When I do a seasonal clothes clearing, I actually listen to tunes that fill my head with upbeat sounds that drown out my internal gremlin voice, telling me stories about why I should keep an item I never wear!

Clearing Your Closets

How to start? Get everything you own out on the bed. Yes, everything. Doesn't fit on the bed? How many clothes and shoes does one Grrl need? Would they all come with you to Argentina? Anything that you can't (or shouldn't!) wear because it's too small, threadbare, has stains — any stains — anything you cannot wear right now for any reason, or that's out of fashion, goes from the bed to the floor. There are wonderful charities that would love these clothes. You're going to feel SO much lighter once they're out of your closet — I promise. So get to it.

Clothing Categorization

Next, separate the clothes you have left on the bed into three basic colors: Black, Brown or Blue. I believe that you then need to decide which two basic colors dominate (for me, that's Black and Brown), and stick with those going forward. Black-based clothing means colors that would go with black slacks: red, white, black, grey. Brown-based might be brown, orange, yellow, ivory, green. When you put your clothes back in your drawers or your closet, hang them by color category, so it's easy to pair up outfits quickly. Do the same with your shoes. If you pick black and brown, you would only need to have black shoes and brown shoes — and not 1,000 pair! Remember, a Bond girl needs to be able to pack quickly and efficiently if her James comes in and says "Work is sending me to Buenos Aires — ready?" If you have your clothing sorted in advance, when you travel, just bring one Base color, bring one pair of shoes (or two, day and evening, or three if you include sandals), and you're off. Shoes are the worst space culprit: If you mix Brown and Black clothing for a trip, you need six pair.

Anything that doesn't quite fit in these categories — jeans, for example — should be hung/folded and put in its own area. And if you have more than, oh, three pair of jeans, you know what I'm going to say, right? Why? Why? Why? Wouldn't it have been better to have saved that money for the trip to Argentina than to have it hanging in your closet, redundant? No more of that, right? And we're not even talking about the shoes and purses, Grrl...

Clothes Ideas from Oprah

First of all, do you love Oprah? I love Oprah. I definitely have an addiction to Oprah. Maybe it's time for O.A. (Oprah Anonymous). I can be the first President.

I time shift Oprah through a service from my cable provider, and some days, after a really hard day at work, I stumble on down after putting on my play clothes in the evening, and I watch 5 or 6 Oprahs (Opri?) in a row.

 *Domino to the Rescue*

As for wading through my own closet, I wasn't strong enough to do this alone. Since Oprah's crazy British Grrls were nowhere to be found, I enlisted my best friend and fellow aspiring Bond Grrl, Allison "Domino" F. She's my Fashion Lifeline, to borrow a phrase from that old TV show *Who Wants To Be A Millionaire*.

I first had her go through all the things I had hanging in my back closet. Hey — I'm not 20, I take great care of my clothes... so I not only had my regular closet full, but one in the guest room. These guest-room-closet clothes, not surprisingly, were the first to go. Since they weren't in my regular closet, I had pretty much relegated them to a back corner of my life anyway. But it was still hard to see them go. REALLY HARD!! I had over a dozen suits, about half a dozen black tie outfits, some nice dresses, a coat or two, you name it. Many of the suits were single-breasted ("It's never comin' back," says Domino), showed wear, or just had to go, per Ms. D.

I think I got to keep two pieces from the back closet. And I didn't even mention to Domino that my James, his daughter, and I had done a ruthless purge of all our clothing, including play clothes and not-my-size clothes, a month or so previously. Can you say SIXTEEN green garbage bags to charity? Wow...

Domino and I took photographs of all the discards to attach to the charitable deduction slip. When you're giving away stuff, don't forget to do this! While she started poking through my current closet, I took all the cast-offs to Image For Success. IFS is a non-profit that takes suits, shoes and the like and gives them to underprivileged women who are getting their lives together. The gal accepting the donations made it all worthwhile. Since everything was dry cleaned from the last time I wore it (1999?), I looked like her angel walking in that door with clean clothes in sizes that "her women" could use. I live in an affluent county, and my bet is that she gets more size 2, 4 and 6s than she knows what to do with. Mine were all in the size 12 range. She even eyed my feet (size 11) and said, "I hate to be rude... but what about shoes?" I hadn't even thought about shoes. So back I went, with my now-empty car, to give Domino marching orders on not only my clothes, but also my shoes.

The harder cut for me was letting Domino sort through my current closet. After the rush of giving all that stuff away though, I decided it was time to be harsh. So I did what I am suggesting here: we brought every single thing out of that closet, and examined each and every piece.

Of the work clothes — thank goodness — many more made the cut this time from my ruthless fashion friend. But I still had a bunch of stuff that had to go, including the dreaded "no, I have never worn that" outfits purchased over a year ago. Just not armfuls of stuff, thank goodness. And a lot of shoes — shoes that were scuffed, or that were just kinda for fun, or that I hadn't worn in a year or so — they all landed in the discard pile. This left only shoes that went with my black and brown clothing schemes, from walking flats through boots and dressy pumps, a pair of Keds, and my sneakers and shower shoes for the gym.

The woman at the Image For Success intake had to sit down when I arrived this time. There were a lot of shoes! I've been the same size for over 20 years, and have basically kept'em all. But importantly, as she said, she "finally had shoes my women can fit into!" (One of the mottos on their website is: "If you can't put yourself in the shoes of someone living on government assistance... can we put them in yours?")

The thing that amazes me is that I'm not a shopaholic. I pity the woman who loves to shop. No, it's more that I have been right around the same size for years, and I take care of my clothes and shoes, so things just add up! When you are doing this exercise, believe me, it's worth checking out a local charity that does something like Image For Success. Check out their websites. Get excited about the women that are going to be able to get a job, because they will be wearing your clothes and your shoes. Read their stories. It's so worth it.

The Opri that I watched last night were all related to dressing in ways that can take 10 years off your looks. Wow — amazing. And all the ideas are applicable to anyone looking to help coax their inner Bond Grrl out.

A few of the Opri had those two crazy British gals she uses, ambushing people and re-dressing/accessorizing them. I have been working on this, myself, for the past few months. No, not ambushing. Re-dressing.

Every few years, we need to take a peek at everything that expresses who we are. Then we need to make an informed choice about whether that outfit, makeup, bit of flab, haircut, or the like represents us as we are, now. No matter how much you might love an outfit... or worse, how little wear you got out of it (*i.e.*, the stuff that's still hangin' in the closet with price tags), it all has to go through the assessment. By being ruthless, you will stay congruent with your Inner Bond Grrl forevermore.

Lingerie: The Dreaded Panty Drawer

Hose. As Oprah says, "Only nurses wear white," so any white hose you have must go. I also personally feel that skin colored or tan hose never look that great. *Sex in the City* made the bare leg acceptable, even in skirts. So I use a self-tanner/bronzer (I'm a white Grrl) and then go bare legged, yes, even with skirts and even on business. So sue me — but I feel dangerous and adventurous when I do it. Sexy me. Oh — your legs are shaved or waxed, right? You're ready to hit the beach when your James comes up the walk with the tickets to Hawaii instead of Paris or Argentina, right? Right...? I don't care if it's December. You're not doing the "bear legs" instead of "bare legs" deal, are you?

Panties and Bras. Hey Bond Grrl, do your undies match? Do you have (she isn't going to say it, is she...?) "period panties"? (Oh NO! She said it!) Do you have "granny panties"? Get them out of your drawer! If you need "period panties," then go out and buy a bunch of sexy black panties, and wear them during your Time. They aren't going to show stains. (She isn't really saying this is she? Yeah yeah, I am.) If you have odd (wo)man out panties or bras — ones where the elastic gave way on the panties, but you still have the bra for example — come on, be brave, let'em go. If you are a Victoria's Secret shopper, so those panties and matching bras cost you Bank, think of how many times you have worn them already, and do the math. They probably have been well worth whatever you paid for them. Now it's time to bid them bye-bye. Then, go to Marshall's or Ross or Mervyn's or Kohl's and get matching bras and panties, or Victoria's Secret if you can afford it. Because if you're wearing shoddy underdrawers, that shows how you feel about yourself. Even if no one ever sees your undies on you but you, YOU are the most important person in this equation anyway, right? Right?!

I'd also seriously suggest going to a store like Victoria's Secret and get yourself measured, to be sure you're buying the right bra size. This is often a huge revelation and it's free. If your breasts are lying under your armpits or drooping, or if you fail the pencil test (putting a pencil under your breast, and seeing whether it stays there or falls to the floor), you need special help. If you're large breasted, you just cannot be wearing a $5.00 bra. I am nearly flat-chested (in dark moments I expect folks to say "Excuse me, Sir?" because of my figure), so I have a whole different set of issues that bras need to address.

Get over the cost of good bras and panties. I mean it. And don't lament getting rid of the ones that just don't work for you. You need to get rid of everything that doesn't make you look and feel GREAT, and, starting from this Inside Out position, build up that sexy Bond Grrl that I know you are! Even if you are wearing these undies under your droopy-but-clean jeans and boxy sweatshirt (because you got rid of the rest of your Play Clothes as we're going to do below, and these were the best you had to keep), you're on your way. Build from the inside, out.

Here's a scenario that will scare you into a good clear-out. You are (gasp!) in that car accident your mom (OK, my mom) always warned you (me) about. The most sexy firefighter in the whole world tries to carry you out of the wreckage — but your dress is caught! The only way to get you away from the car before it explodes is to cut away your dress and carry you to safety! And there's a camera crew, recording every heroic step! (Yeah, that makes it really bad, huh?)

What are you wearing under that dress, grrl?

 Almost French

> Here's another book I recommend to you: *Almost French*. It's about an Australian journalist who falls in love with a Parisian man, and moves to Paris — and her adjustment there. One of the things she talks about is her habit of stepping out of their apartment in sweats, to get the paper for example, without her hair done, etc. Her French boyfriend (now husband) cringed at this. He finally explained to her that this is considered unspeakable in Paris. Why? Because it's ugly. Just like wolfing down too much food too quickly, it means that you don't respect yourself... and you don't respect others and their sense of the beauty around them. Since the French are inveterate people-watchers and lovers of beauty, they pride themselves on making sure they are putting their best self forward, even if it's just to get the paper from the porch. It's a matter of Respect.

Purging Your Play Clothes

OK Grrls, I know you all have your favorite jeans, sweatshirts, T-shirts, and the like. Me, too. Play clothes — clothes you do housework in, garden in, or hang in — are hard to purge when they get a bit tatty. We all make up stories about how we need them for some ridiculous reason, like painting the house, rolling in the mud, or whatever. Even if you are going to be painting the house, you shouldn't be doing it in baggy, droopy-drawers sweats! This shows disrespect for yourself! What if James Bond (or that sexy firefighter) knocked on your door while you were wearing these, lounging eating popcorn and watching your favorite 007 DVD? You might have your hair up and not be wearing makeup — but are you in droopy drawers, too? Oh, so pretty. Come on, be brave: get rid of them.

You'll still have stay-at-home play clothes. They will just be the clothes that you know aren't quite new enough to be going-out play clothes, but you keep wearing them out anyway. Your stay-at-home play clothes need to be OK for cleaning your toilet bowl, but also OK if that firefighter comes by to check on you. Again, think of your current at-home clothes. Would you have a spazz attack if you were to look through your front door peephole, and his handsome face was peering in? Or, what if you were to hear a knock and look through the chain, to find out that you won that Publishers' Clearing House Sweepstakes you entered on a dare? Or — ack! — Oprah's team is standing there?

Close your eyes, take a deep breath, and imagine yourself doing whatever it is that you do in that raggedy old boyfriend shirt and those droopy crotch jeans/sweats. Cleaning the top windows in the stairwell? (Please don't tell me you were going to the Mall that way. Please.) Now, in your mind, get yourself up on that mental window-cleaning ladder, and instead picture yourself in a white T-shirt and your next-to-best jeans. Or some sweats that fit. Don't have any? They all have droopy crotches? You got 'em in high school? Shame on you!

Picture yourself this way, because coming up the walk is your James, with your favorite flowers, your favorite little treat, and airplane tickets to Paris! Do you look like a bag lady? Ohhh, how sexy. I'd be so glad to see you, if I was your James. Not. Come on.

So, get all your play clothes out on the bed. Yes, all. It's easier to take photographs of everything you're giving away if they're laid out on the bed. Again, you want to document it, because you're going to file for a charitable deduction on your tax return for all of it. How do you even start? Take everything in groups. Let's say, first, you take... socks. Do they all match? (Duh.) Holes? Stretched-out elastic? I don't care if they're your Favorites — if they aren't in good shape, they have to go. If they have patterns, are they faded? What about all the single socks you have after doing the laundry, that you hope against hope will magically find their mates again? (I have a picture in my head of rogue socks, wearing a bit of lint as a Lone Rangeresque mask, grabbing hold of the inside of the dryer door and throwing rascally sock-kisses to their mates as the door swings open, screaming "We'll always have the Drawer, schweetha't!" as the *Casablanca* theme swells in the background... but I digress...) If those socks have been mate-less for let's say four laundry cycles, their mates are on the lam, time to put them out of their misery...

Jeans and Sweats

Next come play pants: sweats, jeans, and the like. Does the crotch meet yours? If it doesn't — it's got to go. You think your butt looks big? How much bigger do you think it looks when you have six inches of fabric hanging down off the back of it? Are they high-waisted Mommy Jeans that button under your ribs instead of below your belly button? Those squeeze your insides, and are not flattering to your figure. After I did the Great Jeans and Sweats Dump (old sweats makes great dust rags, by the way), I went to Ross, and got two of the cutest sweat suits for a ridiculously low price. And don't tell me you don't shop in Those Kinda Stores. Get a grip. Why are you spending hundreds of dollars on play clothes? Get something that flatters you, and get it from Target, Ross, Marshall's or the like. Stop spending money that you should be saving to buy espresso drinks at a cute little café in Paris. Believe me, the café patrons are not going to concentrate on your Brands. They are going to concentrate on how good you look!

And by the way, while you're out getting a flattering sweatsuit, get a bunch of white T-shirts or white button-down shirts. You can bleach these like crazy after you do your gardening, housework or what-have-you, and they come out looking fine. Why do you think farmers wear white shirts? If you are in debt right now, still purge your clothes and shoes. Get rid of everything but the Least Bad one, if that's how it is. When you're out of debt, then start building back — but not by going to Gucci! Have you noticed in the Bond movies that the Girls are not bling-wearing brand-flashers? That's because they want to be sure that no one is distracted from their wonderful selves. If you're a big brand wearer, think about why that is. Are you trying to tell people subliminally that you can Afford these brands, even if you happen to have gotten them as knock-offs from a street vendor, or bought them on credit you can't pay off? If so, you're lying.

If you work at home, whether you're a stay-at-home mom or you work out of a home office, you are now going to hold up your hand and swear that you will not ever again spend a whole day in "schlumpadinka" (as Oprah would say) sweats. Go on, swear it! Even if you get into jeans and a white T-shirt, it's better than the sweats schlep!

Now, on to the jeans. Are any of them taper-legged? They have to go. I do not care how new they are, or how much you love them. If you have a Booty Issue — and nearly everyone except a fashion model does — the taper-leg look makes your bottom look ENORMOUS. With those jeans clinging to your calves, your legs come to a point with your booty and hips at the widest point. Give 'em to charity, give 'em to your friend's housekeeper, give 'em to a frenemy (grin) — just give 'em!

If you have capris and you have anything but the slimmest little calves — they gotta go too. I never bought the capri deal myself. I'm tall, so they make me look like I couldn't find pants in my length. Capris cut up a calf and leg visually; they can only really be worn by someone whose legs start at their armpits. Yours don't? I'm sorry — give 'em to a frenemy who loves 'em. Make her legs look like stumps.

 What's a "Frenemy"?

A frenemy is a friend who is really an enemy. We all have these in our lives. They are the grrlfriends who tell us "for our own good" some gossip that is hurtful. They are the ones who say they will support us, and then have catty little things to say when we have a bit of success. They are the grrlfriends who we tell we have gone on a diet, or that we've quit drinking, and who smilingly invite us to take just one bite of a birthday cake, or to join them for margaritas like always on Friday, because "Hey Honey, you look great, don't be so silly!" Beware the frenemy. They're worse than a regular enemy — those, you can recognize because they just try to kill you up front, they don't try to stab you behind your back. Be sure that you remain aware as you unleash your Inner Bond Grrl, and only share with your true friends, not frenemies.

Make your two best boot-cut or flare-leg jeans your play clothes. They always seem to be in style. And get rid of the rest. Take a look at the bottoms of your jeans. Which have the least ratty bottoms? Go for those. Then, if you live in jeans, buy another pair for your Good pair, or just pick your current Most Best pair to do that job for you. You'll wind up with, at most, three pair. And, as I said above, nothing should be above the navel — we're not supposed to be covering our bodies with something that cuts us in half when we sit down! You have poochy stomach? Then do something about it. South Beach Diet, Bob Greene, walking, whatever. But Grrlfriend, covering it with Mommy Jeans to your waist just gives you more fabric over your big booty and pooch — drawing more attention to it! I am not saying to wear jeans down to your pubic line and a crop top, but with lower rise jeans plus a sexy flowing top, you'll actually be able to breathe again!

I get my jeans from the Newport News catalog. They have Tall Grrl length — hallelujah! — and wonderful choices. Their lowest rise is still not scary-pubic-line rise: it's an inch or so below my navel, which means I can sit down without feeling like I'm cutting myself in half. And when it's a poochy day for me, I wear a non-form-fitting (I did not say "boxy") shirt and a duster-type jacket over it, so no one can see my sides or back. Because Newport News jeans are not expensive, and you can return them with no fuss if they don't fit, it's easy to replace the ugly jeans in your closet. Now, if you're carrying debt, we will talk about this later, but no new stuff until all your old stuff is paid for! If you have credit card debt, you are still paying for whatever is on that card, even if you ate it, bought it, or discarded it months ago. So do what you can, but remember to keep paying down that debt and that it's much, much better for your cupboards to be a little bare but as stylin' as they can be, than to keep wearing droopy drawers or to add to your debt load.

Sweatshirts and T-Shirts

Sweatshirts and T-shirts usually share the same problem. Old logos or mementos from long-forgotten trips on an unflattering shirt, stains, hoods that pull on your neck... get rid of them. (And no more buying shirts at cheesy theme-parks on impulse!) If they are at all frayed or stained — gotta go. This was hard for me. I had old Super Bowl sweatshirts that went back to when the Redskins won and I lived in D.C. (Don't look it up. It's embarrassing.) Any sweatshirts or T-shirts with sayings, logos, or the like on them... you know what I'm going to say. Unless it's something cool — an embroidered T-shirt from Nepal, or one with a tasteful little Tahitian tattoo-type turtle in the corner... it's got to go.

How many T-shirts and sweats did I get rid of? My goodness. At least a quarter of a ton. I think this was the hardest for me, because I work at home a lot so I'm in play clothes quite a bit. I'm also apt to buy Ts and sweatshirts at events, trips, and the like. I had a lot of old favorites. Now? I have a lot of new favorites, all from perfectly good Ts and sweats I didn't wear as much as the others. Do it... do it... do it!

You know what helped me the most? I've said this before. I blasted some inspiring dance music on my MP3 player while I went through the clothes I had pulled onto my bed. It put me in an upbeat mood and also made me think, "If I was out boppin' around and a James saw me wearing this, what would happen?" I often leave the house with my hair back in a pony tail, and minimal makeup. But combine that with droopy drawers and an "I'm With Stupid" T-shirt with an old coffee stain... Not good. Definitely not being picked for the next Bond Girl by the movie casting director, that's for darned sure.

My stuff that didn't make the cut went to charity, or to a friend's housekeeper, who sends them down to El Salvador every month. Ts that really had memories for me went (don't laugh) into my rag bag. This way, I actually get to see that shirt again, and get a smile out of remembering the concert, or the bar in the Bahamas, or whatever it commemorates, when I see that rag and I'm doing my chores. Just a thought. Worked for me.

So, you say, what do you wear to clean the toilet bowl, or go to the gym? You want to wear something you can actually move in, of course (none of this Gym Chic nonsense where you're there to look cute, not get your business done). Here are my top three choices:

1. *Race shirts.* If you have run a race of any kind and received a shirt for finishing, wear that to the gym as motivation. If it motivates you, keep it. But only for the gym. If you wear it to Safeway, you're bragging. Knock that off.

2. *White T-shirts or tank tops.* Have I said this 50 times yet? You can bleach the stains out of them easily. I have found some stylish ones in (you guessed it) the Newport News catalog — they come in packs of three for cheap. Go for V-neck ones. Crew necks can make you look like a turtle or that you're wearing your son's clothing — make sure you boldly assess anything you're keeping from a fashion standpoint, not just from an emotional "But, I like wearing these" standpoint (or have a fashionista friend help you).

3. *Colored/Logo Shirts.* Lastly, you could wear a tasteful logo or colored T-shirt that you kept from your purge.

All of these are gym or cleaning or gardening clothes — but only if they are the right size. Don't go out looking like you're wearing your husband's (or son's) clothing!

I want you to look at everything that comes out of your closet like this: Pretend that Oprah's Dream Bus comes to ambush you, because your best friend wrote her to make your wildest dream come true. You (ahem) happen to be cleaning the toilet bowl when they knock on your door. Whatcha in, Grrlfriend? I mean, besides the stylin' yellow rubber gloves? A Bond Grrl is always always always (did I say "always") prepared for the Dream Bus!!!

 *Creative Re-use*

Do you have any triathlon/Race For The Cure/marathon shirts? I recently helped coach some Grrls who wanted to do their first triathlon (and they all finished — Yay!). I gave them my race shirts to train in. Because if you're out running with a few extra pounds on you but you're wearing a marathon shirt, people passing you are going to think, "Hmmm, she might be slow, but wow, she did the Big Sur Marathon!" I know, it's kind of cheating, but it gave the gals I trained a confidence boost. If you are just getting started in a training program, how about asking one of your Grrlfriends that's done a race whether she has a few of those T-shirts that she might give you for motivation? I promise you she probably doesn't wear them that often (I didn't), and she'd probably love to get them out of her closet. But again, don't wear them to the grocery store — otherwise you're bragging about something that you haven't actually done.

Shoes

While you're pitching things and giving them away — what about shoes? What is it with women and shoes? If you are keeping shoes because they're comfy, I'm suspicious already. Do you have what I have heard called "cop shoes" or "nurse shoes," when that's not your chosen profession? Are you clumping around in sneakers all day? Come on, they make your calves look like 2 x 4s! And it's especially time to Get Real if you have more than, oh, two dozen pair of shoes.

Again, shoes can go to charity — whether it's an Image For Success-type place or a relief organization that will take stuff out to disaster victims. Stop your closet from looking like a shoe emporium. For me, at size 11, I don't have the ability to do a lot of impulse shoe buying — and when I find something that really does work, I often buy 2 pair so when one gets scuffed up, I can go to the next. What about you? Are any of your shoes ruined at the back, from driving in them or running down stairs and ruching? Bye-bye. Any that need caps but you never seem to get them to the cobbler? Either take them in — or out they go. Do you have sneakers that are more than a year old? You do know that all the padding/gel/etc. in them is gone now, right? Live a little: if it's in your budget, get a new pair and leave the old ones at the store!

The shoe choices in my closet are down to those that go with my brown-based or my black-based clothing, plus walking sandals, Keds, and a pair of sneakers. That's it. What do I have? Slides in black and in brown, cute black and brown loafers for jeans, black and brown tall boots (short ones cut your calves in half — YUCK!), black and brown work heels, black and brown and white strappy sandals, and black dress pumps in two different heel heights, depending on whether I'm with my James — who is a bit shorter than I am — or if I'm in the mood to strut out at 6'5". Oh — and a cute pointy orange pair of slides that I wear with my brown-based clothes, which contain a lot of orange (my favorite color). If you have five pair of black sandals or pumps or (name that shoe), wear 'em around a bit. If pushed, could you walk, say, five city blocks in any one pair? No? So why do you keep them?

I don't understand friends who have 30 pair of shoes, with many of them just "stand in" or "sit in" shoes. "Sit in" shoes are the ones that are too uncomfortable to even *stand* in for a long period of time, "Stand in" shoes are ones that are comfortable enough to stand in, but that you couldn't walk a long way in — only really allowable for black tie occasions. I have a pair of tall (3") slides that I don't think I would be physically able to walk a long way in — but they are sexy black tie shoes and I can certainly walk from the car and up the opera house stairs in them, and I can stand in them all night. But that's just one pair. Okay, and I have a pair of 6" Lucite stiletto heels (or two...) for pole dancing at S-Factor. Almost forgot (grin).

Be ruthless in the shoe department, grrls. Scuffed? Out. Pinchy? Out. Ugly? Out. If they are brand name shoes — this goes for all your clothes, too — you do know you can eBay them, right? I bought two Armani suits, a pair of Lucky Jeans, and some Manolo shoes on eBay, all for about ten cents on the dollar, because the seller had worn them once, found they didn't fit, and was then stuck with them. If you have the time and ability — eBay your stuff. Why not? If you want to upgrade for a fraction of the cost and you're sure of your size in that brand — eBay is a grand place to start.

Lastly, try to get your shoes off the floor, to make it easier to vacuum your closet. If you have boots and they keep flopping over, you can put rolled up magazines in them to keep them standing straight, and stop them from creasing where they flop over, which ultimately ruins the boot.

Sleepwear

Lastly, go through your nighties, robes, and the like. Are you wearing long T-shirts to bed? Shame on you! How sexy is that? I don't care if you're the mother of five and the last thing in the world that you want to do is have sex or look sexy to your James. First of all, that's just sad, because you're losing out on one of the best things in life. We're going to have a very serious talk about sex later in the book. But if you picked him and love him and want to stay with him — and if you respect yourself — go through those nighties, and (I mean it) pitch 'em. If you're cold at night, get flannel sheets. My James, who runs really warm, got me an electric blanket that goes under the fitted sheet on just my side, so I can be as warm as I want and he stays cool. There are even blankets made for this situation, where the blanket is thicker on one side than the other. Yes, really.

So no more excuses for flannel nighties or sweats in bed. I'd rather see you getting in there naked (did I say that?) than in a long T-shirt with Tweety Bird on it, or your granny flannel. Grow up, honey. I don't mean for you to go out and buy some corset-based Frederick's number where you'll wake up with marks on your body from where it shifted and pinched. No. I mean get some pretty flowing, washable, easy nighties — either right under your crotch line, or if you are feeling Romance Novel-y, longer. They're beautiful, just like you. The short ones won't bind you up when you sleep, and they feel lovely on your skin. If you're working through debt, then at least pitch the ones you know that you would be running to hide, if I suddenly showed up at your door. (Don't tempt me, you never know where I might show up! Maybe with Oprah. Now, that thought will scare some sense into you!)

Restocking Your Closet

Closets are pretty satisfying to clean. The space is small. If you take a look in there and see that everything is a mess, you know you need to clean it up; if it's dirty, you need to scrub or maybe paint it; if it's overstuffed, you need to give some stuff away. But compared to other rooms of your house, you can usually get it all done in one go, unless you're painting. Let's assume you're not going to paint. Grrl, let's get to Honest here, you are not going to get some *The Lion, the Witch and the Wardrobe* closet expansion out the back, so you need to fit your belongings into your space. Don't pretend that the space will stretch to fit your belongings! Here are some ideas to make it a little easier, after you've purged everything:

1. *Use all the same type of hangers.* Hangers are cheap. Get the thick plastic kind, preferably with little hooks on an inside upright, so that you can hang skirts by their hanging straps on the inside of the skirt. (Having all the same color is nice too — I use black.) You might have some skirt/pants presses too, for the skirts and pants that don't have hanging tabs. I know it's an expense to go out and get all matching hangers, but if they match and are thick plastic, they aren't going to get tied up together and bend/break as easily as the metal and paper ones that come from the dry cleaner. And besides, it looks SO MUCH better! By the way, my dry cleaner takes back the cleaner bags and hangers to recycle them, plus uses environmentally-friendly dry cleaning methods. See if you can find a dry cleaner like this, to do a little more to help out our Earth.

2. *Hang your clothes facing one direction.* If you normally hang everything facing to the left, after you've cleaned out your closet, re-hang everything facing right, turning it left after you wear it. Why? Because if at your next purge you still have something in there facing to the right, it means you haven't used it in a Long Time. And so it has to Go. Granted, some things, like black tie clothes, might only get a wearing or two a year, but this at least gives you a head's up as to whether or not you're kidding yourself about wearing everything that you saved after the purge! Sometimes there are items that you are sure you will wear (even though you haven't), and this will dramatically show you what the truth is. If you're keeping a Swear to Wear outfit, just be sure that you don't keep it again after the next purge, if it's still hangin' to the right!

3. *Scarves.* Take one of the paper hangers from the dry cleaner, punch holes in it, and hang all your dress scarves through it. This way, you won't need to fill a drawer with them, or a shelf. You will be able to see them easily, and they take up very little space. I generally do six per hanger. Don't have dress scarves? I find this to be an inexpensive way to change or dress up an outfit, especially if I am traveling. A black shirt with a gold scarf in the evening looks totally different the next day, with a brightly-patterned one.

4. *Keep all your empty hangers together.* As soon as you take something out to wear, put its hanger to the far left or far right of the pole. No exceptions. Every time. That way, you will always know where the hangers are when you put your laundry or dry cleaning away, and the empty ones won't get tangled up in the hangers with clothes still on them.

5. *Your vacuum is your friend.* Use the nozzles that come with it to go after dust! Clean the closet shelves, way behind your shoes, and up high if you have a high shelf. Use the right vacuum tool for the job, and use your vacuum to get dust out of all the shelves, nooks and crannies before you put your clothes back.

6. *Have only in-season clothes in your closet; beware of stains and moths.* Before you take the out-of-season clothes out and put them somewhere out of the way, like in those boxes that slip under your bed, make sure you dry clean or launder everything. I learned this the hard way: I put a bunch of winter clothes away last winter that looked fine, and when I pulled them out, some of them had set-in stains that ruined the clothes! Since I don't put dirty clothes back in my closet, I believe what happened is that I wore the item to a meeting for an hour or so and then put it back in the closet, knowing I could get one more wearing out of it. But I had

maybe spilled something small and clear, or the cat had jumped on me and the small stain went unnoticed — until it sat there for six months in storage! I lost a few shirts I really liked because I stored them like this, so be forewarned. Finally, beware of moths. My James lost an expensive suit jacket and I lost a beloved skirt and blazer to moths that got to our clothes when they were packed away. Throw in some moth flakes — there are even some that don't smell awful. Or you can pack in cedar. Moths hate cedar.

Once your closet is sorted, you'll have more hours in the day to do what you're passionate about. No one is passionate about digging through their closet. (Okay, except for those organizer consultants who get paid to come in and do this all for you.) If you can reach in and match immediately, that's probably 15-20 minutes right there added to your day. Another great way to save time, if you have Dry Clean Only outfits, is to get a number of Stain stickers from your dry cleaning establishment. They put these stickers on stains, to be sure that an area receives extra treatment. If you have these stickers at home, you can put them on as you take a piece off, and stick them where you might have spilled a little spaghetti on your blouse, or kicked mud up the back of your trousers. Then when you take your clothes to the dry cleaner they are already marked, which saves you from trying to remember a little stain here, or spot there.

Seasonal Cycles

In going through your closet the first time, you will find stuff you just need to get rid of, and you should. However, as I mentioned, often there will be some Old Faithfuls that you think you will wear during a different season than the one in which you do your purge. Therefore, if you want to be a bit easier on yourself, separate your clothes into seasons, and keep only the current season in the front of the closet and your easiest drawers. Make sure you utilize the Turned-Around Hanger Trick. Then if, at the end of that season, you haven't worn a certain outfit, you need to pass it along. When the season changes, check each outfit for tears, stains, and the like — and be merciless. Remember: you can't fill a full cup. There is only so much room in your life for clothes, no matter what your grrlfriend with 200 pairs of shoes might think. So clear some out that are just dead energy to you — and make room for something wonderful that will be more like your new Bond Grrl energy!

Linens and Things

Sheets and Pillowcases

Are they stained? Frayed? Get rid of them! On eBay you can get high thread count, luxurious Egyptian cotton sheets and towels, if you feel like really treating yourself, without breaking the Bank. I've even seen some at Costco. In any case, sheets, pillowcases, duvet covers and the like with stains or frays *must go*. If you have a dog or cats, you might keep one old but clean flat sheet to put on top of the bed once you make it, because no matter how much you watch them, somehow "someone" always gets on the bed during the day, right? The best bet for this sheet is one where the matching fitted sheet had to go because of stains or sagging elastic. But you only need one!

I was at a friend's house the other day. Her kids are grown, so it's just her and her husband, plus they have a guest room. She was getting something out of her linen closet, and it was *stuffed* — I mean, so packed there was no room, floor to ceiling — with linens and towels! When my James and I consolidated our homes, I kept my friend's closet in mind as we went through the linens and towels. We sent all the towels that were a little frayed, the linens we didn't like, etc. to Freecycle and/or our local veterinarian. In reality, you only need three sets of linens — tops — for each bed in your house. You might really only need one set for your guest bed. For your own bed, you need one set on the bed, one in your bedroom closet, and then a spare set in your linen closet. That's it! Get the rest out of there!

If you think you might use the linens or towels for rags, you might want to think again. Sheets aren't that absorbent, and towels usually shred. As a final note that will help keep your closet tidy, keep the sheets and extra pillowcases folded into one of the matching pillowcase of the set. This way, when you pull out that bundle, it has the fitted sheet, the flat sheet, and the extra pillowcase/s already in it, good to go. No searching the closet for the second pillowcase that got mashed into the back behind some big beach towels you smooshed in.

Towels

Are your towels faded? Threads sticking out? Brad Pitt or Sean Connery or Russell Crowe or your James-of-choice knocks on your door, because his car/motorcycle/helicopter has run out of gas outside, he has been fixing it, and "Ma'am, I just wonder if I could use your restroom to wash up before heading for the Oscars? I would be immensely grateful." What's he going to find in the bathroom? Hmmmmmmmmmm?

If the towel he uses looks like it leapt out of the rag bag to drape itself over the towel rack, what's up with that?

I stick with white towels. They don't fade, and you can bleach them or spot-treat them and it nearly always works. I'm famous for cleaning my face and accidentally wiping mascara on the towels. Sure, with a white towel you see stains right away — but that means you can get it into the laundry and spot-treat it.

If your bathroom décor doesn't lend itself to white towels, I still suggest you use them. Here's how:

First, when you fold your bath towels, fold them in thirds lengthwise: one third in (long edge toward the middle), the other third over that. Then when you hang the towel, it won't have the side edge out and will look tidy.

Now, take the folded towel and fold it in half over your arm, just like you normally would drape it over a towel bar. Instead of putting the bar through that fold though, take the towel, and tuck the ends down the back of the towel rack, so the fold over your arm winds up hanging in front. This makes the towel half the length it would be if you just hung it over the towel rack like normal, and you see the tidy front fold, not the ends. Very spiffy.

Take a hand towel that matches the bathroom color, and fold IT in thirds lengthwise, so that the sides of the towel are folded in back. Now, hang that hand towel over the regular white towel you've just placed on the rack, so that it runs down the middle of the towel.

Let's say your extra bathroom is red, like mine. This means you have two white towels hanging on the towel rack, and they each have a red hand towel on top. The red matches the bathroom, and the white fades to the background. Then, you can have a small basket of rolled up red hand towels on the side of the sink. These are the ones that guests visiting during the day can use after they wash their hands, so as not to mess up the red/white towels on the rack, of course! I personally put a basket of thick rectangular-folded paper napkins in my extra bathroom next to the sink, with two rolled hand towels in the basket too, to look nice. Folks always use the napkins, but it still looks classy. And, if a friend stays overnight, he or she has a wonderful fluffy clean white towel to use, all ready to go.

Since all my towels are white, I don't worry about having a ton of regular-sized towels that I can't rotate through my house because they won't match the décor. All my body-sized towels are the same: fluffy white, or what I would call nice hotel-type towels. They actually absorb the water, too. (Ever been a guest in a house where that fluffy towel won't take the water off you? That's not your house, is it?)

So when Brad/Russell/Pierce/Sean/James stops by MY house, he can scrub up all he wants. Then again, that towel just might not make it into the laundry!

Pitching the Potions

Now that we're through with the closets and drawers, it's time to get into some of the tougher areas. Tougher than the Closet? Yes, my Baby Bond Grrl, come with me — we're clearing out other things too. Be Brave! As I'm my own guinea pig, I always remind my students that everything I suggest, I have done myself. So I know how it feels!

I am assuming that all of your makeup and potions are in your bathroom. If you have a little bit here and a little bit there — in your gym bag, in your car, under the bathroom sink, in your purse/s, consolidate it all, first. Gather up every bit of every thing that you could call makeup, or medicines, or perfume, or a lotion/potion. This includes everything from the lipstick in the console in your car, on up.

Now that you have everything, I want you to take a deep breath, because we're going to start throwing things away.

Where to start? Well, I believe that you should look at all your bath gels, lotions, toothpaste and the like for Sodium Laureth Sulfate or Sodium Laurel Sulfate. I have read a lot about this, and you can too, thanks to the magic of the Internet. SLS is a detergent used in garage floor cleaners, engine degreasers, and car-wash soaps, because it's corrosive and attacks greasy surfaces. It is also used throughout the world for clinical testing as a skin irritant; laboratories use it to irritate the skin on test animals and humans to test how effective healing agents are on that irritation. There's more, including a University of Georgia Medical College test showing that SLS penetrated into the eyes as well as organs like the brain and liver, causing damage. So is it in your gels, lotions, and toothpaste? It likely is, because it's dead cheap and one drop makes an enormous head of lather. If you are shocked to find out how many of your products have SLS (I was), you might consider a change. Use up what you have, then don't buy more. I know it's fun to walk into a bath and body shop and pick up something that smells good. But if it's linked to possible body damage and isn't great for your skin, is the smell worth it?

While you're changing your potion-buying ways, you might want to investigate whether water (or "aqueous solution of X") is the first ingredient in your current gels/lotions/potions. Water is cheap, too! It does nothing to help your skin, and certainly doesn't lock moisture in. Potions with water listed first are cheaper, because they are… full of water! It's better to spend a bit more, and get a lotion that has something like aloe as its first ingredient. If you want to think about it this way, take a cup of that expensive lotion that doesn't have water as an initial ingredient, then add, oh, a cup or three of water to it. Shake. Looks like more, right? That's basically what you're buying when you buy the water-based product. The real ingredients, plumped up and filled with water in the bottle. And water is another agent that dries your skin!

Finally, you might want to eliminate lotions that have "paraben" or "parabon" in them. This ingredient is often at the end of a long word, such as "methylparaben." This ingredient can cause severe allergies in some people, and is particularly bad for people who have undergone radiation therapy. If you have had dry scratchy skin forever and can't find the culprit, it might be a paraben-related ingredient. My own father was using a *dermatologist-prescribed* skin cream, and for years he was crazy with itching — because that product had parabon in it, and he was allergic! There's nothing sexy about dry skin. You need a cleansing and moisturizing regime and products that are easy to use, and that keep the Skin You're In happy and healthy.

I went through all my lotions, potions, gels and makeup on a day that my James was out. Okay, so I'm weak — I didn't want him to see how many of these there were in the house, the back of the drawer, et cetera! I made a huge pile; first, I pitched any item beyond its expiration date, regardless of how full it was. Then, I surveyed the rest. The Pile Method as a great eye-opener. When I went through my Pile, I found that I had face products (*e.g*, night creams, makeup removers) from a number of different vendors. I admit, I am a sucker for those "perfect skin" ads, so there I sat, surrounded by a Pile including an array of potions. The problem with being a sucker for advertising is that Cleansing Systems are meant to work together. By mixing and matching, you could actually make a chemical dump on your face, with products that aren't meant to work together. I ran my whole collection past the gal who does my facials, who is incredibly in the know. She took the bottles and ingredients and told me which not to buy again, which to replace with what, and the like. I traded being a "buy the trendy thing" grrl for having good skin until I'm 90. And let's not mention how those "Only $39.95 for 3 months" bills mount up on our impulse beauty buys off late-night TV!

So, pick one system, and just stay with it. If your Pile contains a bunch of half-used jars of cleansing creams, day creams, night moisturizers, and the like, what about doing a Spa Day where you invite your Grrlfriends over, to try out all these potions? This might feel better than just chucking them out. But whatever you do, get congruent, and use one system. If you currently use something on your face that works well, stick with it. You must cleanse your face every evening and every morning. You must use a day cream with SPF/sunscreen. The good ones (with at least 7% zinc) turned my face white or greasy; I now use one by Peter Thomas Roth, SPF 30, that doesn't, and I use a cover/base with SPF, too (*e.g*, Jane Iredale). You also should use an emollient night cream (use one with a lovely smell to it — I use one with sandalwood in it that my James adores). Then you want a body cream — if you have a lot of them in your Pile, use them up, but ultimately get it down to one. The rest of the Pile has to go.

Deep Dark Secret

I hate to wash my face. And I hate brushing my teeth, too.

Ooooooooooooh, now you know.

I try to convince myself how good it is for me to do these things — particularly washing my face each evening, after being out in the gook that is in our airborne environment. Especially on days that I have worn makeup or sunscreen. It's awful to leave that stuff on during the night.

Doesn't mean I have to like it.

I think a lot of folks like these rituals. To me, it's something I have to do every day... and I'm not so great with "have to dos."

So I've made it as painless as possible. As for the face cleaner, I finally found one I like. I like it so much, I actually sell it on Mooncrafting.com. It's a foaming facial wash that really does the job and contains only natural ingredients. I also use the matching day and night creams. In my drawer next to my sink, I have a yoga headband to put around my hairline, and a hairclip for the rest. It's all set. It takes about a minute. But I just hate it. I think it's the "hafta" part.

One trick I will share with you is that I also hate flossing, even more than taking off makeup. Because I use a daily conditioner on my hair that takes a minute to set, I keep my floss in the shower. When I put on the conditioner, I floss my teeth. By the time I'm done, it's time to take the conditioner off.

Cleanser, night cream, day cream, wrinkle cream, lip cream... we all scream for eye cream (OK, I take it back, stop whacking me (grin)). I don't want to do ANY OF IT. My facialist recently scared me sober by showing me how dry my skin was. Here's the test. Look in the mirror. Now GRIN as hard as you can — really make your cheeks go up. What happens to the skin of your cheeks right next to your nose? Do you see little lines? Is it really fat and happy there? If not, you are dehydrated, and not using the right moisturizing cream for your skin.

I know, I know, I'm also supposed to be drinking 1/2 ounce of water for each of my pounds, daily — you, too. But I don't. Confessions, Confessions. It's the "hafta" again. And I don't like going to the gym, either. So there.

I will say though, my skin looks phenomenal these days. Because I took my facialist's recommendation and started paying attention. Well, she knows me pretty well, so she phrased it as a Dare. Also, she knew I would be recommending regimes in this book, and she said I had to practice what I preached. So I promised her that for 30 days I would clean my face twice a day, morning and evening — and each time put on moisturizer. In the morning, I put on sunscreen made for facial skin. In the evening, I use a night cream, eye cream, and one specifically for lips because mine constantly crack. I put the night cream on my décolletage area too, such that it is. When I went to see her after the 30 days, she was pleased, but then did a pinch test on the skin on my upper arms — oh my. It does what the Grin Test does to your face. The skin she pinched looked dry, wrinkly, and like I'm 90. So now another part of my routine is slathering Good (not water-based) moisturizer everywhere.

But I don't hafta like it.

Make Up Your Mind

Let's talk a bit more about makeup. You need to get down to basics. Personally, I bit the bullet and moved over to a makeup system that my facialist recommended to me. It's pricey, but now I only use my day cream (with SPF), this base powder (mineral-based, no chemicals), and then a matching blusher. Then I have a long-wear lipstick (L'Oreal has one that is quite amazing in how long it lasts), a compact with 3 different eye shadows that work with my green eyes, mascara, and application brushes. All of these are in one satchel, which also contains a toothbrush and travel toothpaste, my perfume, deodorant, travel hairspray, day and night crèmes, face cleanser, and the like.

I bring the satchel with me to the gym, and of course use it at home, where I put it under the sink. No James likes coming into a bathroom full of your lotions and potions; besides, this way you're prepared to just snatch up your satchel and go to Paris!

You might be surprised that my cleanser and day and night creams are in my satchel. The idea here is that you should not be buying the economy size of anything any more. Sure, you saved a buck or two by buying the 52 oz. size. But all of these products are sensitive to air. They start to go bad the second you open them. Besides, air carriers now won't let you on board with the bigger sizes, and you want to be pared down enough that you don't need to check a bag. And, by having satchel-sized items, you can move onto another system if you feel like it, without winding up with another big pile of partially-used bottles on your bathroom floor!

Nail Polish

One item we all hold onto for way too long is nail polish. You should stick with just two, maybe three, classic colors like red, camel, and pink. If you budget in a professional manicure/pedicure once a quarter or so as a treat for your Bond Grrl self, buy the small-bottle versions of the polish used by your manicurist. It's a little pricier per ounce, but will make it easier to do touch-ups when you're home. Get ruthless — this stuff is just paint and varnish, and it doesn't last forever. After purging (while listening to fierce Tunes to drown out my gremlin voice decrying the money I'd wasted), I am now down to one pale pink, one red that my James loves, and one beige, plus a nail strengthener. That's it.

Cosmetic Procedures

The hardest part is that you're going to throw away some perfectly good items. If you really have an issue with this, make two bags for the items you're not putting back in your drawers: one you'll chuck now, mark the other with a date three months from now. Alternatively, you can have a throw away bag, and a Grab Bag for your grrlfriends, or your grrlfriends' daughters that do dress-up.

If you go the Three Month Bag route, throw into that bag all the makeup, perfume, lotions and potions that you don't really use, but can't bear to part with right this second. Staple the bag closed. If you haven't used them three months from now, out they go. No peeking. If you really do need something from that bag, get it out quickly, and then re-staple the bag. No, you don't get to increase the date! Be strong. If you decide, instead, to have a "Grab Bag" for your grrlfriends, we will discuss that a bit more, below.

This sorting exercise will take a while, but it's worth it. You need to have totally emptied every single drawer, the space under the sink, and the like, so that you have every med, lotion, potion, and such in one big pile. Even the stuff that's in the shower. And yes, I did say every purse, coat pocket, your car, and the rest. Make sure you open zippered pockets — I often find a lipstick or two in them!

Once you've sorted everything into categories and pitched outdated stuff, if you're like me (ahem), you will discover that you have a Fear Factor when it comes to being without some item or another. You might have three bottles of hairspray, or shaving cream, or body lotion, because you pick one up every time you're at the drugstore. Take a good long look, and realize how much money this represents. Silly, huh?

Let me give you my personal example. When I did this exercise, to my horror, I discovered I had not one, not two, but FIVE cans of shaving cream/gel. How did that happen?? Four of them had never been used! I put them in my Give Away/Grab Bag pile. You might find that you have a zillion lipsticks or eyeliners or eye shadows that you were given as promos when you bought your makeup at a department store. Whatever it is, now's the time to be brutal. Pitch it into a Give Away, Throw Away, or Three Month Bag pile.

I particularly like the Grab Bag idea, whereas other students like the Three-Month Bag idea more. (Perhaps it's just a matter of how many grrlfriends you have that would be into this sort of thing.) If something hasn't been used at all, it's perfect Grab Bag material. If it's been used a few times but you know in your heart of hearts that it really isn't You, either throw it away, or throw it into your Three Month Bag if you can't pitch it today. If anything like mascara or sun lotion is three months old or older, you shouldn't be using it, so put a note on your grocery list to replace it, then pitch it. The chemicals break down over time — you don't want to be putting something toxic on your body or on your EYES! Think of all the bacteria that you're pumping into that tube each time you use it. Eee-yuck. And next time you buy mascara, sunscreen or the like, take a laundry marker and date it right on the tube. No more wondering when to pitch it, or conning yourself into believing it's newer than it is.

My Kingdom for Some Hairspray

[From my BondGrrl Blog]

You know, sometimes I crack myself up. Here I am, blogging away at what I actually do believe with regards to looking good, "You never know who you will meet on the street," and all that jazz. And then TODAY, there I am, out in public, slumming around in a shirt that makes me look bony, jeans in an unflattering cut, my hair pulled back, and no makeup. To top it off, a friend called me to come pick something up at his office, so I drove by and there I am, meeting and greeting, looking like something the cat dragged in.

WHAT was I THINKING??

I think we all go through these "I just don't care" days. The funny part about this is, I had also made a date with a friend-of-a-friend, who just moved here from Toronto and is interested in taking some of my seminars. So we're going to go out for cocktails and get to know one another better, since she wants to understand what Unleashing Her Inner Bond Grrl might entail.

She is driving to meet me in my town and said that she'd call me when she was about halfway here. So I just busily puttered about my house waiting for the call, thinking about the book that I'd like to write some day.

In doing that thinking, I thunk, "Um, perhaps we should practice what we preach, Bond Grrl?" SO, I put on some makeup, off with the unflattering shirt, on with a turtleneck and a blue blazer. Put the hair down and brushed it out. (Hence the "hairspray" title — I used the rest of my little travel bottle the other day and hadn't gotten around to replacing it.) So HOW LONG DID THIS TAKE? I timed it, because I was curious. Less than three minutes.

I look immensely — LIGHT YEARS — better. And I FEEL better. So I sat down to blog about it, and here I am.

We all need to remember this. I've made it easy on myself by going through all my makeup, and I having my satchel ready to go. (OK, except the hair spray.) My clothes are arranged in my closet, so I could grab and go. Voilà!

I still have on the jeans — magically transformed by the long turtleneck bottom and longer blazer. And, after taking one more critical look, I pitched the unflattering shirt into the Grab Bag For Friends I keep in the corner of my closet.

I am absent-minded about my appearance — which actually makes me the perfect person to write a book about this stuff. I have NEVER been one to pay that much attention. In fact, I remember in high school, my mother implored me to "just try" some colored blush/lotion on my cheeks, and a little mascara on my blonde eyelashes. It had never occurred to me, and it did look nice.

I realize that paring down might be harder for those who LOVE makeup/primping/etc. Because if *I* had a *medicine cabinet* full of different lotions and potions, you grrls who love the stuff must have a whole *bathroom* full. If you are one of these grrls, all I can say is: Be Brave. And remember that it's all full of chemicals, and by and large if a product is more than six months old (more like three for things like mascara), you shouldn't be putting it on your very very delicate facial skin.

So, here I am, blogging, waiting for that gal to call. And shaking my head at myself, and how easy it is (and how easy to forget how easy it is!) to just take a LITTLE effort and have BIG results.

Maybe I'll just leave early, and buy the hairspray...

Figure out whether you're really going to be able to use all of the items in the Keep pile, once everything is sorted. I will give you another personal example. I also wound up with about four bottles of body lotion, but I use body lotion or oil every day (and so should you). I knew that I would go through those lotions; I just had to know exactly where they were — and not to buy any more! On the flip side, if you know, as I did with the shaving cream, that there is no way you're going to use an item, put it in your Grab Bag pile. You can even give unused items to charity, such as your local homeless shelter. They are always on the lookout for things like razors, soap, shampoo, shaving cream, and the like. Although I haven't tried it, I bet they (or a charity like Image For Success or one for battered women) would also love your unused makeup and cosmetics.

Again, I can't emphasize enough that you should take a good long look at this stuff — because if you, like just about everyone else in America, are in a financial pinch — well, here is an example of good money that's just gone down the drain (or at least, sits in the cabinet underneath it!) Realize that it's time to be serious, Bond Grrl. Then away it goes.

Is That a Black Purse, or a Black Hole?

Since we've been in your purse to clean out the potions, we might as well get it all done.

Paul Kyriazi, in his book *How To Live The James Bond Lifestyle*, recommends that would-be Bonds keep a money clip with cash separate from their wallets. More importantly, he believes you need a specific attitude toward spending and actually handling money in order to be 007 material. Similarly, Bond grrls Plan to Shop — they don't Shop to Play. Stop shopping impulsively; stay out of stores in Emotional Moments. And as a corollary to Kyriazi's money clip and wallet, Bond Grrls shouldn't have purses packed like they are going to Annapurna for a month.

If you are carrying a ton of stuff with you, tell me — Why? It's dragging down your side; it's wrecking your posture. Carrying a heavy purse or (Heaven forbid!) a backpack rumples up your clothes, messes with your spine, and makes you more of a mugging target than a Bond Grrl!

Is your purse a black hole, containing everything for every eventuality? In the movies, Bond Girls very rarely even carry purses. You should be carrying a purse that's as small as possible.

So, what do you REALLY need in your purse? I think that we often wind up planning for every contingency for us, our kids, our man, the woman on the subway... but in reality, we seldom use the things we carry. How many of you have pulled that nasty, unwrapped, bent tampon out of the bottom of your purse saying "ohhhh, now THAT would be pleasant to use!" Your purse has to be minimalist. It should just have the bare essentials in it. What's that? This is what I suggest:

1. *I.D. and Money.* Get rid of the giant wallet with all the credit cards, coin purse, photos of your kids, etc. Yes, I mean it. You should carry one, possibly two, credit cards, your driver's license, your health insurance card and AAA card if you have one, and then neatly folded paper money in a man's-wallet-type holder. Suze Orman goes further and says you need to really respect that folded paper money — it should be folded, all facing one direction, and sorted by denomination. Smushed-up bills in the bottom of your purse with cookie crumbs on them show your lack of respect for that money. If you have Safeway scan cards, your gym card, and the like, keep those in your car, or, for a gym card, for example, in your gym bag. Only things you use every day in the wallet.

2. *No Change.* Are you carrying around a ton of change? If you pay for items with cash, pushing around for exact change just annoys the people behind you in line, and has a penny-pinching air to it. Leave pennies on the counter for the next person who's a little short, especially if they have a Give One Get One saucer by the cash register. Take the rest of your change and keep it in your car ashtray if (like me) you are constantly using parking meters. If not, bring it home and keep it in a dream jar. You'd be amazed how quickly that jar fills up. Out of this "extra" money, pay for little treats like a fragrant bar of soap for you, or a cute card to slip in your James' briefcase or lunchbox. Or, for a small fee, you can put this money through a coin counter at the bank and then put it in your bank account. The idea here is to avoid being the penny-pinching Exact Change Woman at the grocery store. Put that money somewhere that it can add up to Something.

3. *Keys, Lipstick, & Other Little Things.* Your purse could also contain one lipstick (yes, one), a working pen, a small notebook/PDA, a few business cards, your cell phone, a travel-encased pantyliner, a small vial of re-wetting fluid if you wear contacts. That's it. As for keys, I actually only have my car key in my purse. I keep the rest on a ring that stays in my car ashtray. If my purse were to be stolen, the thief doesn't immediately have my home address (from my driver's license), and my house key. This happened to a friend of mine — she got cleaned out before she

could even get home! I learned her lesson! What else could be in your purse? Maybe a comb, though you should NEVER be combing your hair or putting on lipstick in public. What else is in your black hole purse? If it's something you use every single day — keep it. If not, put it in the glove box in your car. (Have you cleaned that out yet?) If you have a cold, you might put a travel pack of Kleenex in there — but not all the time. Same with an extra tampon. The idea is to packhorse as little as you can, because the less you carry in your purse, the more sophisticated you look, and the better it is for your back.

What's my "purse" like? It's a little red leather wallet/business card holder cross-over, on a key ring so that I can clip my car keys to it. In it, I have my driver's license, medical insurance card, AAA card and transit Fastpass in the see-through window on the back, then inside I have the credit cards I use (two related to my businesses and one personal), my debit card, a few business cards, and folded paper money. And that's all I carry. (NOTE: My driver's license is *not* on top in the see-through window; I would rather folks not immediately be able to see where I live.) It's not stuffed, so if I need to go to the library, I can put my library card in there from the car. I have a BlackBerry, which is a phone/PDA combo I clip to my belt, or to the key ring if I'm wearing a dress. Now that I've started using a long-wearing lip stain, I don't even carry lipstick.

As an aside, it's important not to have anything (*e.g.*, this wallet, or a big ring of keys) hanging from your car ignition when you are driving, as it pulls on the ignition and can damage it. That's why my car key clips off separately, and so should yours.

So, that's it. If I'm going somewhere that I need to look a bit more professional, I just put my wallet into either a brown or a black purse, and away I go. As I mentioned, all the other cards I might need such as my Costco card, Safeway card, library card, and the like are in my car, in a zipped bag in my glove box. If I'm going out shopping, I am not going out on a whim (that's how you get in trouble!). So I can get the cards I'm going to need out of that zipped bag, and slip them into my wallet on my way out.

 ## *'Sleek and Prepared'*

I walked into an interview the other day with my car key, a credit card, my driver's license, and $20, all in my suit jacket pocket. Oh, and a pen, and of course my BlackBerry discretely clipped to the back of my waistband, under the jacket. The rest I locked in my car. The interviewer was amazed. It made a huge impression. She even mentioned it to my next interviewer, pointing out how "sleek and prepared" I was, and how I "didn't even carry a purse." Did I get the job? Yes, I did. Was it because of this? Well, I don't know — but I don't think it hurt!

Clean Off Your Desk

If you work in an office, when you go to work on the first day of your week and look at your desk, what do you see? Is it neat and tidy? Is it a train wreck? Are there lots of personal mementos? If you were to up and move to Paris (or, Heaven forbid, were fired), how long would it take to clear up and clear out?

What does your desk say about you? You want it to say that you're efficient, not too emotional, and that you are there to get the job done. You want your personal life to remain somewhat of a mystery. Is there a reason that you have a ton of photos and little sayings and knick-knacks all around your office or cubicle? Do you really need to see all the mementos, tchotchkes, photos and the like to remember what your life is about? Do you put stuff up so that folks will ask you questions about it? This is silent bragging and begging for attention. You should be living your Life and not working yourself to death — so you don't need all those mementos around, right?

I use the same Feng Shui principles that I use in my house for my desk. If you have a small symbol that represents Abundance for you, put that in the back left corner of your desk. A picture of you and your James could go in the back right, representative of Romance. Tokens of recognition and accomplishment go right in front of you, which is the Reputation quadrant. But sparingly.

I have personally learned the hard way that the best thing you can do is to keep your desk tidy and impersonal, because Your Job Is Not Your Life. You should be living your life every second that you're not at work. You want to be able to scoop your belongings into a box easily, and jet if you so desire. In my case, a company that I worked for (where my job was my life) decided to downsize a ton of us without our having wind of it beforehand — so there I was, packing it all up, feeling my "Life" was over. I had a large office, and it took hours and hours. And hours and hours and hours. At another job, a gal was "escorted out" after she sassed her boss one too many times, and then all her emails, her desk, her drawers, and the like were gone through by others. Sure, they packed up her personal stuff and shipped it to her, but in the meantime, they sure commented on the shape of what was left behind! You don't want folks at work to know too much about you. You want to keep your personal life and your work life separate, and your work life spare and organized, whether it's in email, your desk drawers, or the like.

Put forward an organized and streamlined front. A desk that shows efficiency, cleanliness, and some mystery helps separate you from the Gossip Machine. Of course, you might still become a part of it, but only because you are a Mystery. Better than the alternative!

In sum, you want to only have as much stuff as you can manage well. So on your desk, anything that you're dealing with right at this instant should be out in the open. If you're not dealing with it right this instant, or don't use it every day, it should not be out. Things that you use every now and again — say, your tape — belong in a drawer.

If you are a Sticky Note Fanatic, do you have notes stuck on the edge of your computer screen that you haven't looked at in a while — or that you write and then forget? Another mission for you, while you are cleaning out and streamlining your life this week, is to find a little black book, and a pen that you really like to write with. A little black book is very Bond Grrl. Your local bookstore or even drugstore will have lots of options. After you have it, stick those notes into it instead of all over your cubicle or computer. If a thought comes to you, jot it down in your little black book. And if you have a picture of an Aston Martin up in your cubicle as a goal, why not put that in your little black book instead?

Clean Out Your Car

If you saw your favorite heartthrob on the side of the road and he flagged you down for a ride, what would he find when he opened the car door? Fritos bags? McD's wrappers? Shoes? Even if your car isn't spotless, it should be uncluttered. While it might not have been detailed in a while, empty Fritos wrappers or smelly socks is a whole 'nother issue!

Clutter — bad. Preparedness — good.

I live in California — so Earthquake Preparedness is a constant. These days, though, being prepared seems to be a watchword in the entire United States, if not the world. What does "prepared" mean? Well, as an example, you should never let your gas tank get below half full. Because let's say that you're on "E" and then — BLAM! — earthquake. All the stations are taken out. You are in trouble! If you still had half a tank, you could choose when to use the car, or when to walk, at least for a while. Without that choice — you'd better blow up the tires on your bike!

And speaking of Earthquake Preparedness, everyone needs some sort of Preparedness Kit in their car, at work, and at home. Even if you think you are totally safe, you probably aren't. I heard the other day that the biggest and most dangerous fault line outside of California is the New Madrid Fault System, which runs through Missouri, Illinois, and three other states. Yes — St. Louis, potential devastating Earthquake city! Surprised?

You can buy preparedness packs all made up for you. There are lots of lists on websites if you'd like to put your own together — and at least here in San Francisco, you can purchase a Preparedness Kit at your local K-Mart or Costco. Are you ready? If you're not ready — are you really a Bond Grrl?

Week Two: Peeling Off

So, you've cleaned out your closets, drawers, purse, desk, and the like. Don't fill them all back up at once! Remember, when it comes to clothes, a Bond Grrl generally looks classic and stylish, which might mean a black suit with a colorful scarf or a signature piece of jewelry. You don't need much, but you do need quality. If you decide to slowly replace items, spend your money wisely. For example, as I mentioned before, you can find Armani discounted on eBay. Remember, a Bond Grrl is not made of money; she is a Working Girl. Bond wears his expensive suits because he is paid to have them. His gadgets are also supplied. The Bond Girls by and large are laypeople that just got caught up in the story. So as a Bond Grrl, you need to be congruent in yourself, your life, your style. And remember — you don't have a government expense account! While Bond masquerades as various characters, in general, the Bond Girls are who they are; they don't need to have characters or costumes, or flash and bling. They're classy and classic.

So, you've gone through everything. Now you get to have some fun. Throw out all the broken, stained, spoiled, or unusable items. Then gather up everything that's still good (even the stuff you're considering giving to Charity), and put it in a pile in the living room.

Invite some of your Grrls over for a Peeling Off The Extra Layers of Me party. Make them bring some shopping bags, a bottle of wine, some appetizers. Then explain to them that the things in the middle of the floor are all theirs for the taking. Stand back from the squeals and stampede!

That is your Week Two assignment: Get rid of everything that is not put away, after your Week One assignment! Of course, you don't have to wait until Week Two to have your Grab Bag party. You can do it sooner, and then rest during Week Two and admire your clean, de-cluttered Life!

If there is anything in a Grab Bag that one of your Grrls gave to you, tell her ahead of time that you loved it, but that you need to make some room in your life, and you would love it if she would like to have it in her life since she was kind enough to buy it for you. The funniest part is how often the giver gets a pout on 'cause you're giving away that Thing, but then she doesn't want it, either!

At your party, your Grrls can take anything. The rest is going to Charity. Have fun!

A variation on the Peeling Off Party theme is to have an evening with Grrlfriends where you all bring things (especially clothes) that you are still attached to and don't quite want to part with — and swap. Throw everything in the middle of the room, go around and let each person pick one thing and then another and another, like one of those Christmas gift Secret Santa/stealing games. But don't take anything from that Pile that doesn't fit your inner Bond Grrl! Be strong! Have fun, but be discriminating!

Everyone has to swear that anything left over will be given to Charity, or will be listed on Freecycle.org. One of your Grrls might even know someone who would be immensely excited to send these clothes off to her family in El Salvador, or members of her church in a less fortunate area.

 Cast-Off Casting Call

I have certainly been on the receiving end of Hand-Me Downs. I love it. One Grrl's castoffs are another Grrl's treasure. The reluctance to pitch clothes, share, or create external congruency that I have seen in dozens of clients doesn't seem to revolve around an inability to afford to replace clothing. It's usually either due to (a) memories tied up in the clothing they know they need to pitch; or (b) a subconscious stubborn belief that their raggedy-wristed clothing should be Just Fine. Instead of trying to be fashionable or classic, these women believe that others should Want them for what's Inside, doggone it! They wear their dowdiness and frumpiness as a badge of honor. The clients I have had that fall into this category are invariably successful, and/or wealthy. It's odd. They dress down their success/wealth with fat bodies, or unfashionable clothes.

But you know what? That's not really how it works. I think it was Will Rogers who said "You never get a second chance to make a first impression." So if you're in outdated, droopy-drawers, or threadbare togs that don't suit you, sorry to say, but you will be judged on that, first. Not on your awesome Inner Bond Grrl.

Give, Give, Give

As I mentioned, I gave most of my suits/work clothes to Image For Success, a non-profit organization that collects clean, gently used clothing, and distributes it to women who are coming in off the streets, trying to make a fresh start. There is nothing in your life that can be more uplifting — I promise — than giving to others less fortunate than yourself.

Image For Success's last newsletter was immensely inspiring. It contained a letter written by a Grrl who lived in her car. It detailed how she has turned her life around, gotten off drugs — but still needed to get a job, to get out of that car. She explained how hard it was to stay clean, pressed, neat, etc. when everything you own is basically in the back seat.

She said that the first time she came to Image For Success, the volunteers "made her feel like a queen." They had her sit down, then took out business suits, dresses, and shoes, and gave her the ones they thought suited her best to try on. She said it was like being a model in a fashion show. The letter was totally from the heart. The editorial follow up was that she had gotten a job, and was now saving on a security deposit for an apartment. She credits it all to Image For Success. This is the sort of thing that keeps me searching through my closets, being ruthless, and giving.

A while ago, I gave something really good away (by accident) to Goodwill. I went to their sorting facility to try to get it back. Clothing was all over the floor. It was being put into rag bags by the ton. It made me feel sick and upset. It made me sicker that somehow the beloved item I had accidentally given away had wound up there... never to be found. After this experience, I have sought out smaller enterprises like Image For Success, my local Cancer Society or Aid For Battered Women, or The Princess Project, which takes gently used black tie or dress-up clothing, and gives it to underprivileged girls for their proms.

Though places like these can't take used makeup and toiletries, they do sometimes take unused makeup, such as unopened samples. All you need to do is ask.

So now's the time. Give it up — and Give It. If you won't do it for yourself, do it for women like the one mentioned above. Get up right now and Let Your Fingers Do the Walking, as that old ad used to say. Do you have a place like Image for Success, or a Hospice (especially good for magazines/books/sweats/etc.), Princess Project, or the like in your area? I know that you do. Call them up, and find out if they have a pick-up coming near you or a depot where you can take your stuff. I had a bad experience with Goodwill, and so I can't recommend them, but if you check out their sorting facility and it looks good to you, then that's another possibility. Make sure you feel good about where your stuff is going, because it will fuel your cleaning.

Though these charities might tell you that the clothes have to be in fashion, I have found that they don't really mean it. If you have a business suit and it's dry cleaned and in the dry cleaner bag, believe me, they will take it. Put a little polish on the shoes you're bringing in: they will take them even if they have some cuts in them. Do it for our less fortunate Bond Grrl Sistahs — help them get to it and unleash their Grrls, too.

A Place for Everything

In sum, there are veterinarians and humane societies looking for socks with holes in them, to ball up as cat toys. Abused Women's Services, Hospice and the Cancer Society are looking for clothes, books, magazines, and housewares. The Princess Project is looking for formals. These will all give you a tax deduction for your efforts. Or you could eBay your items (or take them to a company that will eBay them for you), then pay down your debt, or save for a trip. Or you could give your cast-offs to friends or Freecycle.org, where "new friends" will come and pick them up at your house, and thank you for your generosity in person!

Then, don't collect any more. If they want to give you a sample pack at a makeup counter, go through it and assess immediately whether you will use what's in there to replace something you already have and are going to throw out. Otherwise, either don't take it, or give it away to a homeless woman or to girls that like to play Dress Up.

A little while ago, I gave away the airplane travel packs I got when I flew on Business, to some homeless guys. They looked pretty darned surprised — and delighted. Wonder which of them is using the Lavender Eau De Cologne and which is wearing the Virgin Atlantic footie warmer socks?

 ### *Clothing Scrapbooks*

When I first went through my clothes to decide what suited my Inner Bond Grrl and what did not, I had a terrible time giving away what in my mind were perfectly good clothes, even if they were obviously dated or I hadn't worn them in a while. Why? Because I had memories attached to these clothes. If this sounds like you, read on. My ever-suffering James came up with a fun idea: he said that I could put on all the clothes one at a time, and he would take a picture of me in them. Then, I could have a scrapbook of the photos to look at when I wanted. But I would have shelves and racks of space, because the clothes themselves would be gone.

I have also suggested this to folks who have lost a loved one and can't get rid of their possessions. Often their lives have stalled, and they can't move on with all the reminders around them. A friend, who is a closet organizer, helped a man who had lost his wife by helping him make a scrapbook containing bits of his wife's things: logos cut from beloved T-shirts, stuff she loved, and the like. Then my friend took care of giving the rest away. Going through the process helped the widower to move on.

You know what? After my James suggested that I take photos of myself in the clothes, I was actually able to give those clothes away, and didn't do the photos. Because I realized that holding onto photos of clothes that held memories was just a wee bit attenuated. But it was a great and thoughtful idea from my James, and so I pass it on to you if it sounds good to you. I decided that if I couldn't remember the memory without seeing the dress, well, maybe it's a memory that's not that important anyway!

Travel Light

A Bond Girl is all about attitude. The only essential Gadgets a Bond Girl has are an open mind, and the ability to realize that her essentiality to Bond revolves around supporting his mission. Again — she has Her Life: Bond has a little knowledge about a lot of things; she has deep knowledge about a few things. As a Bond Grrl, the fewer Gadgets in your purse, desk, car, etc., as well as the fewer attachments, schedules, and commitments that you have, the easier it will be to go to Paris if your James (or your own heart!) says, "It's time, let's go."

Passport To Success

One of the best ways to feel like an International Traveler (even if the farthest you've been is to the next town!), is to get a passport. Unlike a driver's license, a passport has an aura of daring and mystery to it, because its only use is for Travel. For those of you who are just learning to exercise/eat right/etc., that passport picture can be an awesome Goal for externalizing your inner Bond Grrl. When you feel weak-willed, just remember — passports last for a very long time, and you want to look your best in your passport photo! In fact, once you have gotten yourself looking more like your Inner Bond Grrl than a sack of potatoes, you can get your hair styled, go to a department store and get your makeup done for free, put on a fabulous top, and go on down to get that photo taken. Because every Bond Grrl needs to be able to leave her home country, right?

We will start setting Goals in earnest in the next Chapter, but for now, how about jotting down "Get Passport" as a goal in your little black book?

Are You Prepared for Paris?

Your James comes up to you, with that twinkle in his eyes that you love. What's up? He has somehow won a trip to Paris, and you're off in an hour! Or — it's Oprah's Dream Bus!

So, you goin'?

Before you say "Gee, that sounds great, but..." I want you to think about it — to think about your life.

What is cluttering up your life so that you can't go? Whether it's just too many commitments, no one to feed the dog, or not knowing what you could throw into a carry-on in 10 minutes, I want you to take a good long look at your life and how you fit into it. Because all those things and commitments are just bricks dragging you down. And as such, you become a big brick, dragging down your James' flights of fancy. Ouch! Hurts, huh? But is that you?

One of the most important things in your life, as a Bond Grrl, is your relationship to your James. Sure, you're also running your Circus, or your Flying Air Show, or reading the encyclopedia starting at A, like Honey Ryder in *Dr. No*, but you need to be ready to go do those fun things that your James is going to dream up (especially if he reads Paul Kyriazi's book). If it's time for an adventure, you should not be bogged down with cleaning up the elephant dung at your Circus or finding someone else to fly your place in formation! That needs to be taken care of beforehand, so you can easily say, "Let's DO it!"

Getting Ready to Go

Though scheduling hiccups are unavoidable, it's time to do some serious decluttering of your Time and your Life. As the Boy Scouts might say, it's time to Be Prepared. I have a few suggestions, but this really is something that you need to take time to think about personally. Because if you are prepared to be whisked away to Paris or just an overnight in the next town, it's more likely that you will be!

If you have young kids and don't have a contingency sleep over trading plan with other parents or close grandparents, some of this might seem impossible to you. But in actuality, you can either (a) get your kids to have the same sort of adventurous sense and ability to pick up and go (so the family goes to Paris!), or (b) start thinking about making those sleep over arrangements with friends, so you're prepared for later.

Around the house, there are some things that you will need to have organized, too. It might take a while, but will be well worth the effort. All I'm really recommending here is to get some things done that are on your List (I know they are, because they were always on mine!), but which you haven't made a priority. The more things you get checked off on your List, the more prepared you will be, and the more likely it is that you'll get whisked away. Honest. I truly believe that if you start focusing your efforts in a fun direction, even daydreaming about how all the preparation is leading towards that great adventurous eventuality, you draw it closer and closer toward you.

So go room to room in your living areas and outside, and see what would need to be taken care of if you were to be whisked away. Some things can take care of themselves for up to 4 days — some need care every day. Some examples might be:

1. *Plants.* Put all your plants — including plants that you have on your porch — on a self-watering system or timer. These are available at stores like Home Depot, and with a bit of effort you can set up a system that will keep you from having to water your plants constantly by hand. I realize that this might mean laying out some money or, if you're not that handy, negotiating a bit with your James to get it done. Remember — I said *negotiating*. This means that you need to give up an equal amount of energy specifically aimed at pleasing your James, for the amount of energy that he's going to be expending on this task! What you're ultimately doing here is making it easier to spend hassle-free time together. The time you spend each week watering and worrying about plants can now be spent on other things. There are also systems for indoor plants; fancy ones, or simple ones that incorporate a liter pop bottle that you fill with water and screw into a drip system for the roots.

2. *Animals.* Cats, in general, can be left for about 3-4 days if you have a big enough cat box, a self-feeder, and a self-waterer with clean water. Dogs are harder. You will need to have a boarding facility ready to go, or a dog walker/pet sitter already interviewed. The key here is to actually be ready. Your James shows up, eyes twinkling, and says "Darling, you're not going to believe this, but we're leaving for Paris in an hour! Scoot — pack!" or he says, "Just grab your passport; I will buy you everything you need when we get there!" Are you suddenly trying to figure out how to care for Spot and Fluffy, or is there a number at your fingertips?

3. *Light Timers.* I have two lights that remain on light timers at all times: one upstairs, one downstairs, on a randomized schedule. That way these lights come on and off while we're home — but also when we're not. I don't have to worry about setting them if I get whisked away. They're all set.

4. *Mail/Newspapers.* Have a form filled out and ready, under a magnet on the fridge, that will tell the post office to hold your mail until you get home. They have these forms at the post office. You should also have the number of your newspaper service to be able to tell them to hold the paper. Just going to the post office to get a few of these forms and filling them out to be Ready is going to make you smile. Don't put the dates in — you won't know when that Paris weekend is coming up, but when it does, you're set! Just drop the notification in your mailbox on the way to the airport.

5. *Music.* If you and your James have special music that you love to Love to, get another copy of that CD and keep it in your carry-on luggage, or make sure it's in a Playlist on your MP3 player. Then, have the cable that will attach the MP3 player to a CD player or travel speakers, plus all the other accoutrements, stored perpetually in your suitcase.

Your James will be amazed when you have Your Music right at your fingertips. What a Bond Grrl you are! The same goes for items such as any lubricant or Fun Things you might love to use. Keep a travel-sized spare in your travel bag.

Packing

We've already been through your closet and liberated you from clothing that doesn't fit your Bond Grrl persona. When I did this exercise, I also got rid of clothes that wrinkled easily. When you are packing for Paris (if your James doesn't just say "I will buy it all new for you there"), choose whether you're going to go with the Black-based clothes, or the Brown or Navy-based clothes. Once you choose, that's what it's going to be. No mixing and matching. I know it's hard: you want to bring This jacket but also That pair of slacks. But that means double the shoes, Grrls. And that's always where we get in trouble. If I'm going for my Brown-based clothes (which include a lot of orange), I am not going to bring my fabulous red shirt as well. It goes with Black, not Brown. And I also know this means I'm bringing my brown overcoat or raincoat, not the black one.

Think about style — and be ruthless. You know what works best for you. The key is to start with that Black or Brown base, and stick with it — so that you only have the black or brown coat, and then walking shoes and dressy shoes, in the base color. If you mix, you're suddenly checking bags instead of waltzing through the check-free line, your luggage could get lost, you will be schlumping a ton of stuff (or worse, making your James do it), and all that un-Bond-Grrl jazz.

The 'Gym Bag'

Remember when you accomplished getting all of your lotions, potions, and makeup down to one satchel? This is what I call my gym bag, because it contains everything I might need to go to the gym, travel, etc. Mine is a small ripstop bag, about the size of a medium-sized purse. I got it at Target about three years ago, and it's still in great shape. It contains spare contacts, a tampon, small body lotion, deodorant, small brush, hairspray, blah blah. Everything, of course, in the size that is allowed on the plane, with a rolled up zip-top freezer bag in there too, so I can dump everything into it, to get it through the airport scanner. I have another little satchel about the size of an eyeglasses case that has my makeup in it: base, powder, blush, eye shadow, lip moisturizer, mascara, etc. Together, these take up maybe seven inches by five. Very easy. Very portable.

I suggest you make up a Toiletries Essentials kit like this, and use it at all times. You probably still have some lotions and potions that are special and that you use when you want to feel luxurious, such as a protein pack for your hair, or a deep cleansing mask or bath bubbles. But your Toiletries Kit should be set up so that you are completely ready to get up and go at a moment's notice. Think of how much storage room you will have in your bathroom alone! This kit should contain:

a. Your makeup. It should also contain your makeup remover (towelettes are fantastic and easy to pack), travel-sized moisturizers, and a small sunscreen for your face.

b. A travel-sized hairspray, conditioner, shampoo, shower gel, brush, hair ties. If you use these at the gym, be sure that you fill them up at least once a week, on a set day. You want that bag to always be close to 100% ready. Paris? Paris!

c. Contact lens fluid and container, plus an extra pair of lenses. When you get a travel version of your contact lens fluid, it's important to know how many days a full bottle lasts, and to keep the bottle that you have in your satchel full, or have a full one that you can quickly switch out to. I bought a travel size, then put marks on it each day I used it until it was gone, to find out how many days it lasted. You'd be amazed at how long travel sizes last! I would suggest you do this test on all of your travel-sized items, to really assure yourself that they will last you for however many days you need. (Shampoo, conditioner, shower gel, etc.) Those bottles always look so little, but they contain a surprising number of days' worth of product.

d. Eyeglasses.

e. All your prescription medications. If there aren't many, you can keep these in your makeup satchel at all times — this is what I do. If there are a number of them, make a list of what you need every day, and keep the list in your satchel, so you don't forget anything.

f. Deodorant.

g. Two tampons and travel-pack pantyliners. You can purchase feminine essentials at just about any airport, and certainly in Paris. Just be ready to take care of yourself for about a day. You can also fill a Ziploc with about a week's worth of feminine essentials and keep it in your carryon suitcase at all times — this is what I do. (I also keep a swimsuit in there, as this is exactly the sort of thing I tend to forget.) If you have a long flight, using a couple of pantyliners during the trip can also keep you feeling a bit more fresh. I don't know about you, but sitting for ten hours in a polyester seat in the same clothes is not my idea of fun. You can also tuck a few of those feminine cleanliness wipes in your purse, if you have a super-long international flight.

h. You also might want to put in a few small Woolite® packs — the travel packs, not the small bottles — so you can wash out undies if you will be gone for longer than a week. If shorter, live a little: bring laundry home!

Bond Grrl Honeymoon

When my James and I went on our honeymoon, I had a test of my Bond Grrl-ness and preparation at the start!

For the entire week before we left, my James had been telling me that our plane left "around 1:30." Silly me, I didn't check. For us, this means catching a taxi, then Airporter bus, to get to the airport on time: backing that time up equals leaving the house around 10-ish. No worries. I was involved with planning the wedding, and figured I could just get things ready to go the day we left, by getting up a little early.

So the day we were to take off, we got up early — a little before 7:00 — to have a relaxed breakfast and then pack. My James did a leisurely check on our reservations... and discovered that the plane left at 11:00.

YIKES!

So, there we were, and suddenly (before a cup of coffee, even!) we had to get in gear to catch the 7:30 Airporter — not the 10:00 one. My James said, laughing, "Well, I guess this is going to put the 'quick trip to Paris' part of your book to a test, hmmmm?"

Sure, I should have been packed beforehand. I actually had known we were going on a three-week trip for months! But my James was right: this would be a Trial By Fire of my Paris Packing System.

I have lists on my computer for all the basic things that should go on a trip that I might forget, like the cord connecting the iPod to the speakers (the speakers live in the suitcase, of course), cell phone chargers, and our sunglasses from the car. But we didn't even have time to print one out. We had to fly.

I immediately decided to go with my Black-based clothing. First, I threw into the bottom of the suitcase black loafers to walk in, black sandals (strappy, can be dressed up or down, and also easy to walk in), and some black pumps. Next went in three small zippered bags. Two were the Makeup and Gym/Travel Toiletries Bag I've mentioned before (the latter containing deodorant, shampoo, meds, conditioner, feminine products, sunscreen, toothpaste, toothbrush, face wash, etc.); into the last, I flung earrings and necklaces that go with my Black-based clothing. Luckily, I had separated out my jewelry into Black-Navy-Brown as well; this was the first test of my ability to "grab it and pack it."

I didn't need to wonder whether or not I had conditioner or contact lens fluid. It's all there in my Gym Bag. Boy, was I glad to be a Bond Grrl!

Next, I laid out what I would wear on the plane: good jeans, a white T-shirt, a sweater, a fitted windbreaker, plus sneakers. These are bulky items, and so wearing them on the plane leaves more room in the suitcase.

In the suitcase, undies and such went in on top of the shoes and the personals. Socks were tucked into the shoes. As one of my Bond Grrl traits, about a week before I go on a known trip, I pour myself a glass of wine and in a leisurely manner go through and tidy my closet and drawers in anticipation. So all my undies, shirts, etc. were back into order and category (we know how chaos can creep in!), and I had gone through them for spots, stains, and wear. So on Honeymoon Morning, I just opened up a drawer and scooped out what I wanted, then reached up onto the hangers for a few skirts, tops, and a little black dress, and plopped them all into the suitcase. Don't forget: you can do laundry on your trip! No need to bring enough undies to last the entire three weeks — why drag all that around? OK OK — and I tucked in a few Honeymoon nighties from my Grrls!

As part of my Bond Grrl closet clean-out, I had eliminated from my wardrobe anything that needs serious ironing — why deal with that? So I knew that everything plopping unceremoniously into the suitcase would not be a wrinkled wreck when I unpacked.

Next, I grabbed one black purse and my wallet, in which I have a hidden $50 plus the credit cards and ID that are necessary to go to Paris... or is that Nova Scotia? (We went to Nova Scotia for our

Honeymoon.) My passport already lives in my suitcase, as do a bathing suit, sarong and flip-flops, so no searching for them. Also, every time that my James had made a hotel/train/car/plane reservation for the trip, he printed out the itinerary and put that in his suitcase, so we actually knew that we had all our reservations, passports, and the like, from following this procedure.

The packing took a bit less than 10 minutes. And remember, this is from closet to suitcase. (Nearly from *bed* to closet to suitcase!) We didn't have time to hit an ATM, but luckily each of us had that hidden money in our wallets that we never, ever touch on a whim. We were able to catch the Airporter and get to the airport on time!

As we boarded the plane, my James gave me a kiss and said, "I am so glad that I married a Bond Grrl." This made me laugh, but also warmed me inside. Seriously, how many of you could get out of your house in about 20 minutes, packed for a three-week trip, knowing that everything was taken care of?

Are you ready for Nova Scotia?

Go confidently in the direction of your dreams!
Live the life you have imagined.
As you simplify your life,
the laws of the universe will be simpler.
　　　　　　　　　　—Henry David Thoreau

Chapter 2

∞

*'Normal' is getting dressed in clothes that you buy for work and driving through traffic
in a car that you are still paying for – in order to get to the job you need
to pay for the clothes and the car, and the house
you leave vacant all day so you can afford to live in it.*

— *Ellen Goodman*

Clearing Out

Okay, Grrlfriend. Now that you've cleaned out your environs, it's time to clear out your schedule, and clear out your head. Just as you shouldn't have anything in your house that you don't love, if you don't love what you're doing with your time, then it's time to stop doing it. It's as easy as that. And first and foremost, you need to love your self, from the inside out.

If you think about Aboriginal living, what's it all about? Lie around. Chat. Be one with nature. Hunt or gather some food. Enjoy the family and friends. Listen to stories. Have some sex. Lie around again. Laugh. Relax. In a way, this is Bond Grrl living, just with a different style! This is what we're supposed to be doing with our lives.

Inner Appearance

We've talked about matching your Outer Image to your Inner Image. So, what's that Inner Image about? I believe that a good part of what you get/do/feel in life is directly related to your perception of whether you are free, or in bondage.

If you feel that you are in bondage on a certain issue — that you're not free, due to circumstances or responsibilities or anything or anyone else — then you will never be congruent in leading the inner and outer life that is yours. You need to realize that you are in complete control of your Life and your Destiny.

This is all about your perception of your control.

There are certain events that you can't control per se. Hurricanes, for example. When something like that happens, your job in life is not to dwell on it. Adapt to it, and move on. Don't make yourself a victim to it. Don't try to change or fix it.

Same if you're dealing with another person. You cannot change them. Specifically, we can't treat our Jameses like starter homes, where we move in to demolish and rebuild!

Don't get toxic about it. That means stop complaining. Oprah once said, "Complaining about another person and sending bad vibes at them is like taking poison yourself, hoping it will get them sick." I wish I'd said that, because that's exactly right. By sending out evil thoughts and dwelling on what's wrong or talk-talk-talking about it, you're poisoning yourself, hoping it affects another situation, person, or event.

Then, there are certain events that you think you can't control, but you can. You're just being lazy, or haven't learned how to start. Things like time management. Goal setting. Debt reduction. Weight reduction. You can become good at these things, because what it takes is practice. Take that control. Become the inventor of the life that you are leading. When you think about it, inventors are people who look at situations that everyone else thinks "just are" — and then they go about creating a solution to control that thing. (Remember, once upon a time, there was no hairspray, dishwashers, or pantyhose!)

You need to maximize the events that you can control, learn how to control the events you don't think you can, and then have a reality check with respect to events you can't control, and stop putting negative energy into them or blaming them for where you are.

The quicker you do this, the quicker you'll be free. And if I can say one thing about Bond Girls, they are free. They live in exotic locations. They are not tied down — or if they appear to be, it's because they own some fantastic boat, or business, or family, or something else that they are passionate about... so in reality, they aren't tied down at all.

Ten Minutes in Your Power Spot

How to Start? Starting today, you need to find Ten Minutes out of every morning somewhere, to play your day and your life through your head, and highlight the high points and the Good you want to come out of that day. (On the bus to work? Lying in bed after you hit "snooze" one time?) The more you do this, the more you magnetize that good stuff to you. It's only ten minutes — but it's ten minutes solely for you.

This is very important. Don't nod your head, then skip this. We don't find time in our bizzy buzzy lives to really dream like we did as kids. Suddenly, as adults, that dreaming flies out the window of our life — when, as kids, we used to daydream and fly ourselves through it! Picture yourself paying off your bills. Picture yourself at the gym. Picture yourself eating really nourishing, gorgeous food. Picture yourself hugging your James. Go for it: Dream the Dream. Heck, picture yourself on Tahiti! Get your Bond Grrl juices flowing, so you can magnetize that dream to you. Bond Grrls Live Their Passion — but often, you have to find your passion, first!

Next, take two minutes to write down in your little black book the things that come to you during your Ten Minutes — even if you just write down snippets, not the whole story. So if you have a long and involved dream about doing a ballroom dancing competition, just write "ballroom competition" in the diary. It takes less time — and usually, getting students to do the 10 minutes daily is tough enough! But the more that you write and accentuate the details, the more you are magnetizing that event to you. So if you do have time — expound those details in your little black book.

What we're checking on here is what your mind — which is going to be SO EXCITED to be let free to fantasize! — is bringing up. At the end of a month of these ten minute Dreamflights, go back through and see what three things might have been repeated over and over. These are clues as to what your Inner Bond Grrl is dreaming that her Life should manifest. Don't censor her — even if her choices surprise you!

Look deep. If you're dreaming of a lot of Bling, look a little further. Where did it come from? Did you earn it? Did your James give it to you? I don't care right now if things are Realistic. But you want to check and see what in your dreams really Turns You On. Is it the Bling that is making you feel so happy and dreamy

— or is it more that you're lying on a beach? Or relaxing? Or out in the sun? Or drinking a hot toddy after skiing down a slope in the Alps? Don't second guess your dreams. Let them flow. But do realize that any Bling or accoutrements you see are the end results of something; they are not ends unto themselves. That's shallow, and Bond Grrls are anything but shallow. Dig a little and see what Passion resulted in these accoutrements.

The goal of yesterday will be the starting point of tomorrow.
— *Thomas Carlyle*

If you have the ability to spend a bit more time, set up a Power Space in your home. Go around your home, and find a spot that draws you: a spot that you can call just yours. If you're married, this spot can't be your bed, otherwise you are sending out a vibe that your James doesn't belong there! Find somewhere that you can sit, close your eyes, and dream or meditate on some of the pictures, phrases and the like that you have put in your little black book. You can even decorate a treasure box and fill it with items that represent your Dreams and Goals. Keep them in the box when you're not using it though, otherwise they're just dust catchers! Take them out when you have your Dreams, Goals and Prayers time.

Set Aside Space

Why do we fill our lives so full? Do so much for others? Spin, spin, spin?

Is it because if we take it all away, if we're sitting in our own quiet room by ourselves, we feel that we're just a Nobody? Do we feel that we are what we Do in public... not what we Dream, Feel, or how we Live when no one is looking?

This is my question for you this week. We touched on this a bit before, but now that we've progressed to writing, it's time to spend a little more time on it. I think that we often do a ton of stuff because we want people to look at us and say "Wow, look how great she is!" or "Wow, she does so much!" or "Wow, she gives so much to her community!"

The key is though, that as a Bond Grrl, all you do, you must do with and for Passion.

Are you Passionate about all the little chores that you're up to during the day? Or are you doing them so that you can say, "HONESTLY, I just do NOT HAVE TIME to do all your Bond Grrl exercises, I am BIZZY BIZZY BIZZY!" I tell my students this is a coping skill, a way to avoid finding out what's Inside — perhaps fear of finding out there is Nothing inside. Or the fear that you will find out who you are, and you will not like her! The fear that if you stop whirring for a second and contemplate You, that You are nothing more than what you wear, or what you eat, or who you meet, or what you do.

The thing is, that's just not so. I know that you're an awesome Bond Grrl inside, or else you wouldn't be reading this. You may, however, have draped things all over your true self, to avoid thinking about the hard stuff. Like how much debt you're in. Or how much you need to tone up. Or how low-energy you feel, because you don't eat foods that nourish you. Or how stressed out you are, because you do things for others to get their appreciation, not to feed your Passion.

So, be sure that you are making room for your Self in your life, and that you look inside for what is true to you. It can start with just waking up each morning a few minutes early, stretching from your feet up to your head, saying prayers of thanks for being around another day, then giving thanks for the *fantastic* day you are *going* to have. (Set that day up in your head, before you get up!) That's such a good start. It makes a big difference not to just have the alarm go off and SLAM, you're running into your day without thankfulness and joy in your sights.

What about finding a yoga or Pilates class or instructional DVD to do in the morning? I know from personal experience that it's hard to get there, but once you do, you will be so glad you did. Gym time, especially stretching or yoga, is really time for yourself; time to be in your body and present.

Are you going to make room for your Self this week? Because the only way to be ready to be spontaneous (you never know when that ticket to Paris is coming!) is to have room in your life to be so.

Don't Take Flak

What we're talking about here is setting aside space in your life just for You. And that might mean taking that time from time that you're currently spending doing things for someone else. Don't let anyone dissuade you. Don't turn back because someone says that you're lazy, or "It must be nice" to have personal time. I actually get this from folks who "have to work" from Nine to Five. The thing is, we all know that employee bees are NOT working Nine to Five. There are a LOT of breaks in there and a lot of time spent surfing the Web.

I work for myself. This means that some days I only have one project to do for a client — and then, well, no more work. So I might go hiking with a Grrlfriend, and take advantage of a beautiful day. What happens when I tell my 9-5er friends? They heave a derogatory sigh and say in a fed-up tone of voice, "Well,

THAT must be nice." If this sounds like your friends, remember, it's their choice that they are imprisoned in a cubicle during that time, not yours. And it's not your responsibility, either. Don't apologize!

Other people may not understand where you are coming from, but if you start filling in your down time because you feel guilty that you have it, you're building your Life by reacting to something outside yourself. Someone once told me that things like cancer and heart attacks are tied to this sort of whirring around and rushing. Not good! I also heard that our body, which is virtually the same as when we were cavewomen, has only one analogy for perpetual stress: famine. And since your body thinks that your perpetually stressful life means that you must be in a famine situation, it holds on to calories, changes your metabolism, and the like to cope. So stress alone can make you fatter than being in a relaxed life, because of the way your body reacts. Interesting, huh?

So, back to You Time. If people around you don't get this, then don't tell them. Do they really need to know that you're going hiking? In my life, if I don't have any work on a given day, what am I supposed to do? Obsess about it? Freak? Look at my bank account with $32.12 in it? Heck, if I go out hiking, have a good time, get some fresh air in and clean the mental cobwebs out, I'm more likely to be positive and attract good energy. I don't need to tell the 9-5ers that's what I'm doing, if they're going to be sending Guilt Vibes my way!

Sharpening the Saw

I heard a saying recently at a seminar that I hadn't heard before. The seminar had to do with setting your personal goals and aspirations. The speaker stated that it was imperative that you leave part of each day, or at the very least one part of one day a week, to yourself. I have always heard this called "recharging your batteries," but I liked the speaker's phrase better.

The speaker, whom I believe was quoting Stephen Covey, said that this was time to "sharpen your saw." If you're going to be out there, in his words, cutting down the trees that are between you and your goal, you need to take time to sharpen your saw, so you can continue to cut them down quickly and efficiently.

When I use the phrase Recharge My Batteries, it is a code for lazing around on the couch, doing not much of anything, and maybe catching up on a little TV. Sharpening My Saw doesn't have that same "lazing around" quality for me.

So I'm switching my down-time description to Sharpening My Saw. Because just by saying it, I mean something totally different than Recharging My Batteries. Instead of drinking chocolate milk and watching reruns of *Magnum PI* (so shoot me), I would be reading my back issues of *Experience Life* or *Oprah* magazine, or sorting through a cabinet to make it easier to access things the next time I need them. Doing something active (sharpening) versus passive (recharging).

Blocking Out Time

If you have a habit of overcommitment — so much so that you sometimes feel you should *be* committed, just to get some rest! — then you might benefit from having one of those big, month-at-a-glance desk/blotter calendars. On these, it's much easier to see when your schedule is getting completely insane. To use it, block out times on the blotter. Use different colors, and be sure to include personal time. For me, graphically seeing the time blocking is immensely beneficial. I can assess my life, and get clear with where my time is going — and whether I want it to go that way. If you're computer savvy, you can do the same thing in Outlook, but I think it's more beneficial to have it physically there on your desk.

I have two different colors for non-work/personal time. I have one color for Obligatory Personal time — going to the Housing Association meetings, placating that squeaky wheel friend who I just can't quite bring myself to shut off, doing the laundry, etc. — and then another color for personal time spent doing things that make my heart sing. If you do this and find that you have a lot of the Obligatory color in your calendar, remember that this is doing very little to draw in your heart's desire; yet, you're calling it down time or personal time. In fact, depending on how much you dislike that obligation, it might actually be holding you back from your goals. Like attracts like, so if you are hating, disliking or fearing during a block of time, then that hate and fear is being drawn to you like a magnet. For every second you're resonating passion or joy or happiness, you're bringing more of that towards you.

Oh sure, you have to block in work time — but you know, maybe part of your Dreamtime should be on making that work time something you are more passionate about. Trust me on this — if you put your mind to it and figure out what your passion really is, you can find a job that will make you as much money as you need, and feed your soul, too.

If you are working on something exciting that you really care about, you don't have to be pushed. The vision pulls you.

— *Steve Jobs*

 ## Baby Steps...

Getting to that Bond Grrl Lifestyle is actually not that hard — believe it or not. It just takes placing your Bond Grrl high heeled toe on the right path.

Once you find dreams that juice you up, couple them with action — even small actions. In fact, I was watching a movie the other day, where a character said, "We are just little people, and so we can just do little things each day. But what little thing can we do today, that will chip away at this big problem?" Take a step — even a baby step — each day, and write down that accomplishment in your diary and/or on your calendar. Even if it's parking your car farther away at the Mall and walking, that's more exercise than you were getting, and an accomplishment towards your exercise goal. You get the picture.

Make little current promises to yourself every day that support your big passionate dreams. You might make daily promises, weekly ones, and monthly ones, and then something to achieve at the 6 month mark. You could also set goals at one year, three years, five years... but these are more aspirations (things to aspire to) than goals per se. They are too far away to make much of a difference to your life right now and this week. If you don't do some action to make a change for the better every single day, you will always push out the time, until suddenly — SURPRISE! — a month, or a year, has passed and you haven't changed at all. (And who are you going to blame? Your metabolism? Your upbringing? Your boss? Your kids? Your James?) Come up with four promises to yourself that you can cross off by the end of the week, that will bring you closer to your Passion. Then write down some bigger ones, one per week (starting this week), for the next month. Remember: It's all well and good to say that you will lose 30 pounds in six months. But that's just not specific enough or close enough in time for your mind to get around it today. Your goals can't be cloudy, they need to be concrete. So if you're going to have a weight or health and fitness goal (e.g., you want to change the way you eat to match the plan found in a book like Bob Greene's *The Best Life Diet* or the *YOU* books by Mehmet Oz and Michael Roizen, or you want to run a 10k race by the end of the year), your specific weekly and daily goal could be to try one new vegetable every week, and to walk 30 minutes every day.

Heck, your goal for today could be to buy Bob Greene's or Oz and Roisen's or a Debt Diet book, if you've had it on your list since you heard about it months ago. (Go to Half.com — they have perfectly good books available at great prices, and the shipping is cheap. Why not get a Pilates or Bar Method DVD while you're at it?) Specific goals automatically clarify for you if you're succeeding, or cheating. If you didn't walk 30 minutes today, you cheated. Do it now, even if it's dark! If you get to Saturday and you haven't had your new vegetable for the week, better get to the store. Don't cheat yourself. Make those specific goals, and stick to them. That's a measurable, concrete way to your big goal, which is all your brain really understands.

How do I know? Back quite some time ago on New Year's Day, a man named Remar Sutton published a calendar in the *Washington Post*. It started with "Walk 10 Minutes Today." He dared any couch potato to follow it from New Year's Day through Thanksgiving, and then to join him in doing the Bahamas Conchman Triathlon on Thanksgiving Weekend. My friend Leslie and I were serious couch potatoes — but we took the challenge, and in fact, starting from that "Walk 10 Minutes" and the next day's "Find A Pool and A Bike," we ultimately wound up doing a triathlon with dozens and dozens of other fellow D.C.-area couch potatoes on Thanksgiving in the Bahamas. From Couch to Conch: a 1K open-water ocean swim, 25K bike ride, and 5K run. I came in sixth woman overall! The next year, I did the Chicago Triathlon (1.5K swim in the lake (brrr!), 40K bike ride, 10K run). After that, the Big Sur Marathon (26.2 miles/42K). It was the start of my passion for training women to accomplish things that they can't believe they could possibly do — always starting from that first Baby Step.

A goal is a dream with a deadline.

— *Napoleon Hill*

An Example: Blocking Out the Passport Goal

Remember last Chapter, when we talked about having a passport? What about putting PASSPORT about three months out on your desk-blotter calendar as a goal? Put "star" stickers around it. Pick a special color for it, when you're doing your daily time-blocking.

How to start? If you're an American citizen, go to the State Department's website at http://travel.state.gov/passport/get/get_840.html and download the forms. Then paperclip a copy to that date three months out on your calendar. You could also put a copy in various spots where you might "get weak" (the fridge, for example).

What do I mean, "get weak"? Well, if you haven't already completely externalized your gorgeous inner Bond Grrl, you probably feel you have to do some tune-ups before you take that passport photo. Could be lose some weight, eat more nutritionally, go to the gym, bag your old makeup and get a real makeup lesson at the department store (free at most counters or at a store like Sephora), tune up your wardrobe, get a fresh hair cut/color — you name it. So put a copy of the passport form in spots where you might cheat yourself — next to your alarm clock so you won't hit snooze and will go to the gym, or on the fridge to keep you from foraging in there!

I'm giving you three months. That's enough.

Do something *every day* towards that passport goal. Write it down. For example, a passport isn't cheap. So that might be the reason for giving up your lunches out, or your Frappuccino, or your impulse shoe buying. Take the money that you would have spent on those items, and put it in a cookie jar. This nest egg is going to go towards your passport photo and registration.

Although I would generally agree that all this money should go towards paying down your debt first, I personally feel like I'm being "scolded" when I give up everything and only pay that money towards debt. Sure, that debt represents those extras from months, maybe even years before! But by putting a little bit aside from those missed Frappuccinos and Mall splurges towards something like a passport, I feel that I am actually accomplishing something forward, not just filling the big hole behind me. So do use some of the money to pay the debt, but save some to put towards your goal, like the passport.

Back to that photo. Every day, you'll want to do something that moves you closer towards having a fantastic one. You might even use some of your nest egg towards getting color in your hair, if that's something new for you. Be religious about moisturizing your face and neck. Yes, I know this means you're going to have to cut back a *lot* on treats and non-essentials, once you start adding up what it's going to take to get this passport goal accomplished. But you can do it. Honest.

Each time you are doing something that we mentioned from Chapter One (cleaning out your closet, going through and pitching all your old makeup and toiletries, etc.), you could write that down on your calendar as a move towards this goal. Though you won't see much of your outfit in the passport photo, *you* will know what you were wearing every time you see that photo. And what you weren't!

Speaking of hair, how *about* your hair? Have you been going to the same stylist (or Supercuts®) for a zillion years? Start scrutinizing women around you. Is there someone with hair that is similar to yours that has a really stylish "do"? Be brave: ask where she gets her hair done. Often stylists and colorists are different people, so if you know someone who gets her hair colored and that's something you want to consider, then you want to talk with her, too, even if her style is not for you. Remember, of course, that not all stylists are great with all sorts of hair. A woman of color might not get the same great results from a stylist who is only used to cutting Anglo hair, so try to ask someone who has hair like yours. Heck, I have stopped women on the street. Unless they are racing to an appointment (Didn't leave enough time there, sistah? You need to read my book!), they are usually delighted to help, especially when you tell them you think they look awesome!

What about your body, and your face? You want to be radiating your Bond Grrl inside, so set your alarm a little earlier and get some workout tapes, or use that gym membership that you pay for but never take advantage of. Each time you go, put a note on your calendar in your Passport Goal color, because you're going to present a far more toned look facially if you lose a few pounds of fat and gain a few of muscle. This is totally do-able in 3 months. You want to be awesome. You want to radiate "Look at me, I am so hot!" in that photo. Though you might be able to "fake it" if you crash diet for a month before your photo shoot, don't be so hard on yourself. Put yourself first each day in one area that's going to move you toward that awesome passport shot, and take a full three months to do it. It's much more likely to last that way, too.

Now, before the day comes, check out the places around you that will take the passport photo. It's well worth the money to get your hair styled and your makeup done that day — yes, even if it costs you a few bucks — because this photo is going to represent you for the next *decade*! (Yikes!)

Once they snap the photo, *look at it*. If you hate it, pay to get it done again. Make sure that photo radiates your awesome Bond Grrl you. I have great driver's license and passport photos. (Practice what you preach!) People behind me in line will sometimes just reach over and pick them up. They can't resist saying, "WHOA, this is a great shot!" They look from that picture and back to me — usually because I have broken my own rule and I'm standing there without makeup with my hair up, buying a quart of milk (or can of hairspray?) and showing my driver's license to the check-out clerk... but never mind that!

If you already have a passport and you hate the picture, you can apply again, pay a little more, and say that your passport is lost. I did this. My last passport had an *AWFUL* photo of me — Oh. My. Goodness. Each time I showed that passport the person would look at the photo, look at me, look at the photo, then sometimes (if brave) would say something about whether I'd "had a bad day" on the photo date. I had, but it hadn't occurred to me to come back the next day, plunk down another $20, and have a "do over" with the photographer. Since on that old passport I had that awful photograph in the front, it wasn't this wonderful, magical "travel gateway" for me. I stared straight out from that first page, looking like something dragged in from a refugee camp. To get to the "good part" (the pages of travel stamps), I constantly had to pass by the icky photo of Moi.

 Photos You Love

A while ago I went through all the photographs in the house (and in boxes) that had me in them, and if I didn't LOVE that photo of myself — I tore it up. HORRORS! Yes, I really did. And while I was at it, I threw out all the photos that people had sent of their babies at Christmas, all the photos of waterfalls that really aren't that great and didn't make it into the scrapbook, etc. WOW, was that liberating! This was part of Touching Everything in my house. By accomplishing steps like this, I consolidated boxes and boxes of stuff into one or two. How many of you have storage units full of stuff? Time to sort and purge, doncha think?

And speaking of photos, if you're one of the people who would grab photographs as you're speeding out of the door in a disaster, I suggest that after you spend your money on your awesome passport photo, you keep up your "saving ways," and make another Goal to take all the analog ("film") photos that mean something to you to a local store and get them scanned into digital format. (Same goes for old family slides or movies, which you can have put on DVD.) Then they are all in an easily portable CD or three. But only do it if you really would save these if the floodwaters were rising. Otherwise it's a waste of money. I know we all find it heart-wrenching to see people on the news after a disaster has passed, picking through the water-soaked debris of their homes and ruined albums/photos/etc. If at least the photos had been scanned onto a CD or DVD and sent to a friend out of the area, it would just be a matter of printing them all out again.

This process isn't cheap, but if you really love those photos, and that's all you'd save except your family and pets in a disaster, think of it as an "insurance policy" of sorts. As we move more and more to digital formats, that also means backing up your computer hard-drive every week, so that you don't lose those photos if something happens to the computer. (Backing up is never a bad idea, in any case!) And if you have any other items that you would save from your house, go through and make an Emergency list of where these "irreplaceable" things are, so that you (or your neighbor) can grab and go if the time comes and everything is in an uproar. Keep it somewhere prominent, such as the side of your fridge, with your Emergency numbers and the like.

Some of the best money I ever spent was replacing that darned passport. When I took the next photo, I was in a *great* mood. I needed the passport because I was going to realize a Life Dream of driving cattle on horseback through the mountains of Australia. I actually thought I had lost the ugly-photo'd passport, and so got the other. (I wound up finding it later and, ahem, burnin' it. I probably just admitted to a Federal offense. Shhhh...) Now, when I pull my passport out, I just *love* looking through it — at the stamps, but also at Wonderful Me in the front. It gets me excited just to write about it.

So that's one example of how to use a three-month Goal every day to build towards something great. But, it will only really help you if you implement it, a little every day.

Be Early

This section started with time-blocking, and then we moved on to show how time-blocking can help you keep your eye on a Goal. So, what other scheduling tips are there to recommend? Bond Girls certainly show up on time to help Bond, or provide the crucial information, without a hair out of place. Bond Grrls don't overschedule. If you keep space between your appointments, you're not only less frazzled, but less likely to be late. Time yourself on how long it actually takes to get out of the house. (I'm terrible with that "one last thing" bit, myself.) Plan to get lost, or stuck in traffic.

You should be the master of your schedule and things like your e-mail inbox, not vice versa. Find out what your biggest time-waster is, and corral it. If it's e-mail, then tell yourself that you will read e-mail from 8:00-9:00 (and 2:00-3:00, and 6:00-7:00, if necessary) each day, and that's it. Time block it, and stick to it. If people think that you will answer an e-mail right away, they will come to expect it — and then your life runs on their time. Of course, certain things in your schedule can't be changed (a boss's meeting, or maybe picking up your kids at school), but those usually aren't the problem. It's things like getting on the phone, or watching TV, or doing e-mail. Corral some of these, to make room for your Life. Schedule them, time block it, then stick to it.

You should be able to keep commitments, and also factor in the time to write a hand-written thank you for the nice things people do for you each day. I try to write five a day for nice things folks have done. Though you might dash off a "Thanks!" e-mail, it's just going to go into that person's computer Recycle Bin after a quick smile. But people keep handwritten notes for ages, because these days they are so unusual. Be memorable. Be a Bond Grrl.

Two Espresso Morning

> For a time, my grandfather taught in Cuba. He explained that in the morning, the men on their way to work in their Model T Fords would sometimes be hit by a tropical rain deluge. When this would happen, the engines would often sputter, then conk out. So as soon as the storms would hit, the men would carefully pull over, and head into the nearest espresso stand/shack. They would calmly have an espresso, speak with the other men, chat about the rain. As soon as the sun came out, the men would go out and open the hoods of their Model Ts, and then go back for another espresso while their engines dried out. After a time and a bit more of a chat, they would be on their way — no honking, no cursing, no fuss, no muss.
>
> How do you handle the delays that might hit you, over which you have no control? Are you prepared to have a civilized two espresso morning while things right themselves, or do you curse at the rain and take it out on everyone around you for the rest of the day?

Keeping Your Diary

If you're not going to time-block in a desk blotter calendar (which I strongly recommend), you still need to have a way to see progress, that can help lift you in the dark times. It's also a place to jot things when you're at work or on the bus, or a spot to tape a photo of Tahiti! Yes, it's that little black book/diary that I keep mentioning. If you aren't used to keeping a diary (or a blog!) then it's going to be a little harder for you, because it's not already a habit. But you'll get used to it, I promise.

You should be doing your Ten Minutes in your little black book, and recording your successes there, and/or on your desk calendar. Now, one more thing to add. Every single day, twice a day (after you brush your teeth, maybe), starting today, jot down three things you are passionate or happy or thankful about, right in that instant. Just three things that pop into your mind. They can be silly things. Could be your straight and lovely teeth! Could be your James. Could be the smell of your soap. Could be that it's not raining that day. Anything. The idea here is to start building a Passion Portfolio. And don't sass me and procrastinate because you don't have a diary yet. If you have to, start on sticky notes, then ultimately paste them into the diary. Hey, why not write some notes down right here, right now. Just get started! Mess this book up! Underline things, take notes, carry it around, use it however you desire, use it in a way that will help coax your Inner Bond Grrl out.

All You, All The Time

From this moment on, you need to hold yourself responsible for everything that is in your life. From this moment on, you need to stop blaming other people, or circumstances. You need to make a promise to yourself, with the first promise being that you won't let yourself down and bail on yourself.

Think of it this way. Imagine your boss had given you this as a task, and then said, "If you can't accomplish it, you're fired." You'd be cranky, but you'd find some way to do it, wouldn't you? If you had a little fire on your tail and had to get the task accomplished or be mowed over, you'd do it, wouldn't you? So tell me why you let yourself down, laze out, and put off on your Vision?

Be accountable and responsible to yourself. Make the promise, have the vision, and have passion to reach that Life as your goal. It's time to take control: stop blaming, look inward, get your gut/emotions involved, and look forward to giving yourself a present of success.

Yesterday is History. Tomorrow is a Mystery. And Today? Today is a Gift...
That's Why We Call It The Present.
— *Babatunde Olatunji*

Drawing a blank? Here are some long term promises that you could make. Whatever ignites your imagination and makes you feel excited, write it down. Do up some contracts. Remember, it's what *you* want. I don't care if it's a "guilty pleasure," I just care that you actually have some emotion, passion, and colorful daydreaming that goes with it. Can you imagine yourself:

- Smiling as you put the check for the final payment on your credit card bill into your mailbox and take out the colorful *Condé Nast Traveller* magazine you subscribed to by saving money on needless Frappuccinos? Realizing that next month, you can put that payment into a savings account towards an awesome holiday?

- Stepping off the plane on a vacation, smelling the fresh, warm air, as a smiling local puts a lei around your neck?

- Clearing off your desk and packing your last box, with a smile in your eyes as you leave your job for one you are Passionate about?

- Stepping out on a brisk day, bundled up and listening to your favorite tunes, smiling inwardly at how excited you are to be doing your 30th day in a row of walking 30 minutes a day?

- Changing the way you verbalize: for example, referring to exercise as Recess — and your time on the treadmill as building up stamina to Chase the Boys to Kiss them and Give them Cooties?

- Stepping on the scale, watching the needle effortlessly swinging to one pound *less* than the lowest you ever thought you could go?

- Smiling with your eyes and your lips down at a dimly-lit, romantic dinner table, feeling the warmth of your soulmate's hand in yours, feeling in your heart a true, strong, quiet happiness and contentment, maybe an engagement ring sparkling on your finger in the candlelight?

Dream big! When we were kids, we were told not to daydream in class. But getting our dreams going is the only way we are going to embody our new lives. And dream positive — none of these "They'll miss me/appreciate me when I'm gone" tear jerkers. You need to really feel the dream, and don't worry about How it's going to happen. Just concentrate on that feeling. The general, wonderful, joyful, contented feeling. Because a Bond Grrl is contented and satisfied in the life that she has built for herself. Remember: you have built everything that is surrounding you now by your past action (or inaction!). It's just time to harness that going forward.

 Daydream Believer

Research into the brain and the mind/body connection shows that our minds actually can't tell the difference between a real occurrence and one that has been fully imagined. (Have you seen the movies *What The Bleep Do We Know?* **or** *The Secret?* **They go into detail about this.)**

The whole idea is that if you have truly, viscerally and sensually lived an experience in your mind (e.g., you can taste it, smell it, hear it, etc.), then your brain actually categorizes it as an experience it has already HAD.

The Coaching Compass (coachingcompass.com), an email newsletter that I receive, recently said this about the phenomenon:

Picture this... Liu Chi Kung, a world-class pianist in the late 1950s, was imprisoned during the Cultural Revolution in China. After seven years without a piano, he immediately resumed his concert tour. His fans said he played better than ever and wondered how this was possible. Kung said, "I rehearsed every piece I had ever played, note by note, in my mind."

Mental rehearsal, or the process of visualization, can give you a competitive edge. Olympic athletes have used it in training for years and it works not only in sports but for every goal you set.

So, what are you visualizing each day? Are you rehearsing a Mental Masterpiece? Or obsessing over all the things that can go wrong or the agonizing details of how you can fail?

Just remember: your brain doesn't know that you didn't succeed (or fail!) "already." So practice thinking for success — thinking to win, to obtain your goal — and make it easier for your brain to think of you as a winner!

Bond Grrl Baby Steps

I had one of my Grrls mention that she didn't feel like she had any goals — except getting out of debt, which was going to take "a lot of doing," since she had many, many thousands on her credit cards. As I told her, that's just a story she's making up so as not to take control of her own life and path. She does have goals, and I know it. But she gets overtaken by the enormity of what needs to be done. She also can't even say that she promises to herself that she will pay the debt and not use shopping as a depression antidote. ("Promise" is a big word.) This Grrl hasn't even finished all the clearing out stuff that I outlined in Chapter One, and wallows in the Woe Is Me. (How about you?)

I have found — truth — that after your life is clear and uncluttered, something about it spurs you into staying in action on your path. That's why Chapter One is about physically clearing and cleaning, not goal-setting. I'm not sure how this happens, but suddenly, there are Sparks. Things start to go your way. For example, when you are clearing your house, you might find a long-lost Something that you saved in a long-unemptied box or drawer, and had forgotten about. Maybe it's a clipping that intrigued you. When you find that, if you are still intrigued by it, there you go! You have something to work towards! And don't tell me you're too old/fat/whatever. I take pole dancing classes, and I see gals in there who could have said the same thing about themselves. I salute each and every one of them, for signing up. And you know what? Every single one is having the time of their lives!

If you're still having trouble thinking of goals, here are some questions to help you:

1. *What's your little girl made of?* What got you excited when you were a little girl? Are you getting that feeling of excitement into your life, at least once a week? I don't care what it is — go back to your little girl self, and see what she loved. She's still inside you, waiting to have fun with what she did in the past. Does she want to go buy some crayons? Get out in the woods? Go to the zoo? Read adventure books? Ride a pony? Feel that excitement — no promise becomes a reality without energy and passion behind it, and excitement is energy and passion all balled into one. If you can't figure out where your passion lies now, and can't even figure out where to begin, look to your little girl for clues.

2. *What would you do, if you knew you couldn't fail?* What have you always wanted to do, that you didn't (or don't) have the money for? Where would you go? This might be something centered directly around

yourself, though it's far more powerful if it can embody helping others. The more you can imagine helping others (for example, making so much money you can set up a Foundation supporting your greatest passion), the more energy that your goal will have around it. Think of all the folks out there just praying for what your Foundation would do. Once you start it, you will answer those prayers — all those people are pulling your dream into existence, as you're working on pushing it into existence yourself. See how great it is, when your goal embodies helping others?

3. *What could you do, right this second?* What little thing could you do differently right now, to chip away at a problem or contribute to your overall success? Something small, that you could just about get up and do right now? (How's about putting this book down, and just doing it? I'll be here waitin' for ya!) Maybe it's finding the number for the Adult Education at your local community college, because your passion is to be in a different profession and you will need additional training or education. What's another step that you can accomplish this week, after that one? Maybe actually getting a catalog, or going down and talking to the Admissions office?

4. *What can you do, to fatten your wallet?* What additional amount in your bank account every month would let you relax and help you make ends meet? It's probably not that much once you get rid of the stuff you're doing without thinking. Buying a latte every day — ka-CHING — that's like $100/month! What about running a business out of your house, or selling some of your extra things on eBay, or teaching folks about your Passion — whether it's knitting or horseback riding — and having them pay to have you fire them up? These are all easily possible. What about upping the price a bit on things you already might be doing, or charging for them (babysitting, etc.)? S Factor has a work-study program; if you want to join the pole dancing classes and can't afford them, you can work a few hours a week, and receive classes half-off. Many establishments have these sort of creative solutions for the asking. You could also start getting your mind around making some changes in your life that can help make this extra amount a reality to you, perhaps even by starting to take the bus, instead of taxis or driving and paying for parking. Don't look outside for some Prince Charming; a Bond Grrl looks inside and is congruent and resourceful in running and managing her own Passionate Life.

An Example: Abundant You

If you don't feel abundant, you can practice the Money Game advocated by Abraham Hicks in the book *Ask And It Is Given*. Start with an actual (old) checkbook and checks, and for 30 days, write out checks for what you would purchase for yourself with $100, adding $100 each day. So the first day, you buy $100 worth of whatever you like. The next day, $200. And so on. The idea here is to get in the habit of not holding onto money so tightly: to feel magnanimous with that money. And remember — these purchases should be in furtherance of your awesome Bond Grrl self.

Another exercise in abundance, which Paul Kyriazi mentions in his book, was suggested to George Hamilton when he, as a young and impoverished actor, needed to act the part of a millionaire. When Hamilton said he didn't know how to act that part, his director stated something like: "Take a few hundred dollars out of the bank, and carry it around in your pocket. Don't spend it, just carry it — and look around and see all the things you could buy if you wanted, touching that money in your pocket." Hamilton stated that carrying that money around in his pocket made him stand straighter; it changed the way he "walked through life." That's the whole idea.

Remember, concentrate on Financial Freedom versus Getting Out of Debt. Because then you're focusing on the freedom, not on the debt. Focus on where you're going, on what you can do now. Feel the feeling of what it will be like when you are financially free. If someone asks you how you're doing, don't fall into the trap of saying "I'm hanging in there," you need to start now with "I'm doing great." Because you need to radiate prosperity and an optimistic attitude. If your bank has a website so that you can put your bills on automatic payment, do that. Then you won't be focusing on bills every month, and you won't need to focus on what's going out. (Make sure you subtract those checks from your checkbook balance!) If you sit down at your desk and are obsessing about which bill to pay, you are putting energy into feeling that you are just surviving. Take some effort, and get a plan together and into action. And then just let the plan work. A great way to start is to set up those monthly repeating bills (like your mortgage, rent, or the like).

As another example, if you want a relationship and don't have one, start acting As If you do. Create a virtual reality in your mind about a wonderful dinner that you will have with your James: what you will talk about, what you will eat, etc. Don't concentrate on your lack. Concentrate on making room in your life for this relationship, and the Abundance it will bring you. "Abundance" doesn't just mean money. Magnetize it to you. I once heard that our biggest problem is that we get hung up on Reality. As we'll discuss later, Reality is constantly changing. And one way you can change your reality is by acting As If you have the thing that you desire. Relax. Draw it to you.

As an independent contractor, I can certainly attest to the fact that it seems that I get work out of the blue on either days that I have decided to take a day off (as opposed to not having any work to do) or days that I already have a lot on my plate! It's not the days I am worrying, thinking "Woe is me, I will never be able to pay my mortgage." If you relax and keep positive, things will come to you. An analogy I once read is that Abundance is like sand: if you want to have a big pile of sand, just open up your hands and let it pour in. When you try to grab the sand and hold it, you retain nothing and it all runs through and around your clenched fingers.

I remember hearing, I think from Wayne Dyer, a quote from St. Francis of Assisi (patron saint of my town of San Francisco). The Prayer of St. Francis begins, "Make me a channel of Your peace." By surrendering and letting go of how you believe something is *supposed to happen*, the Universe conspires with you to deliver it to you in the way that *it should happen*. Make yourself a channel, and allow it to flow through you. The Universe is the eternal Yes Man. By having no doubt that what you are passionate about *can* work, the passionate and positive feelings you generate *will* make it work. But don't just pray for material things. Instead, really dream about, feel, and thank the Universe for the amazing, useful, and passionate life that is coming to you — and then let it deliver. Just become a channel for that Reality to come into existence through you.

Wayne Dyer also agreed that it helps when you desire something more for others than for yourself. Dwell upon how getting what you want will benefit others. For example, upgrading your look and how you act into a relaxed Bond Grrl confidence will inspire and uplift others, even if you're just walking through the Mall. If you meet people's eyes and smile, that smile is infectious, and you have increased the good energy in the world. Or, by building a business of your Passion, as we discussed before, you could employ people, speak and inspire others, and set up a Foundation. Yes, you.

*f*Empowerment®

 ## *Quick Checkup: Are You Meeting Your Goals?*

Hey, have you even SET them?

Have you made a contract with yourself? And signed and dated it? Have you made that promise to yourself?

If you have, have you accomplished your first goals? Have you set some new ones?

You are in charge of your own destiny. Before you became determined to unleash your Inner Bond Grrl, you might have floated through life, just taking what came your way. It may not have been your habit to set goals and make promises to yourself. Maybe you spent a lot of time concentrating on how other people, or circumstances, were constantly in your way.

Time to change that!

Since you started this book, what can you look back upon that makes you proud and happy? Do you see your accomplishments? Were you everything that you could be?

NO?

Guess what. Every minute, you get a chance to start again. So put some emotion and passion behind your goals. Get excited, get angry with yourself, get SOMETHING — but get going!

What motivates you? Go through some magazines and cut out representations of what you're aiming for. Now, we KNOW that you're not going to get the castle on the estate in three months. But if it inspires you — snip it out. What about some pictures of money to represent abundance and paying bills, or a picture of someone who is not model-thin but who looks fine, to represent a slimmer you? (An old photo of yourself, super happy and fit, would be the best! Did you find one in your clean-out?) If you can truly visualize the promise you've made to yourself, it helps your mind to make it come true. And remember, every single book we read, every magazine, every TV show we watch or radio program we listen to affects how we feel, which affects our energy. I have given up any show that makes me feel less than joyful. Do I read the newspaper? Not the front page. Listen to the news? Nope. It's all death and disaster and hype and such. That energy will stick to me all day, and I choose to have my own reality that I attract and expand.

Look. It's not easy. I know. I have days when I just want to go back in the comfy rut I'd been in for a long, long time. But the difference between success and failure, someone once told me, is that the successful person picks themselves up one more time after being knocked down. Similarly, the folks out there who are successful — guess what? It didn't just happen upon them. I personally envision Oprah when she was working for a local radio show and attending Tennessee State, writing down goals, maybe taping them up on her wall, accomplishing them, then aiming a little higher, a little higher, and continuing and continuing. Can't you see it? You can do that!! It is never, ever, too late to Live your Life. Life is not a spectator sport — you need to participate!

Close your eyes. Envision the excitement of getting a check in the mail with enough left over so you can support a charity that's meaningful to you. Envision the calm that surrounds having all your debts paid, and the emotion of giving a significant amount to others in need. Often, we have gotten ourselves "in need" (debt) by buying clothes/purses/stuff that we never really use. We buy to fill up a black hole inside. OK, now I am going to get serious with you. Imagine instead that all that debt on your cards had gone to the women in the Congo. Do you realize that if you'd done that, you would be considered pretty much a saint? Do you realize you could save women's lives? Do you realize that "a latte here, posh jeans there" could have gotten women out of terrible, horrible situations?

Once you have your thoughts and your feelings/emotions in line, time to get your actions moving in that direction, too. Because, as I believe Reverend Michael Beckwith said, "They will come and take your furniture away while you're 'visualizing,' if you don't pay the bills."

Accomplishing Your Mission

Abraham Lincoln lost eight elections, failed at two businesses and had a nervous breakdown before becoming our 16th President. The road to success is always filled with detours, speed bumps and potholes. To minimize their impact you must be prepared, learn from your failures and accept that change is inevitable.

— Kathleen Brady

What strategies do you need, to accomplish your mission of becoming (to steal a phrase from the military) All That You Can Be? You need to be willing to make deals. You must be willing to ask for what you want, work towards it and for it, and to stand your ground for what you believe and are passionate about. And you must never give up — it's only too late if you don't start now.

Know in Your Mind... Know in Your Soul... Know in Your Body.

I went to a seminar the other day, and the speaker told a story that I think is applicable to Bond Grrls in training. She said that her minister held a forum of his current parishioners, to brainstorm how to help make new parishioners feel more comfortable. The minister said that one of the things that people often do, trying to make a new person feel comfortable, is to ask, "Are you new here?"

It's an easy question, but it could be insulting — what if that person was going to evening services for years, when you were going to day services? So after discussing other things that one could say, the minister decided to do some role playing, and asked the speaker to take the role of the greeter, while he would be the new parishioner.

She said that in the role play, she walked up to him, asked his name, asked whether he'd like to come to the coffee after the service — and the next thing out of her mouth was, "Oh, are you new?" She said it got a big laugh because she is a professional speaker and there she was, saying just what she wasn't "supposed" to say!

Her story illustrated the point that when you're trying to embody a new concept, there are a number of steps that you will need to take before you really "get" it. You start at "I know that" (intellectually). So you might *know* that you have to give up smoking, but you only know it in your head. The second step from there is "I know *how to do* that." Here, you have a script or program to follow, but you still might mess up because you haven't practiced it. That was the issue with the speaker's role play — she had to practice (and make some mistakes along the way), before she'd really changed. At this stage, you're willing, but it's still not really in your body yet. Lastly, you move to "I *do* that." When you reach this level, you have not only changed how you think, but it's also just what you do. In fact, you have so embodied the concept, it is actually now part of who you are.

So, when you're making a change, it's just not enough to say "I know that" or "I know how to do that." You have to practice it and when you slip up, laugh, and know that's how it's going to go, until you've embodied that change. Just keep at it, because you have to get through all these levels to get to the end.

Success Through Goal-Setting

What follows is from an article by Brian Tracy (BrianTracy.com). Brian Tracy is an amazing and powerful speaker. He is kind enough to broadcast podcasts, seminars and newsletters for free from his website, just to help you become a better you. I can't say enough about Mr. Tracy and how he has inspired me.

I have found that students often can't distinguish between a wish and a goal. The quickest way for me to explain it is that a wish is not measurable ("I want to be rich"), whereas a goal is measurable and specifically quantifiable ("I want to have $1 million in the bank by 10 years from today.") I have often read this article by Mr. Tracy to my students, as there is no way that I could explain true goal-setting better than he has here. He has been kind enough to give me permission to share this with you:

> The ability to set goals and make plans for their accomplishment is the master skill of success. It is the single most important skill that you can learn and perfect. Goal-setting will do more to help you achieve the things you want in life than will anything else you've been exposed to. Becoming an expert at goal-setting and goal-achieving is something that you absolutely must do if you wish to fulfill your potential as a human being. Goals enable you to do the work you want to do, to live where you want to live, to be with the people you enjoy, and to become the kind of person you want to become. And there is no limit to the financial rewards you can obtain. All you have to do is to set a goal (for example, for financial success), make a plan, and then work the plan until you succeed in that area.
>
> The payoff for setting goals and making plans is being able to choose the kind of life you want to live. So why do so few people set goals? According to the best research, less than 3 percent of Americans have written goals, and less than 1 percent review and rewrite their goals on a daily basis.... I think that there are five basic reasons why people don't set goals.
>
> <u>The first reason is that they are simply not serious.</u> Whenever I speak with a man or woman who has achieved something remarkable, I learn that the achievement occurred after that person decided to get serious.

Until you become completely serious and totally determined about your goals, nothing really happens.

The second reason why people don't set goals is that they don't understand the importance of goals. We find that young men and women who begin setting goals very early in life invariably come from families in which the importance of goals is emphasized. The discussion that takes place around your family dinner table is one of the most powerful formative influences in your life. If your parents didn't have goals, didn't talk about goals, didn't encourage you to set goals, and didn't talk about people outside the family circle who had goals and were moving toward a higher level of achievement, then you very likely grew up with the idea that goals are not even a part of normal existence....

The third reason why people don't set goals is because they don't know how to do it. One of the greatest tragedies of our educational system is that you can receive 15 to 18 years of education in our schools and never once receive a single hour of instruction on how to set goals. Yet we find that in certain schools where goal-setting programs have been introduced since first grade, young people become excited about goal-setting — even if the goal is only to increase the scores by 5 or 10 percent over the course of the semester, or to be on time every day in the course of a month. Children become so excited about achieving goals that by the third or fourth grade, they love to go to school. They get the best grades. They are seldom absent. They are excited about themselves and about their lives....

The fourth reason why people don't set goals is fear of rejection. The fear of rejection is caused by destructive criticism in early childhood and is manifested, in adulthood, in the fear of criticism by others. Many people hold back from setting worthwhile goals because they have found that every time they do set a goal, somebody steps up and tells them that they can't achieve it, or that they will lose their money or waste their time. [Note from Sandy: This is a frenemy!]

Because each of us is strongly influenced by the opinions of those around us, one of the first things that you must learn when you begin setting goals is to keep your goals confidential.... Share your goals only with others who are committed to achieving goals of their own and who really want you to be successful and achieve your goals as well....

The fifth reason why people don't set goals — and perhaps the most important reason of all — is the fear of failure. People don't set goals because they are afraid that they might fail. In fact, the fear of failure is probably the greatest single obstacle to success in adult life. It can hold you back more than any other psychological problem.

The primary reason why you fear failure is simply this: You probably do not understand the role that failure plays in achievement. The fact is that it is impossible to succeed without failing. Failure is an indispensable prerequisite for success. All great success is preceded by great failure. If you wish to fulfill your potential, you have to be willing to risk failure over and over and over, because there is no way that you can ever accomplish worthwhile goals until you have fallen on your face so many times that you have eventually learned the lessons that you need for great achievement....

Setting well-defined goals enables you to channel your efforts and focus your energy toward something that's important to you. Goal-setting gives you a target to aim at and enables you to develop the self-discipline to continue working toward your target rather than becoming distracted and going off in other directions.

Let me share with you five keys that will help you to reach your goals more effectively. Each of these keys starts with one of the letters in the word goals. Whenever you find yourself getting off the track, simply repeat the word "goals," and think about how each letter stands for a key that just might apply to your current situation.

G stands for Get to It. Sometimes, the only difference between a successful person and a failure is that the successful person has the courage to get started, to do something, to begin moving toward the accomplishment of a specific goal.

[You] may have a long-range goal. In order to achieve it, you need to sit down and make a list of all the steps that you will have to take to get from where you are to where you want to be. Then begin with the first and most obvious thing that you can do on that list. Complete it, and then start on number two. Don't worry about the long term. Just concentrate on the obvious first step that you can take. Surprisingly enough, everything else will take care of itself. The Confucian saying, "A journey of a thousand leagues begins with a single step," is so popular in so many languages because it is so true.

The second letter, O, stands for Opportunity. Successful people do not wait for opportunities to turn their goals into reality; rather, they make their opportunities, because they are perfectly clear about the kind of life they wish to create. Once you have taken the time to decide exactly what you want, you will experience an endless flow of opportunities that will help move you in that direction....

A stands for Ability. Many people hesitate to set high, challenging goals because they lack the ability necessary to turn those goals into reality. But remember that we all lacked knowledge and experience when we started out in our careers or fields of expertise.

Do you remember when you started your first job? You probably felt a little clumsy, inadequate and unsure about how to do it well. As you progressed and got more experience, you became more and more confident, and in many cases, you did an excellent job without even thinking much about it.

Since you gain the ability necessary for high achievement through knowledge and experience, if you increase the speed at which you acquire both of those, you increase the speed at which you move ahead.

The letter L stands for Leadership. Leadership is simply the ability to get results. And you begin to get results when you accept full responsibility for yourself, for your job and for the outputs required in your position.

You demonstrate leadership when you refuse to make excuses or blame anyone or anything for the problems you are having. The acceptance of the responsibility of leadership enables you to move ahead and take action.

When you are not satisfied with your job or income, and you sit down and make a written plan to change it, and then take action on that plan, without waiting for anyone's approval or permission, you are behaving like a leader.

The final letter, S, stands for Stay with It — have the resolution to persist in the face of adversity until you succeed. Between you and every goal that you wish to achieve, there is a series of obstacles, and the bigger the goal, the bigger the obstacles. Your decision to be, have and do something out of the ordinary entails facing difficulties and challenges that are out of the ordinary as well. Sometimes your greatest asset is simply your ability to stay with it longer than anyone else.

When you look around you, you will see that all achievement is the triumph of persistence. You will see men and women everywhere who are struggling with and overcoming adversities in order to accomplish something that is important to them. And so can you.

So these are the words and phrases to remember in setting and achieving GOALS:

- The first is Get to it! Get started; take the first action at hand.
- The second is Opportunity. Begin to prepare yourself now so that you will be ready for the opportunities that will inevitably arise.
- The third is Ability. Resolve to learn what you need to know to live the kind of life you want to live.
- The fourth word is Leadership. Take charge of your time and your life, and accept responsibility for your results.
- And, finally, Stay With It. If you stay with it long enough, nothing can stop you from finally winning!

Amen to that! Brian Tracy is very inspiring: I suggest one of your goals for this week might be to download one of his podcasts, or purchase or borrow a set of his audio CDs. He, Tony Robbins, Oprah and other motivators will keep you on your path when you feel tired and you want to stray!

What's Your Excuse?

What's your excuse for not taking steps right now to unleash your Inner Bond Grrl?

Whatever it is — Stop.

I actually don't care what it is. And I say that in the most loving fashion... but I do mean it.

I saw a TV show once where people are told to act as if they only have 72 hours left to live. They are given a set amount of money (not a lot), and told that they have 72 hours to do whatever it is that they would be sorry to die without having done. They have to do it all themselves: the show doesn't set things up for them. It's so emotional to watch what these folks accomplish!

See, the deal is, you can do it, too.

What if you were always moving toward those things that you're passionate about? What if you were to live as if it's your last 72 hours? How do you know that it's not? (Okay, no fair burning all your bills since they'll never get you...) It's your job to get the passion and emotion behind those dreams, set a plan, and then let the Universe provide the way.

Do You Have "Destination Addiction"?

Dr. Robert Holden invented this phrase for folks who live in the Not Now. They always live for Tomorrow. Tomorrow, they will be happy. When the kids are out of school. Or when they get their degree. Or when they pay their bills. Of course, once the new day dawns, they are living for the day after that... when tomorrow comes, they have set a new destination, farther out along the timeline. Do you have Destination Addiction? How's about starting to feel happy, right now, today? You were created Happy. It's just a matter of finding that inner Happiness by laying down your burdens, stress, and the like, and enjoying what is going on right this second. Yes, right now. Put the book on your lap, close your eyes, take a deep breath, and just enjoy what Is; enjoy the Goodness that is You.

You Must Be Present to Win

Stay in the present. Do not live either in the past (mired in your failures or letting dust gather on your trophies), or in the future (when everything will magically be easy without you making current changes to effect that future). Then, it's the Universe's job to deliver. The Universe is like a restaurant — put in your order, and then you need to wait; your order is coming. You don't second-guess as soon as you put in your order at a restaurant, and worry about whether or not it's "really coming," or get up and go to another restaurant after ordering, because the food isn't magically on the table immediately. You put in your order for something that looks really tasty to you, you trust in the "system," and it comes without further effort on your part. (And you certainly don't get up and block the way to your table!)

Remember, psychology has shown us that the subconscious is a Yes Man. And there is nothing more powerful than Gratitude. It is the most uplifting energy that there is. So, you want to say things like "Thank you, Universe/God/Christ/Allah/Mary/Yahweh/Source for that new car that is coming to me right now!" Not in the future. And you do not want to finish off with "...but it's too expensive"! That just sends out great, positive energy to the Universe ("Send that car, bay-bee!"), and then shoots it right down with the negative. Your subconscious, which is your own little Source flame inside you is, remember, a Yes Man. So it will first say "Yes, a new car!" Then, it will say, "Yes, it's too expensive!" See what I mean?

Haven't you ever had *no hope* of something happening, but sent out a huge prayer anyway, letting go of (a) how it will happen and (b) that it won't happen? And then somehow a miracle occurs? If you think this has never happened to you, you're just not paying attention. Or you put it down to Lady Luck. Take some credit for the fact that you helped create that luck! It doesn't have to be something big, but the second you get your emotion/passion/heart and soul behind what you're passionately desiring, and leave it there by not second-guessing — it *will* happen.

*f*Empowerment®

Now, I'm not saying that it's going to just happen with prayer. Let me tell you a joke that embodies this. A man is totally down on his luck, and the only way that he can figure out how to get out of the mess he's in is to win the lottery. So every day, he goes up to a mountain, gets on his knees, and prays, "Dear God, please, please let me win the Lottery!" This goes on for a while (you know how those jokes go), and one day he gets up onto the mountain, and as he's bending his knee, saying his prayer, "Dear God, please please let me win the Lottery!," the clouds start rolling around. The clouds break, and a deep voice calls down from on high, shaking the Earth, saying, "Buy… A… Ticket!" So, you might smile at that, but remember, you can pray all you want for something, and be excited and grateful and ready, but if you're not taking action (if you're sitting on a couch eating potato chips and praying for a great body), you're not going to get it.

The Universe is always looking for ways to make that which you put a lot of emotion/energy into happen for you. This is what *The Secret* outlines, if you have seen that movie or read that book, but this realization has been around for years and years. The first instance I can remember reading about it was in Napoleon Hill's *Think and Grow Rich!*, published in the 1930s and one of the best-selling books of all time. "What the mind of man can conceive and believe, it can achieve" is one of Hill's hallmark expressions. Just be sure that while you are asking for something you desire, you aren't spending a lot more time and energy negating what you're praying for. An example would be praying on the one hand for a new job or a new relationship — but then spending your time gossiping about how "bad" your current job or relationship is. Quit it! Not only is gossiping just not a Bond Grrl trait, but all it does is tune you into that negative energy — and attract more of it. Stop. You get what you're concentrating on. If you're talking about dirt, then that's what you'll get, dirt — and other things of that same energetic resonance. It will totally overwhelm what you are positively praying for.

As a corollary, if you are seeking your James, don't concentrate on what you "don't want." How many of us do that? Instead, concentrate on being completely joyous in your own life, and then have wonderful daydreams about dates with your James. You need to love yourself first; you cannot look for love in someone else's arms until your lovin' arms take in you, first. Then, when considering your James, get all warm and fuzzy about it — about how you will talk for hours, about his quick wit, about his sense of honor, etc. But in the meantime, remember that the more you are doing things you are passionate about and the happier you are in your life, the more you will be attracting the same. The more you are dogging guys and complaining — the more of that energy you get. You get what you concentrate on.

A Bond Grrl has a 100% fabulous life — and then James comes in. James doesn't "fix" her life (far from it), or "gather her up on his white horse" and ride off into the sunset. (I think that the stories we heard or saw as little girls did some serious damage to a lot of us in this area.) The key here is to remember, at all times, that you are One Hundred Percent Fabulous without anyone or any-bling-thing else. It's about You, nekkid, present, perfect. Yes, I do really believe that so long as you have that joyous twinkle in your eye, that's all you need to attract everything to your life.

This is why you need to de-clutter your life, too — because anything that is surrounding you should draw out joyous, passionate energy from you. Does it all? If not, get strong — and get rid of it. (But you already did, didn't you? *Didn't you?*) Stop making excuses that there's no time to de-clutter. All that Stuff is just negative energy blocking you from getting the life of your dreams — the excuses are, too. Get congruent with the energy you want in your life. Get *passionate*! Pay attention to the way the things (and people) around you make you feel. If you're livin' in the past, my sister, you're missing out on the only true reality of life, which is The Now.

 ## *WYTIWYG: A Not-y Issue*

In a later Chapter, we will talk about the concept of WYSIWYG (pronounced "Whizzy-wig," it stands for What You See Is What You Get). When it comes to the Universe, What You <u>Think</u> Is What You Get.

I read a story about Karl Wallenda, the patriarch of The Flying Wallendas, the most famous high-wire/tightrope act in the 20th century. Quoted as saying: "Life is being on the wire, everything else is just waiting," Karl Wallenda fell to his death off a high wire in San Juan in 1978. Interestingly, his wife tells a story about how, for the first time in his life, her husband started obsessing and dreaming about falling, before this stunt. Was it prescience — or did his subconscious hear all the "fall, fall, fall" (attached to a strong emotion: Fear), and carry out these instructions?

My best grrl, Domino, recently told me that her motto and the phrase she had pinned to her computer at work is Failure Is Not An Option. So — what's the mind hear? Failure. Instead, I mentioned to her that perhaps a better aphorism would be Success Is The Only Option.

I remember when I was doing some runway modeling, the word we were not allowed to think of was "Trip." Right before we went out, we were always told "Walk Tall!" We were told that the "brain can't hear negatives," and so by saying to ourselves "Don't Trip," we were really sending the signal to our brains to do just the opposite.

A final way to illustrate this the following: Ready? I want you to think about a giraffe. Got it? OK, you're focused on that giraffe, I want it in your mind's eye so strongly, the giraffe could walk right into your room right now and you would not be surprised to feel its hot breath on the back of your neck. OK? Set? Now, do NOT think of an elephant. Whatcha thinking of? OK now DEFINITELY do NOT think of a purple elephant! See? You had that giraffe in your sights, all set, 3D, and bloop! All gone. You're going to see that elephant for a while, now, too. (Sorry!)

So make sure that you are concentrating — and getting emotions behind — verbs, actions, thoughts and deeds that you want to manifest into your life, not the "Nots"!!

Keeping Time Free

I have been reading some of Dr. Laura Schlesinger's books. I think she's pretty strident, but I happen to agree with most of the things she says. In one of her books, she made the point that if you're using words like "overwhelmed" or "overcommitted" you need to just stop, and fix it.

Easy for me to say, huh? Well, no, not really. I have, in the past year or so, winnowed myself off of various boards of directors, out of friendships that weren't uplifting, out of clients who bum me out (even if they pay me), and the like. I have practiced saying "No" when someone "needs" me to do some thankless chore that really they just don't want to do themselves. I am getting used to being called Selfish, when in reality, that word means that I'm not letting someone else get *their* way with *my* time.

Take a look at your calendar. If something doesn't either make you money or give you lots of fun, why are you doing it? I called this "Obligatory Personal Time" above. It could be PTA meetings, boards, coffee klatch dates, "water cooler" talks, lots of things. If you sit around sniping and moaning, especially about your James, is that what you want to be known as? A whiner? Is that what you want to attract to yourself? The more you do it and talk about it, the more you're going to keep getting the same.

Women in particular don't give themselves breathing space. We are constantly go-go-go. Why? We came here to this life to have fun. Period. Somewhere, it seems, we got weighed down with Doing, not Being. We have to lighten that up.

Are you weighed down, either by your own Attitude, or by your Things? Remember, you attracted your attitude, your worries, and your things into your life. You might have built all this up over a number of years; maybe it's going to take a while to release it. I heard Oprah say once that "True forgiveness is giving up the hope that the past could have been different." How true. You really must forgive yourself and your past hurts, to move on. Remember, whatever happened in your past made you who you are today. Every hurt has a help in it. (Or, as my friend Mike used to kid in terrible situations, "Every huge pile of horse [manure] has a pony attached to it somewhere.") When considering your past, remember that the things you carry with you now have lead you to become more self-reliant, more independent. They have done their job though, and it's time to lay them down. I have a quote on my desk from Rev. Dr. Michael Beckwith that says, "If this crisis were to last forever, what qualities would I have to grow to have peace of mind?" You can do it. Then let it go, if you really are determined to get congruent with your inner Bond Grrl. She's free.

 ## *Keep Your Options Open*

It's important not only to keep your time fairly free (not booking every second), but also to keep your mind and your options open.

Enjoy the journey, and don't get too attached to any outcome. Because if you're attached to a certain outcome, you will be unable to see any other paths that might actually wind up being nicer or better for you.

On our honeymoon, my James and I had pretty much planned out what we wanted to do for each bit of our trip. We had one portion that we couldn't move: a riverboat cruise down the St. Lawrence River. The rest of the trip (I thought) was all set, too. Until, oh, the middle of the trip.

My James, who does the driving, said that he thought that it was going to be just a bit too hectic to hit an area called the Charlevoix. We would need to get off the overnight train early — at about 5:00 a.m. in Quebec City, instead of 8:30 a.m. in Montreal — to do an approximately 300 mile loop through the Flavor Trail of the Charlevoix. Being big lovers of good food and drink, this had sounded fantastic.

But there we were in Nova Scotia, and though the food might not have been Flavor Trail quality, WOW, was it ever beautiful. We were staying at a fabulous B&B that we hadn't even found online — we had made a wrong turn and kept going, winding up at the Bayview Pines Country Inn (bayviewpines.com), where our hosts Chris and Jo were wonderful, and the views just stunning. (The Universe, working her magic again!)

So my James, sitting there the morning we were to leave the Inn after a lovely breakfast, said, "Why don't we just stay here for a little while longer?" Mind you, the only part of the trip I had actually researched was the Charlevoix. My job was to plan the wedding, so he gave me just that snippet of the honeymoon to be responsible for. Most important thing I did that morning? I kept my mouth closed and thought about it for about 30 seconds.

Because the first thing I wanted to say was, "This is the only part of the trip I actually know anything about... I spent a lot of time and effort... blah blah blah blah blah." I thought about it, and I realized that he was right.

We would cut about 300 miles of driving out of our itinerary — and spend time in this lovely place that the Universe had provided to us, instead. We could enjoy the overnight train trip without having to worry about immediately getting on the road again. And we could have an extra day in Quebec City — one of our favorite cities in the world.

So, instead of complaining or talking about all my wasted effort, I said, "That sounds like a good idea, tell me about what we'd do instead."

My James was so relieved! Before I started living my Bond Grrl lifestyle, I was much more a regular girl. I would have whined and moaned, I would have pressed to do what we were supposed to do. I would definitely have pouted. I might have done a little foot-stamping. Just a little. With my lip out. And my arms crossed.

Instead, I said, "Good idea."

So guess what? My James said, "Let me see." While he spent some time on the B&B's computer, re-booking our entire trip, I was able to work on this book. He found stuff that he thought I would really like. He kept coming in and saying, "So, queen bed with a view of the ocean, or suite with a view of the gardens?" Stuff like that. He booked us into nicer accommodations. I am not sure, but he might have felt a little guilty about changing our plans — but I didn't say a word, you see.

He knew what he would have felt like, if he had spent a lot of time and effort on something, then had new plans sprung on him. I mean — come on. We all hate it. So by my not complaining, he went out of his way to make the new bit of the trip really really nice.

How great is that?

So when things start to change, don't hold onto your old rut just because. Don't talk about all the wasted time you spent. And, Grrl, never make a scene just to make the other person feel bad. That's all you'd be trying to do, right? Make them pay for your wasted time? Breathe, think, and then go with the flow.

You never know. You might have your motels in the Charlevoix turn into a luxurious spa outside Quebec City!

Take stock of your present situation — honestly. Are you overweight? Don't have two pennies to rub together? Overbooked? Whatever it is, it's time to appreciate and love yourself in your current situation — because you can't change it right in this very second! Take stock, and stop lying to yourself. Most of the people I know are living in the past, or for the future, and so they completely miss out on the present. Look at your present. Thank yourself, your Higher Power, or your Magnetism for what's good in it. And then dispassionately examine what's Not So Good. You attracted that too, it's yours, now time to go about changing it. The first thing to do is change your Attention into Intention — pay Attention to the way you talk and act, and Intend to change your present into a healthy, happy, optimistic and passionate near future.

Can You Say No?

If you're overcommitted, start practicing and saying No. Get out of obligatory commitments that you hate... and be ready for Fallout. Because if you say No to something you don't want to do any more, someone else is going to need to pick up the slack.

 ### *Send the Bottle Back*

I heard a very funny seminar a while back about being comfortable with wine and wine tasting. One of the things that the speaker suggested was that everyone, on the next bottle of wine they order, should send the bottle back after they taste it.

Yeah, I gasped too when I heard that.

He said you can't do this with a glass of wine, but if you order a bottle, and you don't like it, you have just taken the tiniest little sip out of the top of it (because at a good restaurant, of course, they just pour you a taste, not a whole glass). The restaurant can always sell it by the glass, or behind the bar. So what the speaker said is to send it back, saying "No, that's not going to go with the food. I'm sorry, but we'll have [another wine] instead."

If the waiter freaks out, which he probably will, calmly say that you would like to speak with the manager, and then just explain that you know that s/he will understand, but the wine isn't actually to your liking, and since you know they can sell it behind the bar, you'd rather have [some other brand].

Now you're going to ask me if we've been brave enough to try this yet, and we haven't. But I thought it's the perfect analogy for the whole Saying No thing. It's going to take practice. First — the wine. Next — Mom's Taxi Service!

If you hate your chores around the house, get a housekeeper, and pay for her by eBaying all your dust-catching shoes, teacups, CDs, and the like — or cut back on the Frappuccinos. Do not put this stuff on your James instead. Are you always the taxi service for the kids on your block? Stop it. If chores aren't fairly divided, then just take your own kid and have some quality time with him or her. Listen together to some goal-oriented CDs you got at the library. Do you hate the PTA? Quit. I don't care if you're the only one that gets anything done there. If that is taking time away from you and your James, or you and something you are passionate about — just quit. If you are passionate about the PTA, of course, more power to you. Go for it!

I believe it was the awesome Dr. Maya Angelou who said that, in the end, it is not how much you do for others that they will remember, but how you made them feel. Are you just doing, without loving it, without a passion? Stop.

Go Ahead — Cancel

What if you have said Yes to a bunch of obligations that you realize you aren't looking forward to? Then it's time to call and cancel. No excuses. If they ask for an excuse, just say that you overfilled your commitments accidentally. Then be quiet. Don't lie (that it's your mother's funeral... again). Obviously, you don't want to leave anyone in the lurch, the way you would if you rejected a *glass* of wine you'd already tasted. But if they're not counting on you to do whatever it is, get out of it if you're not all hot and juiced to go.

Getting out of obligations is a real problem for some folks, me included. Give it a try. I just did this today, in fact. I went to the gym and worked out this morning. Then, coming home, I realized that I didn't feel that great, and I was just not going to be able to do what I had planned for the day. Which was a lot! So, I called, apologized, and cancelled. None of these were appointments where someone was counting on me — an office meeting, lunch with a friend, swimming with a friend, a class, and two other appointments with potential new clients. I called them all off, came home and slept for five hours! Now, if I had been following my own advice and making a bit more time for myself all week, might I have avoided going flat all at once? Maybe. Probably. Lesson learned.

Listen to yourself, and from now on, don't order something or do something to please others or make their life easier. Only put something on your plate (whether literally or figuratively!) that you're juiced about. I know, some stuff is going to be on there that isn't your favorite — I have some work to do right now that I'm procrastinating about, too. But the idea is the more you do this, the more room there will be on that plate for things that are actually healthy and energizing for you.

Defending Your Life

I heard someone recently talk about why it's hard to let go of our excuses and get out of the Blame Game. She said that when we say "I can't lose weight, it's my metabolism," or "My James doesn't appreciate me," or "I am too overwhelmed to do this," or "My boss doesn't understand me," we are telling a story, and taking a stand. If we decide to do something that will contradict that story, or we find out that what we have said is not necessarily the truth, we must first admit to ourselves that, in a way, we have been "lying." Subconsciously, it's hard to change, because it's human to want to defend our "story." Think of a little kid with chocolate all over his face, who is asked if he was in the cookie jar: He will swear on a stack of Bibles that he wasn't, even if faced with clear evidence of the contrary. Remember this, when you find yourself taking a stand and defending your life; are you just defending an old and outgrown story?

Darkest Before the Dawn

In trying to get congruent with your Inner Bond Grrl, you may reach the point where you are doing so many things, that there are not enough hours in the day to get it all done. Or enough days in the week. You will have your old commitments, which ultimately will peter out, but haven't quite yet. And you will have your new congruent Bond Grrl commitments, which you're trying to sneak into the day, too.

Just don't give up. I do think it IS darkest before the dawn, as the old saying goes. Even if you are taking baby steps, eventually you will reach the tipping point where you still have a lot of your old life and responsibilities, PLUS the new stuff you're aiming towards. After that, the new will start to outweigh the old.

I try to take one day at a time, but sometimes several days attack me at once.

— *Jennifer Unlimited*

When I first started my change, I worked on the things that I had you do first — going through clothes, makeup, drawers, and the like and getting and keeping them congruent with my Inner Bond Grrl. Sure, I didn't have any new clothes to fill in the gaps — but I figured I have the rest of my Life to fill in the gaps. I also took time to examine my old Life, to be sure to only take with me what I really needed, but also not to discard something that could benefit me in the future.

I remember the day that was the Darkest — it was definitely dark. I wasn't sure I had made the right decisions, at all. But that was the tipping point. I talk about it a bit later in the book. Within a week, after mourning a lot of things I had needed to unload from my life to move forward, I felt lighter, happier, and so much more relaxed. Because I actually knew and felt in my heart that I was moving back onto my own true Path.

If you are feeling that too many obstacles block your Path, sometimes a good burn is in order. Take a piece of paper, and for ten minutes or more, write what feelings of Stuckness you want out of your life. For example, if you feel that your Boss is completely unreasonable, don't write his/her name on the paper and burn it! No, write how that boss makes you *feel*. (So, perhaps, write "disempowered.") If you want to leave a relationship that has lost its passion, don't write that person's name down, write what's stopping you. Is it fear? Loneliness? Then — burn baby, burn, and release!

Just remember to keep feeling your way down the Path — because after that dark patch, the sun will start to rise over the horizon!

 "Overwhelm-ment"

I heard this term at an Abraham Hicks seminar, and I fell in love with it. I can often find myself in this state if I don't watch out. Not very Bond Grrlish of me, is it? Yeah, I know.

Because I know that our time here on Earth is limited (no pretending on that one!), I have a habit of wanting to try out everything that I can — right now.

I get the idea to try something, whether it's a new hobby, an athletic event, or the like, go full bore into it, then I find out about and want to try something else, try to hold onto the previous one too, and... well, you get the picture.

I have a habit of taking on new projects and making businesses out of them. Instead of having hobbies as a way of relax, I generally will take up a new interest, and try, by doing it, to make at least enough money to cover my costs.

This is probably where a lot of my overwhelm-ment comes from. I am overcommitted not so much to things I hate, but to things that I want to do. But there are only so many hours in the day. The things that seem to fall out of my life are the non-money-related ones, or the ones that take a bit of effort to stick to. Like, oh, the gym! And these are the things that are supposed to keep me balanced! Also in my overwhelm-ment, I usually eat poorly, because I'm nibbling, not making meals. Also not good.

I am lucky, though. I realized a while back that life is way too short for complaining, moaning, spending time with drag friends, etc. I had a painful re-alignment process about this, but I did it. Though I'm an attorney, I'm a transactional (contracts) attorney, not a litigator who fights in court. So, the idea of hurting someone's feelings upsets me. But the thought I kept coming back to is that, if I didn't "hurt" another's feelings/drop them as a friend, or ask them not to send me whiny or mean emails any more, I would be hurting myself or dragging myself down. Them, or me.

I still have people in my life who aren't the most uplifting, or who are big complainers, but in general I have relegated them to a very tiny portion of my time. I suggest you think about this, in clearing out your Time, to make room for your Life.

Can You Say Yes?

Are you afraid to live your life? NO is the start — but then YES has to follow. You have to get rid of the stuff you've accidentally magnetized to you, but then proactively fill your Time and Life with what you desire and are passionate about. This means you need to know what you want — which is why you're doing those meditations and deliberations! So many people are just sleepwalking through life, because they think it's easier. Or they're actually saying Yes, but then are fearful of being rejected by the Universe, so they take one energetic passionate step forward, then two steps back by fretting that they "don't deserve it" or "will never get it." We only get one go-around, and it's time to Say Yes and Be Vibrant about it. Be your own Chooser and pick the life you want. No more Victim. Say YES!

Banishing Negative Thoughts

So, what happens when you leap and say Yes to a Dream, but just as you get ready to launch, the gremlin in your head starts whispering the Guilt, Fear, or Victim noises? The best way around this is to remember that magnetic law of Like Attracts Like. What this means is not so much that specific thoughts of an Aston Martin, if they give you great joy, are going to materialize an Aston Martin (though that definitely could happen), but more generally, Joyful Energy begets Joyful Energy. So, thoughts of that Aston Martin are not only going to materialize that Aston Martin, they're also going to materialize all sorts of other wonderful situations, events and things that resonate at that same energy for you. So if you hear your gremlin picking at you for dreaming, be ready. Choose something that makes you happy, every time you think about it. This could be your James's smile; kittens and puppies; your niece's giggle; whatever. When you start having negative thoughts, you resonate, then magnetize to you, like a tuning fork, any other negative thoughts of that same energetic resonance. To break that magnetism, you need to have an equal and opposite positive thought like the ones mentioned above — what I call a "kittens and puppies" thought — to bring that higher vibration to you and halt the negative pull in its tracks.

Negative thoughts are just that... thoughts. And thoughts can be changed. It is a choice. It is not involuntary. So, when I find negative thoughts creeping into my head, I make a conscious choice to change my thought. I find something for which to be grateful for in that moment that works every time and there is ALWAYS something in our lives for which to be grateful.

— Linda Miller, lawofattractionsecrets.com

The Deer in the Road

[from my BondGrrl blog]

Last week was just Bad. A deer came barreling down from a hill beside our neighbors' house. Instead of hitting the deer, I swerved and hit the neighbor's BMW. (NOTE: HIT THE DEER, it's only a comp claim on your insurance.) 15 MPH is still HARD: Cars are "hurt," airbags go off, the whole sheBANG. Then, my James dropped my notebook computer (which is my life), frying the motherboard. So the screen and wireless card didn't work. (Thank goodness for Dell In-Home Tech Support.) As if that wasn't enough, I decided to up my law practice rates by $25/hour and my "pays the mortgage" client said, "Nope."

So, what did I do? I went to my S-Factor pole dancing class. I called upon my Inner Bond Grrl, to come and just take me away!

Then, I spoke with a very wise woman, Susan Bird, who is one of my fEmpowerment trainers (you can read about her at BeABondGirl.com). She reminded me that one exceedingly good thing that happened last week is that a spurious (*i.e.*, unfounded) lawsuit against me settled. Yes, they got some of my insurance money, but if you go to court, it will cost you Bank in lawyer fees, agony, etc. So, you pay some, then are supposed to blow it out of your energy field. That's basically what my lawyer said about it.

What Susan reminded me is that you get what you concentrate on. So, though the lawsuit was over, the angry, hurt, vengeful energy I was generating against the guy suing me and against the System attracted equally bad energy. (See, even us coaches do it.) Hence, once that lawsuit was over, BANG I get hit by some SERIOUS things, bang-bang-bang!!!

Susan said that this was The Universe reminding me what magnetism is all about. (Gee, and was I in the middle of writing this chapter, too?) What You Think Is What You Get. You Get What You FEEL. If you are FEELING angry, fearful, vengeful, etc., you're drawing that to you like a magnet. You become a tuning fork for any energy of like resonance. So even if the thing you're angry about resolves itself, other "like-energetic" things are still speeding your way, until you change your resonance and flush them out of the pipeline, so to speak.

As a kid, did you ever do that science experiment with tuning forks? If you start one going and one next to it is the same tone, it will start resonating too, even though you never touched it. That's what this is all about. If you are resonating on revenge, or what you're going to "do to him" who "done to you," or you are with a James who is keeping you in fear or keeping your stomach in a knot, this is all I have to say to you — Stop. I am living proof, Grrls. You are drawing to you other events attuned to that same energy. So the second that James is out of your life, or you stop being vengeful, IT WILL NOT STOP. You have put that other stuff in the pipeline, and you're going to reap the "benefits" of your energy for a while until it clears OUT. Meanwhile, you certainly need to be careful not to dump more stuff into the pipeline!

So what's it mean to you? Set aside that 10 minutes a day and concentrate on thoughts of "kittens and puppies." Get yourself to FEEEEEL great! Do that Inner Visioning of you in your gorgeous, passionate Bond Grrl Life. Don't cut it back! Dream Dream Dream — Go! If you don't put yourself in this place Every Single Day, at least part of the day, and your day is made up of Go Go, Frustration, Hit My Head On The Wall, Pissed Off, Get The Kids, Hate My Boss, Hate My Life-ness, well Grrl, that's what you

continued

> will Get More Of. Sorry, but it's true. You get what you resonate and that is a FACT I have just been hit on the head with, and re-learned.
>
> Let me give you one more tidbit on this. Susan is a hypnotherapist. In fact, she does personalized, energy-raising CDs. She works with you so you're resonating, at least for the period you're listening to that CD, at a higher, more happy and joyful, passionate level. By spending the time listening to a CD like the one Susan makes, or just listening to your own Daydreams, you break the chain of the Bads.
>
> So Susan did "energy work" on me. I definitely did think in the back of my mind, "This is not going to work." BUT — while doing it — I concentrated on feeling and believing that it WOULD. (That "Be in the Now, give up the How" thing.)
>
> So what did I find in my e-mail when I got home? The client that said You Are Cut Off, No More sent me two contracts to review. Working with Susan, I had decided to give up my fear of that, specifically. Because I have a low overhead, I came home really believing that, by not working with that client for so many hours a week, I would have more time to work on my fEmpowerment business, which I adore. Let it go and... in it comes. Wild, huh?
>
> I am also driving a friend's car, while mine is getting fixed. It's a beater, and really slow. And a stick shift. You know what it's making me do? Slow Down. (Driving this car at 55 MPH is like taking my life in my hands, but it's free, no rental fee!) In my own car, I can go 80 and still be filing my nails, talking on the phone, juggling balls, daydreaming. That is not good. This car is bringing me back into Present Focus.
>
> Remember — It's ALL Good.

Sometimes, it's too hard to leap from a negative, depressing, or fearful thought ("I will never, ever be out of debt") into the equal and opposite positive thought ("I feel like a millionaire"). So work your way there by going to that secret "kittens and puppies" thought that always gets a smile from you — whether it's your dog licking your eyes, a perfect football spiral, the smell of cut grass, maybe even the idea of kicking your enemy/boss all around town! The second you start thinking of that, you have broken the resonance of that negative thought, and have started the climb away from it. An Evil Smile is still a Smile — so Revenge is better than Depression! The next thought might be something a bit better, then a bit better — in the end, you're back driving down the road in your Dream Aston Martin, out of the clutches of that negativity and feeling like a millionaire. Just don't try to take too big of a leap; be prepared with that "kittens and puppies" thought for when the negatives creep in on you, and Dream!

Clearing Your Memories

What about all our "baggage"? One of the best ways to clear those I Am A Loser memories is to make them ludicrous. Each of us has done something or had something done "to us" in our lives that will pop to our minds at an inopportune moment — something horribly embarrassing or uncomfortable. If possible, the best thing to do is to laugh at it, or make it even more ridiculous than it was. Remember that by bringing up that memory and dwelling on it, you're resonating at that energetic level again. You need to stop it from having such a hold on your Psyche — and one of the best ways is to poke fun at the memory.

Nobody can make you feel inferior without your permission.

— *Eleanor Roosevelt*

You're definitely older now than you were when Whatever-It-Was happened — chalk that event up to your naïveté, see it for what it was, and realize that, usually, it was not half as bad as your inner critic gremlin will want you to remember. Could it make a great funny story? All comedians make up their best skits out of events that are at least partially true, and usually self-deprecating. If you can Clear the Memory, especially an embarrassing one, by making it into a story, you're going to get people to laugh at it. And there is nothing that dispels bad energy better than laughter, or at least just bringing these memories up to the light of day and consciously releasing them.

If you want to make a memory go away that's holding you back, you need to get a hold of it first. Bring it out, examine it, and look at the Truth of it. Rid yourself of its energy, which is only magnetizing more of the same to you, when you worry that memory like a dog worries a bone. It's just a memory. It's past energy that's stuck in your Psyche because you keep coming back to it and don't let it free. You are letting that Past define you forevermore. Because if you go over and over something in your mind, your mind doesn't know it's not your Present. (Remember the concert pianist example?) So thinking about some Loser event from the past makes your mind tag you as a Loser now. Time to dissipate those thoughts, flush them, and move on. Sure, they will come back to you in down times — but try to fight with laughter, with reminding yourself that you're not guilty, or with whatever it takes. Actively define who you are, and actively dump who you are not.

True happiness is of a retired nature, and an enemy to pomp and noise; it arises, in the first place, from the enjoyment of one's self, and in the next from the friendship and conversation of a few select companions.

— *Joseph Addison*

 ## Integrity

> This morning's quote from abraham-hicks.com read:
> It does not matter what path you take,
> but it does matter if the path you are taking
> is something you believe is appropriate.
> NOTHING is more damaging to you
> than to do something that you believe is wrong.

In exploring and expressing your inner Bond Grrl, you must sort out what you, personally, believe is appropriate behavior. NOT appropriate because "They had it coming," or because of an "eye for an eye," but rather a true and honest, grounded feeling of propriety about your action.

Come on — you know when you're doing something that's not motivated from your heart. As the book *Excuse Me, Your Life Is Waiting* said, you need to check, every time you do or say something, to be sure that it makes your heart sing. We're not talking about what "makes you feel good." You might convince yourself that just one more piece of chocolate cake is going to make you feel good when you eat it — but in reality, it doesn't make your heart sing, does it? It just fills a void. Similarly, you might do something out of revenge, which makes you feel GREAT when you do it (or so you say). But does it make your heart sing? No. It ultimately makes you feel rotten, and you wind up "defending" your actions — especially to yourself.

If you are about to do or say something, have a heart check to see if it's really in tune with who you are. Not a gut check — though a gut check that gives you a sinking feeling would be a big N-O! Does what you're going to say or do make your heart sing? Does it make the corners of your eyes turn up a little in a smile? Well then, GO for it!

But if not — don't. It's damaging to you: you're only attracting more of the same to yourself, and, as they say, revenge is a bitter and cold meal that you eat alone.

Let Go of Grudges

And, while you're clearing those memories, clear those grudges out, too. The French say, *Pardonner, c'est libérer un prisonnier... et decouvrir que le prisonnier, c'était vous.* ("To forgive is to set a prisoner free... and discover the prisoner was you.") As you dwell on poisonous energy, it resonates in your body, magnetizing more of the same to you. Are you actually glad to be unhappy? Because everyone gets something out of holding a grudge, being unhappy, and the like. I remember when I was in college, a friend's mother, who was a psychologist, told me this. We told her something that we hated that was going on in our dorm, and she said that we were getting something out of it, or else we would change it. In fact, it was true: While I thought about how Unfair she was and how she just didn't Understand, late that evening when I mulled over what she had said, I realized that I was getting something out of it — I got sympathy by complaining about it. I didn't like that realization one bit. And so, as soon as we got back to the college, I did what I could to change it. That was probably my first small step towards becoming a Bond Grrl!

If you have been careful about picking who is in your life, you have people that are also moving towards their highest potential; who are not just in your life to give you what you need. That would make you a user, not a friend. Some of this comes down to understanding the word "relationship." People often don't understand how to be in relationship to one another; they only give what they want to get, or they only give to get. Remember, you have a lot of different relationships in your life for a lot of different reasons. If you don't, maybe it's because you hadn't been educated on how to have a good one. A relationship takes concentrated effort. You can't be a good friend to too many people, because a good relationship takes work, effort, and time, and each of you has to give back to the other in an energetic, uplifting way.

And if you're in a healthy relationship, then don't hold grudges. (If you're not, get brave, dump it.) I saw a bumper sticker the other day that said: "Why take life so seriously? It isn't permanent." That sums it up. Stop holding onto negative thoughts and grudges related to the past, and *especially* related to folks in your Present. Just surrender. Let go. You need to be the person you want to attract. Think of a Bond Girl. Is she someone who holds a grudge and refuses to make dinner because Bond didn't take out the garbage? Is she passively aggressive because Bond doesn't ask about her day when he comes home from a hard day at work himself?

Try this. Make it a Goal in life to quietly make others feel wonderful by feeling wonderful yourself. Like a true smile from a stranger in the mall — the more you spread that feeling around, the more you will get it back.

 ### *Resonating Hate*

I recently read an article written by a martial arts expert. It pointed out that when we have an illness, or when we're fat, we often send Hate to our bodies. We Hate that sickness or illness or fat. What he said we should do instead is look at it from a cellular level. Your little cells are dying for you. White cells are dying to save you when you are sick. They give 100% of their lives, against that illness. Or when you are heavy, those cells are protecting you. Often we get fat because we are upset, and we eat more, and those cells gather up those calories to pad us against all that external upset.

What he said was to stop concentrating on the negative. He said to spend at least part of the day thanking those cells that are giving their lives for you when you are sick, because to them, their entire existence is gone to save the bigger You. Same with the fat cells: if you project hate on them, they hang in there because, "WOW, there is some nasty hateful energy out there, we better protect the bigger body from that!" So thank them for protecting you, and tell these cells instead that it's all right now, time to go.

I loved this article. I started practicing this when I recently had quite a serious illness (cat scratch fever). All those cells were fighting against the bacteria that had entered my leg. Every single one of those cells has my entire DNA for the entire Me in it. So, in truth, each of them is Me, just at a tiny, tiny level. And they gave 100% of their lives to save the bigger Me. Thank you.

Thanking fat cells is a bit harder when you're putting on your jeans and the back fat is gushing over the belt loops. But for me, I eat when I feel stressed, or I feel that the world is tough, or that I lack something. So I started talking to these fat cells, explaining how much I appreciate them doing their job to protect me, but it's time to go now. In talking to these cells, I am convincing the Big Me, too.

Letting Friends Go

The hardest things to shed are friends (and so-called friends). But just start by making yourself your own highest life priority. Stop going out with the squeaky wheels that you don't like as much as those you think of as your True Friends, or like less than just having some time to yourself. It's better energetically if you talk to them frankly, instead of being passive-aggressive and hoping they choose to go away. However you do it, shed, shed, shed. And make sure that your quiet True Friends, who don't ask that much of you, but just Love you, know that they are always in your thoughts. Have you noticed that you sometimes wind up spending far less body-time with these True Friends; that the squeaky-wheels use up your body-time, but your mind is disconnected when you're with them, thinking about being elsewhere? Time to get congruent: spend your body-time and mind-time together, either alone and goal-dreaming, or with your True Friends.

What Grrlfriends Are For

So once the Frenemies and Obligations are gone, how many True Friends can you really have at once? Don't forget you also need to plan time for mentors/teachers, students, and family and other positive people in your life, time for yourself, and ample room and time to be a friend to your James. This last one is immensely important: you must book time in your day, every day, to be available to listen to your James and his dreams. We will go into this a bit more later, but you are going to be his One True Friend — his guys are all going to be trying to one-up him, even if he thinks of them as his friends. You're really the one who will know him and be his Best Friend.

On the flip side, your true grrlfriends, not your James, are there to boost your serotonin level, which women need a lot of! Grrls love to chat, talk, dream, wander mentally — men, not so much. This chatting boosts your serotonin, and blocks Overwhelm. For more on this, read John Gray's *The Mars and Venus Diet and Exercise Solution*. Remember, of course, not to share with a frenemy who is going to rain on your parade. You also should not be sharing with your friends any details of your life with your James that are not going exactly right. Remember — Bond Grrls just do not diss on their James, period. Otherwise, our grrls remember it, and when things are going well, they still hold it against him. The things that pile up in memory always seem to be the bad things, not the little sweet things that balance it out — perhaps because we only talk about the former, not the latter? Time to rein that in, Grrlfriend.

In my opinion, women often are way too free with their time when it comes to their grrlfriends, with the upshot that their alone-time and their James-time suffers. If you have a James in your life, and it's the right James, then that's your core relationship. The bull's eye on the target. That's where you want to put the most relationship-related energy and effort. In this bull's eye is also time for yourself, and for pursuits that give you passion — such as teaching, or being a student, meditating, or anything that gives you Joy. Second, if you have family, including kids, those get the next level of your energy — or as much as you can stand. I'm not saying to grit your teeth and deal with your nasty Aunt Nellie on her terms. All of this presumes that you're going to speak up and be congruent with what makes you happy, not waste your time and life trying to please others, regardless of whether you are blood-related to them. But you do need to weight helping your son with his homework, for example, above a Girls' Night Out.

On the next ring of time and energy are your friends. You're going to have some best friends. One is your James. Then, you're going to have maybe 2-3 Grrlfriends, tops, that are of the b.f. (best friend) category. As you can see from this example, there is *so* little time when you're leading a planned life, not just floating through it; you really must rid yourself of people of lower energetic vibrations, who love to hang out with you because you bring *their* energy up. Our time on this Earth is finite: spend it with a purpose. And no matter how much I wish it was different, no one is going to hand you more than 24 hours in any single day, or an extra day per week.

 Reason, Season, or Forever?

Ah, friends. Some friends, you have for a Reason, such as the gal you train with at the gym. You see her every day, you share a ton of stuff on your morning runs, you really like each other — but perhaps you're not all that much alike. When the training ends, you'll drift apart. Though there isn't any malice or ill-will, the Reason that you spend so much time together is specific: for example, it might be training for an AIDS Walk together. If you do another race, you might look her up and companionably spend time together again.

Some friends are in our life for a Season. These are the folks that are there for a specified, longer bit of time: college friends, friends at a certain job, or other moms at the school. Again, you get along great, do lots of things together...but you're together until that Season of your life ends, not forever.

Other friends are Lifetime friends. They almost always start as Reason or Season friends, but there is just something about them that keeps them in your life. They make you feel great, relaxed, and at ease. Sometimes you'll have more Energy aimed at that friendship, sometimes less — but neither of you really minds. When you see each other, you just pick up where you left off. No worries.

As your life continues, you gather up and shed friends. Unfortunately, sometimes when the shedding happens, or when you feel it should happen, the person on the other side of the relationship might believe that you two are Lifetime friends. It's tough if there is this disconnect. It usually means a lot of drama, as that person come to grips with the fact that you mean more to them than they mean to you. It's not really any different from when that boy you were madly in love with told you he "wasn't that into you." But sometimes it can be easier to hear this from a boy, than from a grrlfriend!

Real Friends vs. Frenemies

While you're taking stock, who in your life is really a Frenemy? Who is smiling in front of your face, and stabbing you in the back? Time to distance yourself as much as possible from them, too. Part of being a Bond Grrl is Traveling Light. Traveling Light also means getting rid of the so-called friends who talk you down, make you purchase things you don't need, gossip about you. The energy vampires, the complainers, and ones who sabotage your dreams with What Ifs. Get them out of your life.

Quit Dishing the Dirt

In sum, you need to take a look at your friends. Are any of them (Am I going to say this? Yes, I am.) like Lint Balls? I am not talking about Frenemies. No, I'm talking about the friends that cling to you like a Lint Ball, suck your time, and make you feel guilty not to spend time with them. It takes time and concerted effort to get yourself free of them.

You might want to make a Friend List in your little black book. Who do you spend most of your time complaining with? Write them down as Dish the Dirt (DTD) Friends. Now, you're a Bond Grrl, you know what I'm going to say. It's time to fix what you're complaining about, and stop complaining. Putting energy into a negative like that just draws more of it to you. So, once you stop with your complaining, listen to what energy is bombarding you from these DTD Friends. One way out of these relationships, once *you've* quit your complaining and sarcasm, is to gently tell them you're not going to listen to *their* whining and negative energy, either. That's going to winnow out a category of folks that you do Wine and Whine nights with, and the like. By quitting these W&W nights, you bring yourself closer to your James (by not moaning about him). Because it seems that nearly all these sorts of events devolve to how wrong everyone's Jameses are, right?

Are there any people left on the original DTD Friends list? If so, you might move them into Reason or Season friends. Be honest with yourself, and look at the friendship from that other person's perspective; do you believe that your reasoning matches theirs? If you feel that they believe you're a Lifetime friend and you know you're not, make sure to be honest, but kind, with them. Because it's going to end at some point, and you do know it.

Lastly, which friends, when you get together with them, make your heart sing? These are likely your Lifetime friends. Why is it that you don't see them that often? By making room and clearing out the Frenemies and the DTD Friends and friends that (be honest) you just don't have anything in common with any more (Reason or Season friends where the reasons and seasons are long gone), you're going to have more time and more energy for people and events that actually add energy to your life.

 Personal Triage

I recently went to a Tea at the Four Seasons in San Francisco, where San Francisco District Attorney Kamala Harris spoke. I was in the middle of this chapter, and her words struck me like an arrow. Ms. Harris stated (or so say my hasty, napkin-written notes!) that if you only have ten minutes in a week to call your friends, "do a little Personal Triage, first. You might want to call the friends that make you feel good, and who 'get' what you're doing, instead of absent-mindedly calling the ones that make you feel guilty for not calling because they're old friends and you 'love them.' Maybe some day those folks will catch up, maybe some day they will 'get' you. But make healthy choices for yourself, and be a jealous gatekeeper of your precious time." Amen to that!

Shed Gently

Now, there's a difference between shedding the Energy Vampires and dumping folks who have loved, supported and helped you, because you want to move on to bigger and better things and you think that they are not part of your New Big Picture.

There are gentle ways out of friendships — really. Move, for example, from attending the coffee klatch of complainers, to asking some of them to accompany you to things that you want to do. Especially events that your James might not want to attend, like going to a gallery opening or a ceramics class or a Chick Flick. If you realize that you don't want to see more of that person or they don't want to join you in something you find supportive of your inner Bond Grrl, then that's a big clue. It's time they go.

Often the best way to do this is to do what you should be doing — making more room in your life for your James and for yourself. Then, tell the friend that you can't do whatever it is that she wants you to do, because you're spending time with your James. You might lose her; you might not. But it's a start. And if she complains that you are choosing your James over her... well, so, yeah, tell her that's right, you are. Are you curling up next to *her* on a cold night?

Hey — I have had my share of big blow-ups in this area. I'm not as good a shedder as I'd like to be. I hate friendship blow-ups, especially when a friend who believes the friendship has a high energetic value suddenly realizes that you don't value it like she does. Ick. But after the uneasiness, you're going to be more free. You should really be aiming for this streamlined life, where everything and everyone in it makes you happy and excited. That's what being a Bond Grrl is all about. I know it's tough, but you'll feel so much better and have so much more quality time after you do! Now, get to it! Brave Grrl! Bond Grrl!

Be courteous to all, but intimate with few, and let those few be well tried before you give them your confidence. True friendship is a plant of slow growth, and must undergo and withstand the shocks of adversity before it is entitled to the appellation.

— George Washington

Chapter 3

*Be more concerned with your character than your reputation,
because your character is what you really are,
while your reputation is merely what others think you are.*

— *John Wooden*

Creating Yourself

Who are you, when no one is looking? Why do you want to unleash what's inside? What made you buy this book? What has made you read this far? What is it that ƒEmpowerment® can bring to your life? We've talked so far about getting rid of what you don't want. You've even set some goals and promises about what you want to change. Now it's time to focus on creating your Bond Grrl self in the space you've made.

A Name for Your Image

We all have names that we were born with. Names that have managed to accumulate a lot of Baggage throughout our years. If you wonder what I mean, just stop for a second, and hear in your inner ear the voice of your Mom shouting at you, using your full name, or maybe your first name AND your middle name. Ohhhh, bad things were comin' down...

 One Grrl's Answer

This quote is cut from my first web student, Mica. I had been teaching my Bond Grrl seminars in person in the San Francisco Bay Area, but a friend suggested that I start putting the ideas online. So I started a blog. I wasn't sure whether anyone would read the blog, but it became a great way to get my thoughts and teachings down into words. Then, one day, I had a reader! That first reader was Mica. She was my initial online Baby Bond Grrl, and is very, very dear to my heart. This is what Mica said:

"I'm starting my New Year's Resolutions early. Some are: getting in shape, get my finances in order, be a better parent, be a better Grrlfriend, a more understanding best friend and by doing these things become a BOND GRRL!! I read somewhere that it's hard to make New Years Resolutions and keep them at the beginning of the year; that it's better to set them when it's more convenient for you. That you should start goals when you know you have the time and energy to work on it. Also, set goals during a time frame that works for you. A year might not work so set shorter goals of 6 months, 3 months or maybe 1 month depending on you and what you want to accomplish.

With the help of Solitaire [AUTHOR'S NOTE: That's me, more on this in a second], the founder of Double Oh! Productions and fEmpowerment training, I am going to complete my quest to be the Best Bond Grrl I Can Be.

Just a few weeks ago, I didn't know what a blog was. I've heard about them on the news, but I didn't know how serious it was. You can get/give all kinds of info from all over the world with a blog. People talk about what some may consider their most private lives. With that being said, that's how I met Solitaire. She is very smart and gives a lot of good information about everything. She's the Bond Grrl I want to grow up to be!

Now, I'll speak more about being a Bond Grrl and why every lady should be one. My teacher Solitaire said that Bond Grrls represent feminine strength, beauty and resilience. They are strong-willed, smart, dangerous, elegant. Timeless, intelligent and not naïve. She said that, "...Confidence and feeling comfortable with yourself are very, very attractive attributes. And due to this confidence, a Bond Grrl can (and does) do anything." I've always had a hard time trying to explain things to others (my words don't always come out right). But, Solitaire explains Bond Grrls and the keys roles they play in their James' lives. To be a Bond Grrl, you need to be completely in charge of your life, and find out what you are passionate about, and then pursue that."

As you become fEmpowered, you are choosing your image — deciding which parts of You you love and want to keep, and which parts you will help to fade away. Your cleaning exercises in Chapter One and your goal-setting exercises in Chapter Two should have given some form to this idea. In experimenting with your Inner Bond Grrl, you might even want to try on some traits that you like from other people. One of the best ways to try on a new image is to come up with your Bond Grrl name.

You want to pick a name that addresses one of your issues or goals. In other words, pick your Bond Grrl name based on what you want to address or aspire to, in your life. I chose the name Solitaire. That name is actually used by a character in one of the Bond movies, but that's not why I chose it. I chose "Solitaire" because one of my issues is that I am often driven to please others, without considering my own true feelings and needs. (The *Runaway Bride* syndrome.) But in the card game of Solitaire, you play by yourself, for yourself. The metaphor of the name resonated with me. It reminds me to be playing the Game of Life to please myself, even if no one is watching. Solitaire plays for her own enjoyment.

I do actually believe that I was put on this Earth to help others. But a negative corollary of this is that I can wind up looking to other people for approval, instead of looking inside and finding approval and satisfaction there. Or I can work myself to death helping others realize their dreams, putting my own on the back burner.

This might not be the best name for you, of course, if you're kind of a loner, or if you already think that the world revolves around lil' ole' you! You might want a name like Bridge. (Just kidding!)

One gal in one of our seminars chose the name Bubbles, because she felt that she was way too serious. She looked very serious (kind of broody), but when she was called Bubbles it made everyone laugh — even her. Another gal in a sensual dance class, who was very giggly when nervous, didn't want that to come out when she did her sensual dance. She picked the name Sultry. If you're sultry, you are not giggly.

My mom's Bond Grrl name is Nicole, after Nicole Kidman, whom she believes to be the most glamorous, poised woman she has ever seen. (My mom is more the vivacious, Meg Ryan type.) So, what's your internal image? Time to think about it. What's your Grrl's name? Vixen? Sultry? Lavender? Honey? Sophia? Let's start drawing her out — by naming her.

Now, the idea is to start embodying that name, when you go about your daily life. What would, for example, Sultry do when faced with an embarrassing situation? She would probably not turn red and duck her head, and giggle or put her hand in front of her mouth.

Once you've chosen that Bond Grrl name, don't forget, you can change it! My first Bond Grrl name was Sheena. I wanted to be a little more Wild than I was in my regular life, and that name embodied it for me. Once I had Sheena in my life, I wound up choosing another refinement though, and that was Solitaire. In working to embody Solitaire, I am working to this day on spending at least a bit of each day doing things just for me. And she has the wildness of Sheena in her, too!

If you can't think of your name right away, start exploring, with the help of your diary/little black book, some adjectives that describe the qualities you want to develop — words like "sultry" or "elegant" or "exciting" or "effervescent." For me, Solitaire conjures up terms like "independent," "sensual," "self-reliant," and "self-contained." Write these down every day for a week in your little black book, and see what develops for you.

 ### *Baby Bond Grrl And Her Adjectives*

This was Mica's post, when she was working on her adjectives:

"So, my Bond Grrl teacher said that I (we) need to come up with adjectives to 'embody' my inner Bond Grrl self. So for the past several weeks I've been coming up with some that describe me now and how I want to be. I haven't come up with many and some came from Solitaire. I tried not to use adjectives that describe how I look. Here is my list:

Me now: Overwhelmed, passionate, crazed, sensual, depressed, mysterious, clutter bug, confident, faithful, respectful....

What I wanna be: Savvy, sultry, happy, adventurous, aware....

I'm sure there are more adjectives that describe me and I'm going to do this exercise with one of my Grrlfriends to see what we can come up with but, this is what I've come up with now. I have them posted in my cubicle at work to nurture my Inner Bond Grrl.

Now I know that my adjectives are suppose to match my life style. I admit that now, I feel like I'm just an overwhelmed frazzled businesswomanmotherI'llmaketimeforsexpleasetouchmedidyoutakeoutthegarbage woman. But my quest has only just begun, to becoming the Best Bond Grrl I Can Be."

Mica ultimately chose a name that, for her, represented the attributes she wanted to embody. I won't go into how she got there — that's a private journey for each student. Like Ruby Skye, Gold Rush, Sophia and dozens of others, Mica smiles at her name, and it embodies her awesome Bond Grrl self! And as my first online Baby Bond Grrl, she is one of the students attached straight to my heartstrings; through our coaching relationship Mica got out of the gossip-mongering of an old, dead-end job, and is now in a job that is furthering her inner Bond Grrl. Mica is a single mother, a dedicated Bond Grrl to her James, and an amazing, awesome, intelligent, wonderful grrl. She lives in Chicago, so we have never met in person. My vow to her is that *when* (not *if*, right?) I am on *Oprah*, she will accompany me. And, truth be told, I cannot wait! I have now had other online students, but Mica has a special place in my heart and always will.

Balancing

Having some trouble with this exercise? You could try this — ask your two best friends to write down the adjectives that describe you as you are now. Ask them, "When you're describing me to another person, how would you complete the sentence, 'Oh! You'd really like [your name]! She is...'" What do they come up with? Boisterous, strident, adventurous, bold, life of the party, wild, loud, crazy, fun? If that's what they say, how about concentrating on some balancing "yin" adjectives for your Bond Grrl self? If your friends describe you as helpful, giving, nurturing, generous or a Wonder Woman, then it could be that you're not thinking of yourself first, and as such, you're probably overextended. These friends think of you as the first person to go to to get help, or to give them something. So in that case, it's time to think about working on saying "No," and a Bond Grrl name that's a bit more aloof.

See what I mean? The deal here is to be balanced — your Bond Grrl name should embody adjectives that are in opposition to those your friends come up with to describe you. By the way, if you're feeling really brave, you can ask your friends to complete this sentence, too: "Oh, I'm not so sure that you'd like [your name]. She can be..." This will give you further insight into your persona. If you're going to do this exercise, don't forget to just say Thank You to your friends, don't argue with what they say!

Mission Possible: You

One of the Goals that my Bond Grrl students come up with time and again relates to their bodies. I know we've all heard the saying: Your Body Is Your Temple. But honestly, one of the problems with our bodies is that they are generally so forgiving! You eat that junk food, you don't go to the gym for a month, and though you don't feel so great, there isn't actually a mechanism that gives you a good slap "upside'yo'head" when you're approaching the point of no return. Like that Temple, you weaken the structure of your health, some termites get in, some dry rot... and then one day, the whole thing comes down and no one can figure out What Happened. It was happening a little bit every day. And unless you start investigating and repairing what you still can, the same sort of dramatic result can happen to you. I am not only talking about your body itself, but also your attitude and your spirit. If every day you're concentrating on toxic thoughts, and eating toxic food (no matter how "good" Revenge might feel, or that chocolate cake might taste!), then that non-Joy is like that dry rot, slowly affecting your Temple. So let's investigate where you are in this respect — and get some commitments to change what you can, to unburden your Inner Bond Grrl from unhealthy habits!

Eating

Think about what you eat. Does what you put in your mouth match your Bond Grrl adjectives? If not, stop it. OK, yeah, fine, you live a life where that's impossible. I do, too. I put about 1,000 miles on my car a week, and I'd love nothing more than to stop at Burger King and snarf down a milk shake, burger and fries. I used to, and then wonder, "Gee, how come my clothes are tight and I don't feel so great?" Respect your body, Grrls, and get a grip. You can take one or two hours at the start of each week, and put together healthy snacks that you can bring with you to your job or in your car, and provide to your James or your kids. By thinking ahead a little, you won't get hungry, which is what leads to snacking on junk. As an example, if you were to just eat two raw almonds every hour (and make each almond three little bites, eating them consciously instead of tossing them down your throat), they will act as an "appetamer" to keep your appetite down by keeping your blood sugar more even between well-balanced, planned meals. I did not say a handful of almonds! (Yes, I did come up with that word, "appetamer." I believe that foods that we call appetizers are either really appeteasers or appetamers. An *appeteaser* makes you hungrier than you were before — sugar or easily-digestible carbs do this. You wind up worse off after eating them. An *appetamer* has enough protein or difficult-to-digest carbs that you can eat a little bit, and take the edge off until your next planned meal.)

There are so many wonderful books out there that can help you with eating (and no, I did not say "dieting"). I particularly like *The Volumetrics Weight-Control Plan*, and it even came in #1 in *Consumer Reports* magazine when they did an issue on Diets. Books like this, Drs. Oz and Roizen's *YOU* books, Bob Greene's books, and the like actually discuss the "Why" of eating. They are all great, and available on BeABondGirl.com — or, if you don't mind having a used book, get them on Half.com. Once I understood a bit more about Food as Fuel, it was easier for me to have will power around scarfing down a gigantic piece of chocolate cake. Just eating a bit slower, or keeping my blood sugar even by eating the almonds, has helped my will power (read: brain chemistry) more than any self-help mantras I might repeat as I gaze longingly at the candy dish. Remember, your brain (your will power) runs on chemistry, which comes from the Food you eat and the Beverages you drink.

Eat like a Bond Grrl. Eat like who you're becoming.

We are indeed much more than what we eat, but what we eat can nevertheless help us to be much more than what we are.

— *Adelle Davis*

Guilty Pleasures

I love eating. What can I say? My James and I are both good cooks, enjoy food and wine, cooking, entertaining friends, and the treat of going out to eat now and again. It's all good.

WELL... not ALL good. I suppose we all know that the problem with loving food (and perhaps with American-sized portions) is that somehow it mysteriously leads to our clothing being a size too small when we try them on the next season!

The book *French Women Don't Get Fat* inspires me. It has recipes that taste great and aren't that difficult, and the little bits in between are fun to read. I think that the author, Mireille Guiliano, is spot on with her observations.

I was looking for a breakfast recipe in this book this morning. In the recipe search, I came across a chapter entitled "Bread and Chocolate." It reminded me of issues that students, friends and roommates have had in the past.

In this chapter, Guiliano talks about American women's overwhelmingly difficult relationship with chocolate (the whole chapter is on bread and chocolate). To her, one of the biggest problems is that American women eat chocolate and other treats *en cachette* ("in private"). The idea of eating on the sly and having guilty pleasures, per Guiliano, is antithetical to the French.

In France, if you get pleasure out of something, then it needs to have a place in your life. One needs to "maximize the rewards of pleasure while minimizing the costs." Guiliano discusses how "guilt-ridden scarfing" seems to typify American women's relationship with chocolate, whereas in France, one takes a morsel of chocolate as almost a religious experience; savors it on the tongue; eats it "on purpose."

This leads to a discussion of "sensory awareness" with respect to food. If you are "scarfing" your food, you are very unlikely to be able to reap the rewards of taking the time for all your five senses to revel in that dish. This can lead you to feeling cheated. Again, to quote Guiliano, "To know how to appreciate that burst of delicate flavors, that supreme smoothness of texture as it melts in your mouth and begins its way down your throat, is to me a great accomplishment of sensual eating. It's an experience that could not be more remote from eating a Snickers bar on the run."

What is your relationship to food? Are you scarfing food on the sly? Are you standing up at the sink, eating without a plate, fork, and napkin? Are you eating in the car? If so, and you wonder where the pounds have come from, it's time to make eating an experience that you're proud of, and that you take pleasure in every day. Slow down. Gaze at a food's beauty. Sniff, then inhale its essence. Taste and savor. You are likely to eat less, and enjoy more. For more on this subject, check out the website mindfuleating.org — in their "Living CAMP" section, you can practice mindfully eating chocolate (or a banana, or even a donut). This is a great "reality check" on how you are addressing food, and reminds you to thank everyone in the "food chain" when you sit down to eat. Did you know, for example, that it takes 8-10 months to grow a banana? Each banana is cut and carried by hand, separated by hand from other banana bunches, crated and transported carefully to avoid bruising, shipped from a foreign land and monitored closely... how's about thanking all those people, and even the banana tree, that gestated that banana longer than your mother gestated you? Take stock of your relationship with food.

Nibbling

When it comes to food, the word that I can't hear without cringing is Nibble. Nibbling is just a cutesy word for grazing; for eating constantly. Usually, a Nibbler nibbles food not because it's something delectable that she wants just a morsel of, but instead, it's something to keep her mouth and hands busy. That would be all well and good, if Nibbling was done on things like celery, with little caloric value. But no. It's usually cookies, chips, bread, and the like, where every Nibble is chock full of calorie-dense carbohydrates without much nutritional value.

I cannot say that I am not guilty! The other day, we had some pita chips in the house after a party. I don't throw this stuff away because it is "wasteful" in my mind (you know, all those starving children in Africa that your (my) mother talked about, growing up, to make us (me) clean our (my) plate(s)!) So what did I do? Nibbled my way through that whole darned left-over bag of chips. Yikes! Was that congruent with and supportive of my Inner Bond Grrl? Can you see a Bond Grrl scarfing down pita chips or guiltily eating a big handful of M&Ms, then looking both ways to see if someone's going to catch her? Um, no.

Four vows that I follow are:

1. Not to eat anything in the car but a couple of almonds to tide me over.

2. More particularly, to sit down and eat at the table, with a plate and everything. And preferably with candles and a sexy jazz CD. Remember, a Bond Grrl is sensuous: She's all about indulging her five senses.

3. Not to eat and do anything else (*e.g.*, watch TV, talk on the phone).

4. Put down the fork between bites. Chew every bite before picking it up again.

This stuff shouldn't be so hard. I mean, the last thing that I want to suggest to myself or anyone else is to keep a food diary. What a chore. I also can't keep a promise, like the one suggested often by Oprah, to stop eating at a certain time before going to bed. I wish I could, but my James gets home very late, and eating together is one thing that we enjoy, but after dinner, as I get up very early, he usually tucks me into bed!

Anyone can embody the 4 vows above, and it can go a long way towards eliminating the casual nibble-eating that insidiously packs on the pounds.

Often part of nibbling/eating what you shouldn't revolves around a lack of planning. If I don't have food in the house or haven't thought about what I'm going to eat, I wind up getting hungry and looking longingly at the Drive-Thrus. Also, somehow eating outside the house (especially Getting your

Money's Worth at all-you-can-eat buffets!) is a recipe for chowing down. This just means not having consciousness around the ritual of eating. There can also be psychological reasons behind eating — in other words, you eat because something's eating you. Nothing points this out better than Oprah's Foreword to Bob Greene's book, *The Best Life Diet*. If you haven't read it and weight is an issue for you, you should.

I was at a seminar the other day that included lunch, and sat down next to a gentleman who had made himself the most beautiful plate of food from the buffet line. It looked like it came right out of *Bon Appetit* magazine. I looked at mine, heaped high with a bit of everything, jumbled on the plate. I said to him, "That's really quite a beautiful plate of food you have there." He smiled and said that by laying things out and thinking about what he was eating, he ate less. What a great lesson. The next time I was at a buffet, I did my best to do the same: to have an artistically beautiful plate of food, which by definition, means less food. (You can't pile food vertically on the plate a foot in height, if you're aiming for beauty. Trust me on that.) I also concentrated at that next buffet on eating slowly (that's #4 above!). I told myself I could go back — but only after savoring each bite. Your stomach doesn't get the signal from your brain that it's Full until a long time after that first bite. If you eat too fast, or eat unconsciously, you can wind up being overfull well before your brain sends the "stop eating" message. What happened on that occasion? I couldn't believe it. I was too full to even consider dessert. Truth.

What's another trick to help you eat less, and enjoy it more? I find that heating the dinner plates is a great trick. Heating the plate keeps the food hot, so you can eat slowly and not worry about the food getting cold. If you have a microwave and microwave-safe dishes, you can put a wet paper towel on top of the plate (or between two plates) and put it in for one minute. This will heat the plate right up. I also use a smaller sized plate, so it looks more full with less food. You can also have a cup of broth-based soup before you eat, which will help fill your stomach before the meal. These may seem like small tricks, but they help me, and they are pretty painless to implement.

And then there's Exercise…

Feed your body for the wonderful and expendable thing it is. If you feed it junk, it's going to act like a car that you've filled with watered-down (or, worse, sugared!) gas. And if you don't exercise, it's like trying to make that car go after it's been sitting in the garage gathering dust for a month, or a year. You have to run the engine each day, to keep the parts lubed (so to speak).

The one thing about eating right and getting exercise is that you know you should do it. So, do it. Don't complain that you're too busy to eat right or exercise. Being a Bond Grrl involves preparedness, health, enjoyment, energy, zest. Being able to do what's asked for. Don't exercise? As a start, park farther away from your destination and walk part way. Get active. And I actually take a page from Dr. Roizen and Dr. Oz's book *YOU: On A Diet*, and believe that, come rain or shine, you should walk for 30 minutes every single day, at a minimum.

Juicy

We started by discussing your Bond Grrl name. So let's say you're eating right, and you're moving your body. You're healthy and happy. But you don't look like a runway model and are never going to be there. So let's come up with some adjectives that you can embody, instead of bumming about your figure. How about "luscious"? How about "juicy"? (Stop laughing.) Would you call a twig-figured model either "luscious" or "juicy"? I sure wouldn't. If you're going to carry around a few extra pounds, whether it's for now or forever — work it into your adjectives. Remember, get those adjectives in your black book! What other words do you want to embody, besides Juicy and Curvy? Savvy? Sultry? Mysterious? Happy? Exciting? Adventurous? Sophisticated? Aware? Smart? Confident? Chic?

What Men Want May Surprise You

While on the subject of Your Body, I would like to share an article that I found on bellaonline.com. The article was called *Sex Appeal and Real Women — Be Proud of Your Curves*, and it was spot-on with my thoughts and teachings with respect to body image. The author stated that women always find innumerable things they would change about their bodies, the biggest being that they feel "too fat." However, their Jameses state, when asked if they'd change anything about their wives: "I wish she was more understanding; had more time for me; was willing to travel to an exotic location for vacation; watched sports with me; etc., etc." Most men have nothing bad to say about their wives' physiques.

It's not about Victoria's Secret bodies, Grrls. It's about time and attention.

Let's get our heads around this, Bond Grrls. This is what they want — let's give it to them. How hard is it to want to travel with your James to an exotic location, or spend a little time with him? Especially when he obviously thinks that you're beautiful and sexy... as is?

Walk The Walk...

When I hear people use this phrase, they usually mean "Be congruent in your ideas and your actions." But to me and any nascent Bond Grrl, this means just what it says: you've got to work on the way you walk, and the way that you talk (more on that, below).

I know this sounds mundane. But you know what? Having a fabulous walk and a fabulous voice is never going to leave you, once you have Bonded (so to say) with it as part of your New You. Whether you're schlepping around the house in your chosen, less-droopy play clothes, or you're out on the town with your James, the Walk and the Talk are going to be part of your new signature. So, let's get down to it.

I want you to walk across the floor. Yeah, really. But wait just a second — don't get up yet. When you walk, pay attention to what you feel like in your body. Don't change anything; just do it. If you have a full-length mirror available to walk towards that'd be great, but you can do this by just paying inner attention. Now, scoot.

Back? These are a few questions I have for you:
1. Do you walk quickly, or slowly?
2. Do you take little steps, or do you stride?
3. What part of your body do you "lead" with? Your head? Your chest?
4. Are your shoulders forward?
5. Where are your eyes?
6. What does your stomach feel like? Your butt? In? Sticking out?

Do you need to go again? Have at it, but feel what you do, without changing anything. Now I want you to come back and really think about the above and how this possibly conveys your Self to others around you.

Pace

Do you walk fast, as if you are going to mow people down if they don't jump out of your way? As if where you are going is much more important than where you are now? Do you walk so slowly that grass grows under your feet, implying you have nowhere to go at all? Your pace should fit with your Inner Bond Grrl adjectives. What were they? Bold, adventurous, seductive, sophisticated, demure, alluring? I am pretty sure that they weren't aggressive or disengaged, or mopey and dejected.

*f*Empowerment®

If you walk very quickly, you emanate the energy that what is going on around you isn't nearly as important as where you are going. But it also gives off a whiff of poor planning. Even if you're excited to go somewhere, you don't want to go at a pace that gives you shin splints. If you have banked and planned your time so that even a traffic jam is accounted for (it's always better to be too early than to arrive late), then there is no need to rush. You're there to "Bond" with your environment; to see and be seen.

Let's try a little example. I want you to get back up (sorry, today is exercise day), walk really quickly across the floor, and do it with a relaxed, easy smile on your lips and in your eyes, while appreciating everything around you. Maybe you don't even need to get up. Even imagining that is pretty impossible, right? I don't believe it can be done. To appreciate and radiate your Self, you need to move at a speed that allows you to admire your journey — and allows others to admire you. (Yes, really!)

On the flip side, walking super slowly, or looking down, can be viewed as "troubled." You can be perceived as inward-looking and inattentive to your surroundings. Again, this is not the Self you want to radiate!

So envision, then develop a pace that really reflects and incorporates your Bond Grrl adjectives. Next time you walk anywhere, let your pace speak confidence without briskness. Set a pace that reflects that you are on a fabulous journey; that will make people want to know where you are going — maybe even make them smile at your radiant, confident face! Yes, that includes the grocery store, though there, walking slowly and looking down might mean looking for the right box of cereal!

A Giant Step for Grrlkind?

What sort of steps do you take? I had this subject brought up to me by Somatics teacher Madeline Wade. She is one of my seminar teachers and an amazing resource. (You can see her on BeABondGirl.com.) In a very basic way, Madeline explained to me that Somatics is a method to build a personal presence that says "Yes!" to your desires. How?

First, you need to become an effective observer of how you move through the world. Next, you become comfortable with your own power and presence. Ultimately, you learn how to reflect your awesome inner Bond Grrl on the outside! Believe it or not, you can learn how to transform internal, self-limiting beliefs and habits by enhancing your body skills. As your body goes, your mind flows — and vice versa.

A Somatics coach can help you uncover the small ways your body currently moves, that can project a different image than the one you might want to portray. One thing that I had to work on was the length of my steps. Why? I am over 6' tall. And I took baby steps. In fact, when in heels, it was very obvious how small my strides were. You would hear a "clickclickclickclick" to each one of my James' steady "thunks." I hadn't noticed it until it was brought to my attention by Madeline. She noted that — for my having legs that just about came to her armpits — I walked with a stride even shorter than hers!

First, she made me walk with my normal stride. Then, she made me set a very exaggerated stride, without taking Giant Steps like we used to do in grade school games. She asked what that different pacing triggered in my mind. That's what this training is all about — finding out what comes to your mind as you change the way your body moves. I am a certificated Authentic Movement instructor, and Somatics is a different but sister track to studying the body/mind/soul connection.

I related to Madeline that by taking tiny steps, I felt more feminine. I have been tall all my life — always head and shoulders above the crowd, you might say. But it wasn't until I started talking with her about how gigantic and unfeminine I felt as I lengthened my stride, that I started realizing that there is really a LOT that's lodged in the way we move, hold our heads, and such.

With this learning, I wound up modulating my stride, so it's about twice as long as it once was. When I tried it at first, my Gremlin Voice kept whispering how gigantic and unfeminine I was, even though I was just taking a stride that matched my body! You might not have this issue, but your stride does need to match your body. If you are taking too long a stride for your body (this might happen to a short person who constantly feels she has to keep up), then you'll look rushed, and certainly not poised. A tall or heavy grrl who takes tiny little steps is also going to look unbalanced. If you're like me, you may be doing it because you're trying to take the steps of a petite woman and somehow imagining that you're a foot shorter or 100 pounds lighter. Don't do it. Be congruent with who you are now.

Body Positioning

This is a big one. What part of your body do you "lead" with when you walk? Where are your shoulders? Where are your eyes? What does your stomach feel like?

First, let's talk about your posture. No, I'm not your mother. But how do you hold your shoulders? No one can slump like a tall girl, take it from me!

Have you ever seen a skeleton, maybe hanging in the corner of a Biology class? A skeleton's shoulder blades are FLAT on the skeleton's back. Think about the way that you sit or the way that you walk. Is the bottom corner of your shoulder blade poking out backwards? That means you're hunching. You can find out this way:

1. Sit in a chair, relaxed but straight.

2. Now reach back with your right hand, and put the back of your hand (not your palm) up and lay it on your left shoulder blade. If you're not that flexible, you will just reach to the bottom of the shoulder blade; if you're more flexible, you might be able to reach the whole back of your hand onto that shoulder blade.

3. Where is the bottom point of the shoulder blade, in relation to your spine? It should only be an inch or so away, and in the same vertical "plane." Try this: roll your left shoulder forward. See how that shoulder point moves away from your spine, and sort of sticks up and away from your backbone? Now, concentrate NOT on rolling your shoulders back (they will do this anyway) but instead on moving the bottom points of your shoulder blade towards your spine. If you roll your shoulders up, then down and back so your chest goes out a bit, this will bring the points even closer together.

This is how the points of a shoulder blade actually hang on a skeleton. So if yours are not in that position, your muscles and your posture have conspired to draw you away from the correct neutral position. By slumping for years, our muscles get pulled out of shape. One muscle stretches forward and gets longer so the shoulders can easily slump, while the opposing muscle that would hold the shoulders back into their more natural position shortens. If you've been a slumper for a long time, it's going to feel very, very awkward to get your skeleton into the right position, with your shoulder blades flat, and your shoulders back and down. But you have to get to it!

As an exercise, when you're next walking, think about those wingtips of your shoulder blades. Think about them pointing back towards your spine (or pinching it — without actually forcing them back). Now, often people trying to help with your posture will say, "Stick your chest out." Having a size A-B cup, I would almost always counter with "What chest?," but my better-endowed sisters have even more of a problem. Their slump often comes from carrying around all that weight forward. Whatever your anatomy, I want you to think about keeping those shoulder blades towards one another, and those shoulders down and back.

So why don't I concentrate on the chest? Because one of the things that I have noticed is that often when women walk, they either walk with their forehead, chin, or their chest out. Walking "from your chest" looks aggressive; walking with your forehead or chin forward usually means you're looking down, and it just doesn't cast a good light on your face.

So where should you walk "from"?

From your pelvis/hips! I suppose that I'm supposed to make a knowing Bond-type comment here, but I will demur. What does walking from your pelvis entail?

1. Stand up, shoulders rolled up, over, down and back. Now concentrate on your stomach. I don't want you to suck in your stomach (though that will happen). Instead, think about drawing your bottom ribs up away from your hips — elongating your whole torso. Yes, this will make your stomach suck in, but in a different way than if you just held your breath. One way to help with this is to place the tip of your thumb on your bottom rib, and your forefinger on the point of your hipbone. (Think of the front clips of suspenders.) Now, without using your breath to do it, *e-lon-gate* your lower spine to draw these fingers away from one another. It will also naturally draw in your stomach. Keep breathing!

2. Next, think about your tailbone. If you want to, feel the end of it. Your tailbone should point toward the ground. Once you realize how swaybacked you might be (the "booty out" position that is awful for our lower backs and points our tailbone towards the back wall), you're going to feel you can't walk at all with your tailbone tucked where it belongs! It takes practice. Often it involves tucking your buns under, which will ALSO suck your stomach in automatically. You do not want your booty to stick out. You can't have the Bond Grrl walk with your sacrum dislocated. Your booty has to be part of your back, no matter how much Junk you have in your Trunk.

3. OK, so you're relaxed, stretched, tucked under. Now I want you to take a step, but **NOT FROM YOUR FEET.** (Whathuh?) Take a step by turning your hip on a horizontal plane. What this means is that your step should start up at your pelvis, and you should step forward not by swishing your booty from side to side up and down, but by pivoting your hipbone in front of you, staying in the same horizontal plane. To demonstrate this, put your palm against the side of your hip, with your fingers pointing forward. When you step forward, you don't want your fingers to move up and down. They (and your hipbone) originally point toward the wall in front of you. After the step, your fingers are pointing slightly to the left (if you moved your right foot) of that point, but at the same distance from the floor. Your foot/leg will

naturally follow, but you can actually only move your hips on this axis if you have your ribs pulled up, booty tucked under, and stomach in. This is called Walking The Line.

4. Remember, keep your shoulders down, but elevate your ribs up and away from your hips. If you are hunched down so the bottom of your ribs is close to the top of your hips, it's very hard to move your hips back and forth down the Line. Lifting your ribs gives you more room in your torso to turn your hips the way that you should, by pivoting them horizontally around the axis of your spine.

This is difficult to put in writing! Imagine having a line in front of you, running between your feet. As you move forward utilizing the steps above, walk with one foot after another on that line. Try it. Keep your hips on one level plane. See how, if you were to swish your booty, you would fall off the Line? If you are a Stomper and walk with your feet on either side of the line (not "on" it one after the other), then you're not pivoting your hips. They only pivot if you walk that imaginary Line. (If anyone has ever said that you "Walk like a truckdriver," that means you're a Stomper and are walking down both sides of the Line.) Finally, if you're walking the Line, you must hold your stomach in, tailbone down, ribs in, and all that jazz. If you're too heavy to be able to actually physically walk a line, one foot after the other, then just do your best; the idea here is to have something to work towards.

It's going to feel weird, no doubt about it. But this is The Way a seductive walk starts. Not swishing your booty from side to side like a streetwalker — instead, what you're doing is pivoting on the axis of your backbone, so first your right hip comes forward with your right leg, then your left hip, and so on. It's the way a woman's pelvis is actually meant to walk.

Another way to visualize this is to imagine two walls on either side of you, snug and right up next to your hips, You Walk The Line, and don't bump into either one. You just glide on down them, not bump from one side to the other. Women often think that a "booty swing" = a sexy walk, but from the front it looks juvenile, and from the back it looks trashy. Walking the Line looks sophisticated, whether you're wearing sweats (you know, those nice, clean, non-droopy ones, right?) or black tie. And there is Nothing a James likes better than to just Watch You Walk.

This is the graduate level: Lead with your pelvis, as you walk the Line. What does this mean? Very subtly, lean back away from your pelvis. This is how models walk. It means that your pelvis arrives first and your chest arrives just a split second after. This is the gold standard of sexy walks. I will admit to you I'm not that great at it. It takes super abs. But just by mastering Walking The Line, you're going to look just as good coming as you do walking away, and better than 95% of the other grrls out there.

 ### *Something in the Way She Moves*

[From my BondGrrl blog]

Yesterday, I was out running errands in San Francisco. I seldom get into the city and it's a shame, because it's sooooo good for people-watching!

I happened to be in town in a pair of trousers that are JUST long enough. These trousers were such a steal that I bought them even though after the hem was let all the way out, they JUST brush my shoes.

So what's up with that and why is it important? Because I had an "Ah-Ha" moment over it.

Have you ever been wearing trousers that are like this — "just about" long enough? If you have, then you know you have to walk a little bit slower, turning at the hip and Walking The Line. If you do, and the trousers have any sort of bell at all (you can't get away with too-short trousers if they are peg-leg!), you can keep the bell from moving. When it moves, that's when the trousers look too short.

So you glide a bit more. As for me, I definitely didn't try to dash to cross any yellow lights, because by striding out that fast, the pants looked too short. (I checked in all the store windows.) I took long enough strides, but at a slow, sort of foxtrot pace.

Perhaps the key to Walking The Line is to walk as if we are wearing trousers that are just long enough!

...And Talk The Talk

Now that we've covered the Walk... how's about the Talk? What does your voice sound like? Not whether you talk fast or whether you talk slowly. Not whether you always seem to be the one talking, or whether you leave your listener breathless just waiting to hear from you. No: what does your voice actually *sound* like?

I want you to talk. Yes, just talk. Read this paragraph aloud if you want to. Put your hand on your forehead — your nose — your throat — your chest. Where is your voice coming from? Can you tell?

Now, let's find your Bond Grrl voice. Come up with a pitch or tone (like "ahhhhhh" or "eeeeeee") that is as high as you can make it, so that it reverberates in your forehead. You might need to sit up if you're reading in bed. Keep toning, but lower the pitch of your tone, so that it travels down your face, into your nose. Use your hand, to feel where the tone vibrates from. Now keep toning (take a breath if need be), and bring it down lower so that it vibrates your chin, to your throat, down to your chest, and finally, comes to rest down at the base of your sternum — the area that would be just below the middle of your bra. Go ahead, do it. I'll wait.

Now, try again — read this paragraph with your normal voice. Do you get a better idea of the pitch of your voice? Usually, our voice comes from our throat; sometimes (if we have a nasal voice) it comes from our nose or, if we have what's called a "throaty" voice, it originates in the upper chest. Got it? Now, read this paragraph out loud from here on, and concentrate on reading it from that space that you found below the middle of your breasts/bra strap.

OK stop laughing. Do it again.

THIS is your Bond Grrl voice. Not all the girls in the movies have this voice — but you should. It's sexy as heck. And because it's coming from so low down in your lungs, you can't support a huge stream of talk. You actually have to slow down, which gives your listeners a break. Also, you can't shout — because that voice lower down in your lungs means, again, less air support. That's better, too. Having your James lean forward to listen to you instead of leaning back getting his ears blown off by your barrage of words is a lot more sexy.

When I remember to use my "authentic" or "congruent" Bond Grrl voice, my James really notices. I speak slower. I also have more of a chance to choose my words. He says that he is automatically more interested in what I have to say, just due to the pitch of my voice.

If you're at a big gab sesh with Grrlfriends or teaching at a seminar, there is no chance you can hold up your end by speaking in that authentic voice. So what does it mean if you find that you can't converse in that tone? That, likely as not, you're either lecturing, gossiping, or talking too much. Are you letting your hair down with your Grrlfriends and nagging, or running off at the mouth? If you can keep your ear out for your new Voice, and use it in all of your social relationships, you will soon discover (maybe to your dismay) how often you lose the Voice because you "have to" talk faster or louder than your Voice will support. I have friends that talk and are fun and entertaining — but I can't get a word in edgewise. I myself, when wound up, can get this way. I'm not saying that you're not going to slip; I'm just saying to be vigilant about it from now on. Choose!

If you have the urge to mouth Marlene Dietrich's torch song, "Falling in Love Again, Never Vanted Toooo, Vhat am I to Dooooo, Cahn't HELP it," you're not alone. Every time I get back into the swing of using my Voice after a period of mindlessness, I laugh when it comes out of my mouth. I always hear that torch song in my subconscious. Granted, I never heard the real thing, only a mock-up of it on old *Hogan's Heroes* re-runs — but if you know the song, I bet you are going to feel the same way!

You should also notice how fast you speak. You want to speak at a rate that is a bit faster than the normal rate. This makes you seem engaging and exciting. Not so fast that the listener is still concentrating on word two when you're on word 20, but not so slowly that they are jumping in to fill out your sentences. In fact, a recent article in the *Journal of Consumer Psychology* about word pace in advertising, entitled "Hearing Voices," noted that speaking "with faster-than-normal syllable speed and low pitch produces fewer negative ad-directed cognitive responses, along with more favorable ad and brand attitudes." So, according to that article, by finding that lower pitch, and speaking at a slightly faster than usual speed (though not like an auctioneer), you engender "favorable attitudes" towards your Brand... which would be You!

An Example: The Magic Voice

I did some training with real estate agents recently. One of the gals was a bright, eager, rarin'-to-go 23 years old. She pouted that she had a very girlie voice, though she wanted to come off competent on her outgoing message. So she had me listen to it, to give some feedback.

She did indeed have a girlie voice — she definitely sounded young on her message. So we went through finding her authentic voice.

I made her read some real estate listings until she could hold her hand on her chest and feel her Voice coming from that part of her. She (like everyone!) laughed a lot doing it... but when she found that Voice — wow! She sounded like a competent adult. She is just starting her career; she wants that outgoing message to sound competent and confident.

Once you find your authentic voice, listen to it. Record your voicemail message, then play it back. Don't she sound AWEsome? In your authentic voice, you're going to not only sound a little sensual (hey, that's not bad!), but competent, relaxed, and reliable. Like Magic.

Give it a try. See where your voice is coming from. And then use it. If you're in a crowded restaurant, don't shout to be heard. Make them lean forward to hear what you say. It will make you choose your words more carefully. Stay in that Voice — and see how much closer that alone moves you towards your Inner Bond Grrl.

> *I can't say I'm going crazy*
> *But you make a pretty good case...*
> *And you never fail to amaze*
> *It's your voice I hear drivin' me wild...*
>
> — *38 Special, "The Sound of Your Voice"*

Love To Laugh

Remember the "Laughter" song from *Mary Poppins*? It starts something like this:

> I love to laugh
> Loud and long and clear
> I love to laugh
> It's getting worse ev'ry year!
> The more I laugh
> The more I fill with glee
> And the more the glee
> The more I'm a merrier me...

I recently spent a long weekend at a seminar with a lot of people. It was a Vintners' Holiday at the Ahwahnee hotel in Yosemite — yes, veddy nice. Interestingly, the whole laughing thing came up at the affair. There were a few receptions, with people generally drinking wine and having a good time. Lots and lots of laughter. As Mary Poppins continued in that song:

> Some people laugh through their noses
> Sounding something like this "Mmm-mmm-mmmm-mmmm..."
> Some people laugh through their teeth
> (Goodness sake)
> Hissing and fizzing like snakes [hissing sound effect from Mary]
> Some laugh too fast
> Some only blast — BWAAAA!
> Others, they twitter like birds [twittering sound]
> Then there's the kind
> What can't make up their mind [combo of all the sounds]...

The song goes on as Uncle Albert states that when "things strike him funny" he can't "hide it inside... and squeak — as the squeakelers do..."

When I saw *Mary Poppins* for the umpteenth time as a teen, I came to the unpleasant realization that I had one of those braying laughs — interspersed with a snort one and a hissing one. Oh dear. So Pretty. I immediately started paying attention to an acquaintance who had what I felt was a really fun and catching laugh, and I mimicked it. Now, that IS my laugh, unless I am caught completely by surprise.

I had three people come up to me at one or another of the Ahwahnee receptions, to tell me that my laughter "made them smile," and made them "want to come over and listen to" whomever I was talking to. In other words, my laughter led them to the person I was interacting with — making that person more "attractive."

I laugh a lot. Even at bad jokes. I also pay attention to my laughter (even if it's a little laugh), and I make sure it gets to my eyes; that it's not just a polite "heh heh" laugh while my eyes stay dull or roam the room.

So why are we talking about Laughter? Because, my Bond Grrl, I think this is another immensely important trait for you to be cognizant about and congruent with. In the book *What Mona Lisa Knew*, the author points out that laughter/smiling/etc. is one of the best ways to defuse tension and get people to listen to you. I would add that having a pleasant — even an infectious, if you can manage it — laugh is one of the best traits you can have.

As I mentioned, when I was in college, I paid attention to, then changed, some parts of myself that people might think of as automatic (laughter, walk). I wanted them to be more attractive. The more supposedly "unconscious" the action, the more of an effect it has on others. Since people won't think that you have practiced having an attractive and infectious laugh, that goes a lot farther in making you attractive in their subconscious than anything that might seem more plan-able. Similarly, practice your walk until it's completely unconscious. If you love your laugh, your voice, or your walk — don't change it. But it's always good to be open to new things, so do give these exercises a try.

By the way, I even changed how I sneeze. Yes, really. It's possible: there are mouth sneezes and nose sneezes and big and little ones — and with enough effort you can fix how you sneeze and never run the embarrassment of a nose sneeze that is, let's just say, full of "surprise."

I don't think I've ever actually seen anyone write about this stuff, but for me, I know that it made a big difference in how I am received — especially the laugh thing. Thanks to Mary Poppins!

When Bond Grrl Eyes are Smiling…

Yes, I'm going to talk about the way you smile, too! It starts with this question: Do you smile with your eyes? Your eyes are the "windows to your soul." Everyone has heard that. But how often, when we are talking to someone, do our eyes dart around like a bird after seeds — or focus on some mythical cloud or angel up and to the left? Your eyes should be looking straight forward, but not locked. If your eyes are locked on something — like your James rushing forward to scoop you up into his arms! — people will often actually turn around to see what you're staring at. You want your eyes to be soft, and really just sort of "present" at all times even if you're walking down the street.

A smile is the shortest distance between two people.

— *Victor Borge*

 ### *Laughter in the Wild*

When we were on our honeymoon, my James and I stayed at some wonderful B&Bs and inns. At one of the B&Bs, we came down for breakfast, and as one does, ate and chatted politely with the folks that were at the table with us. Well, one of the gals looked at me, then LOOKED at me. It felt a little weird. We were talking about where we had been sightseeing, and what we all had been doing before meeting at that breakfast table.

When we said we had been down in the Maritimes area of Canada, she nodded to her husband and said, "I *knew* it! Were you in Peggy's Cove two days ago?" We smiled and said Yes. Well, I'm tall, so maybe noticeable that way — but it had been a cold and blustery day, so I probably looked just like everyone else muffled up in jeans, parka, hoodie, etc. I couldn't figure out how she knew me.

She went on, saying that she and her husband were walking along the main road in Peggy's Cove, and then she "saw another couple standing and taking pictures and having a good time," and that woman's laugh "was so infectious, catching, and attractive" that she actually stopped just to listen to it, and it "made her feel happier the entire day."

Guess who the woman was?

Me.

She said that it wasn't until I laughed at one of the other couples' stories at the breakfast table that she knew that I was "that woman."

How about that? I told you that how you talk, walk and laugh is not only important to your attitude, but can affect those around you. She said she was "happy the rest of the day" just from hearing me laugh.

Get out there, make the world a happier place! Smile with your eyes. Listen. And laugh your attractive laugh!

Make Someone's Day, Even If It's Just Your Own

Like "kittens and puppies" thoughts, smiling with your eyes can instantly raise your spirits. It's hard to think of something nasty while you are smiling with your eyes. You can not only raise your spirits with that smile though, you can raise the whole world's spirits.

Next time you walk in a crowded area, pay attention to how few people, in America at least, meet your eyes. Or if they do, it's someone who might be trying to menace you, or catch your eye to get you to give them a quarter. I want you to practice walking confidently, with a smile in your eyes. A mall is a great place for this. I know you can do this. That smile doesn't even have to be on your lips if it's in your eyes. Scan the people who are coming toward you, and find a person that feels safe to you (an older man maybe, or a woman in a business suit). Now, think as you look at them, "I'm really interested in you!" Just think it for a second, but really concentrate on it and quietly concentrate on them, smiling with your eyes and letting it touch your lips. Sometimes they will even come out of their reverie for a second. Sometimes they will even smile back!

Once you have gotten that acknowledging smile, look down and away (what I call the shy look). This is your mystery look. But here is the secret. KEEP SMILING as you keep walking. They won't be able to take their eyes off you. You'll see this out of your peripheral vision. You know why? Because by continuing to smile as you keep walking, you are signaling to them that their smile just made your day. You are signaling to them that *their* smile has made *your* smile last. Keep walking, keep that smile touching the corners of your mouth until they can't see you any more.

You have made their day, because they think they have made your day. And you know what? It will make them smile more. And that will lighten up a little bit more of the world — bit by bit by bit.

As a side note, if you keep your eyes on someone after you have had the acknowledgement (instead of looking down and away), they're actually likely to approach you and wonder if they know you, or think that you might be able to help them with whatever is going on in their mind at that moment! Again, just practice and walk... with shining, happy eyes, think, "You're so interesting," nod or smile, look down and away, then on you go. You don't want to draw them in.

This is what I imagine happening on a day that you're really in your Flow. You're walking in the mall, and by the end of the walk, you will have had 20, 30 of those encounters. You'll get a little jet of energy from each encounter. Then, one (or more!) of those people that you encountered is going to carry that energy on to perhaps make 20 or 30 of those encounters of their own. How great would it be, if suddenly everyone in the mall was really looking at each other with a quiet, happy, shiny feeling, that "I'm really interested in you!" look, even if everyone kept walking? I think we would feel more knit together. I also think it's harder to harm someone whom you feel, even if just for an instant, has an interest in you.

What sunshine is to flowers, smiles are to humanity. These are but trifles, to be sure; but, scattered along life's pathway, the good they do is inconceivable.

— Joseph Addison

Chapter 4

Do not fear death so much, but rather the inadequate life.

— Bertolt Brecht, *The Mother*

Bond Grrl Training

Get Ready for Action

The life of a Bond Girl is never boring. Sometimes (at least in the movies), it's almost too exciting. I'm definitely not suggesting you should go out and get shot at or get taken prisoner by an arch-villain. But living a fEmpowered life means being ready for adventure.

What kinds of adventures have you dreamed about having but never felt quite ready to do? Traveling? Riding camels in the desert? Hang gliding? Pole dancing? Test-driving an Aston Martin? Swimming with dolphins? If you let go of the things (and people) that are holding you back and get clear on your Bond Grrl goals, you can have those adventures — with or without a James.

Back in the Introduction, I mentioned some things I think that Bond Grrls (and everyone else) should be able to do: Swim. Jump. Walk over a bridge spanning a canyon. Drive a stickshift. Climb a ladder. Hold on. You might want to add "gallop a horse," "ride a motorcycle," "shoot a gun," "climb a rock face," "SCUBA dive," or something else to this list. Remember, you don't have to be an expert. It's Bond's job to be the expert. You just have to not be an Eek Girl. So get out and try some of them — especially if they scare you!

Do Something You're NOT Good At

I have tried SO many things, because I thought they looked cool and I wanted the experience. Biplane flying. SCUBA diving. Martial arts. Yachting. Golfing. Tennis. Blah-ti-blah, you get the picture. I was never much "good at" any of these things, but I sure had fun giving them a go. Remember — regardless of what your religious beliefs are — you only go around once in this body, at this time, in this place. Make the most of it!

What else might you try? Anything you like. Just don't get Obsessed with it. I know, for example, a lot of folks who golf, and they have to be Grrreat. They get all bent out of their happiness if they aren't. It's actually kind of funny — they "complain" about their handicaps, et cetera. What about enjoying the lovely course, and the companionship of your foursome? I can be out golfing with my friends Jan or Leslie or Flo, and golf is just a wonderful reason to be outside, enjoying the day, laughing, teasing, and chatting for a few hours. If it's your Passion then okay, be serious but don't be a wet blanket; if it's not quite your Passion, don't be a pain in the neck and, as one wag stated, don't make golf "a perfectly good walk, ruined by a little white ball."

I remember this one interview I had for a job. The Big Wig interviewing me said something about his "high" golf handicap. I think it was a 10. Zero means you play a perfect game, and handicaps go up to 40. You get to subtract your handicap from your strokes at the end, and the lowest score wins. So in reality, a newer player with a high handicap could play Tiger Woods and BEAT him, because Tiger could play a scratch or perfect game, and the newbie could hit like 20 over par, but then the newbie gets to subtract their handicap. If their handicap is over 21, they just beat Tiger. Okay, so my handicap is FORTY. So this Big Wig is all on about his "high" 10 handicap, and I am laughing inside. Finally, I said, "I have a 40, but I love to get out there; I pick up the ball when I'm playing badly." Hello, it's a *game*... that you're supposed to *enjoy*...

Fine. So I didn't get *that* job.

I remember another time at a party when the conversation drifted into the subject of martial arts, and I said (true!) that I wasn't all that great at it (my knees aren't all that good, though I have a number of years of training in both fencing and karate, plus a little aikido and ninjutsu). Or maybe it was riflery, where I am left handed but right "eyed," and so I have to pretty much lay my face over the sights to get a good shot. By mentioning stuff I've done but am not particularly good at, I have these funny stories I tell "on" myself that make the listener laugh and loosen up. Then I ask them what THEY do/like to do/etc. By sharing a bit of a self-deprecating story, you've also given them an opening to share something more personal about themselves — to let their guard down a little. It'll never happen if they're on guard to see if you can one-up them, or if you perceive that they're trying to one-up you.

Though it's not who you Are, what you Do often helps keep your conversation engaging. Every year, you should try new stuff that you think might be cool. You want to fly a helicopter? Go to a school and get them to give you a "demo" lesson for half-price. But don't make it more than it is, and please, do not brag. When I was getting my pilot's license, you know what? I didn't care that much for it. I realized I was doing it to impress the guy I was dating (who flew at the barnstorming show I worked for on weekends). So I didn't keep it up. I have some great experiences, but they are just that. Not a Passion, just something I've done.

If you try something, you can chat about it if it comes up in conversation. (You should not be the one to bring it up!) If you can not take yourself too seriously and find the humor in your experiences, this is often endearing to the listener. In fact, they'll often think you're downplaying your expertise, even if you're just telling the truth! However, watch out: if you get deeply into something (you turn out to be crazy about diving, or flying, or what-ev-ah), then don't turn into a Bore. Because people outside that interest group want to hear what you've done — in a story that lasts like 30 seconds. So, unless you're in a room full of equally avid folks, chat a bit then move on, and do what the listener is hoping against hope that someone in the room will do: Ask about Them!

Mind you, in some things, I am fairly good. When people ask what I do, I always say "a little of this, a little of that" and then pick whatever I feel like talking about. If the person I'm talking to is an attorney, I never tell them that I am one, too. Almost invariably he (usually a he) will go on about how Important what he does is. On. And on. And On. And... If I get tired of it, I will smile and say, "Oh, yeah. Did I mention I've been an attorney for 15 years, and been in on some of the most important stuff that's gone on in the software/Internet arena, as a law firm attorney, then general counsel, then running my own firm? Oh, I think I forgot, and told you I am a masseuse. By the way, I think I hear my mother calling."

ƒEmpowerment®

Yeah, OK, fine. That's not nice, but I'm not always nice. Sometimes I just like to see their jaws drop. But it's usually when faced with someone puffing up their importance and talk-talk-talking about What They Do. Can you see Bond doing this? He might drop a little bombful of knowledge (the vintage of a champagne, or the brand of a whiff of perfume), but he doesn't go on about it — and certainly doesn't talk about himself, ever.

In sum, have experiences that interest you. You only get one chance this time around! If you hate it — quit. Then make a little story of it. If you love it, great, but be humble. And most importantly, get out there! Do it, Do it! Something outrageous! Find a "demo" every few months at some SCUBA store, or a school of some kind, and make them do whatever they do with you, for free. What can it hurt? Then be strong, and unless you loved it, don't get sucked into (ka-CHING!) lots of lessons!

Now, you're not going to say you don't have the time, are you? We cleared all that up a couple Chapters back, right? If not, please have a re-look at your Life, because this is the only Life you get this time around. (Of this, I'm sure.) And if you don't make the most of it, and live to your highest Joy, then the World will be dimmer for it.

Motorcycles & Sportscars

One thing that I believe everyone should be able to do is drive a manual car. If you don't know how, do you have a friend who has a manual, and would be brave enough to teach you? When I first learned, oh dear, I was really awful. I was going to University in England, and the only car I could afford was a manual car from the 50s (with a choke, and everything — oh, and of course right-hand drive). I used to measure how well I had done driving that day by how many times I stalled on the way to school! In fact, it became a friendly running joke in my classroom. As the only American, I had had a bit of trouble breaking into friendships; the British are incredibly friendly and cordial, but slow to true friendships. Personally, I prefer this to folks who come on like your best friend when they first meet you! Once I started poking a bit of fun at myself (and took it well when they did too), it broke the ice.

Why do I believe you should be able to drive a manual car? Because you're a Bond Grrl! No, really — because I think that everyone needs to be able to do things that can get them out of trouble. You might be out with your Grrls, and realize that one has had too much to drink. (That'd never be you, since you don't need to wash your Life away with alcohol, right?) She has a manual car. Can you say to her "Hon, let me just drop you off at home, I want you to keep having fun here but I want you to be safe, too. I'll drive you home, then take your car home with me, and get it back to you tomorrow morning so you can drive me back home, okay?" Or, what if a friend calls you at 3 a.m. that she has rolled her car, she's frantic, and needs someone to pick her up? This actually happened to me when I was in college. In my case, I lived in a dorm, and, though I didn't have a car, one of the other girls was willing to loan me hers — but I couldn't drive her stick-shift. I wound up having to call another friend who I knew could drive a stick, to come drive me out to save the first friend. (The gal with the car sure wasn't going to get out of bed at 3 a.m., though she was willing to loan her car!) I also read recently of two young girls who were kidnapped, and were able to get loose and actually get in the kidnapper's truck and get back to safety. One of the teens said matter-of-factly to the press, "The one thing I am thankful for is that my Dad taught me to drive a stick, because [the other girl] had no idea, and we'd probably be dead now."

I actually have also taken motorcycle lessons — I took them because I thought it would be cool, but also "just in case." In California, there are inexpensive Basic Rider classes. They supply the motorcycle, and even help you pass the DMV test. So if you're at all interested, this might be an avenue for you to explore.

In sum, I believe that driving a manual car or a motorcycle is like swimming. It's something everyone should know how to do, even if you never really practice it all that much. And it could, theoretically, save your life some day.

Body Presence

What might you investigate (perhaps a class at the local community college?) that could help you really get into your body? We often disassociate ourselves from our bodies, and pride ourselves for our minds. Then, we feel uncertain in the Skin We're In. What about yoga? Belly dancing? Pole dancing? What about even taking some beginning massage classes, where you take turns giving and getting massages? (This is how I started, and wound up obtaining my massage certificate!) There are classes to make you feel strong (judo, karate, Pilates), or sexy (belly dancing, pole dancing). Explore all sides of your body presence and remember, your body is the greatest tool you have. Because you *Are* a soul/energy; you *Have* a body. (How many of us think we "Have" a soul, indicating that we believe we "Are" our body?) You need to take care of, appreciate, and explore her, in all her glory!

Blind Woman Dancing

[From my Bondgrrl blog]

There's a blind woman in my ballroom dancing class. Wow. She has a great, sunny outlook, and is a fantastic dancer. I wind up holding her arm when we do some of the floor exercises at the beginning of the class — whispering, "Two more steps and we're at the wall," and whatnot.

We are taught fairly complicated steps, but we get to WATCH the teacher do them and follow along. She just holds onto the wall and waits patiently. Then, the instructor comes over and dances the steps with her slowly, to get her to feel the pattern we are doing. She gets it each time. I don't know how she does it! Is that the Bond Grrl spirit, or what?

The guys in our intermediate class aren't that good (barring a few). I have trouble following them because they aren't getting their feet quite right, or they don't really lead. If, as a follower, you already know the steps to the routine, you can look okay without being led — but that's not what's supposed to be going on out there. I often wind up frustrated because the guys are looking at their feet, or not leading, or have their arms down so I am not "held right" — stuff like that. How does she do it? I wonder if when dancing with her, she brings out the best in those guys, because they know that it's truly important that they lead and watch out for her. And in return, she trusts them to take care of her. But even when (out of the corner of my eye) I see that she's not getting a strong lead and winds up lost, she always has a good attitude about it. She's always having fun, laughing, and making the leaders feel like it's all Just Fine. Are we all so gracious?

Ballroom Dancing

While ballroom dancing isn't going to save your life, I feel that just a bit of formal dance training is desirable for any Bond Grrl. If your James wants to take you to swank night spots in sophisticated cities, you should be able to look good out there on the dance floor. Not many people really know how to dance any more — though some of the shows like *Dancing With The Stars* have started it on a comeback! So you'll stand out more if you can do a few steps. There are many places to take dance lessons. Dancing is good exercise, it's fun, and you and your James can do it together. Often, dance studios will have so-called Wedding Specials where you can get a package of private and group dance lessons for two, at a low price. That's a great place to start.

I believe that everyone should know the standards: Waltz, Foxtrot, and then maybe Cha-Cha or Rumba. If you learn Nightclub Two-Step, you can look good dancing to slow music when everyone else is just hanging and swaying. Me, I have the ballroom part covered: I'm looking for a class that will teach an old white bird like me some Hip-Hop!

The Universe Delivers: Hip Hop!

I edited the above paragraph in the last hours before finishing the edits for this book. My edit actually just involved adding the last sentence, about wanting a Hip-Hop Class.

I really would quite like to learn Hip Hop: Love the dance moves, like a lot of the music. So I had it on my mind, while heading to my S-Factor pole dance class this afternoon.

I am in a new class at S-Factor, at a new time. I joined a class that has been together for a while instructed by Denise, a teacher I adore. One of the gals from the class was missing, and in introducing me to this class, Denise stated that the missing gal would be back next week; she "has a performance going at her studio this weekend."

What studio?, says I.

Her Hip-Hop Studio, says the class.

Yes, really.

Ask the Universe... Don't worry about the How... Be curious, be excited, and just let it happen. Hip-Hop, anyone?

Feeding the Mind

One of the quickest ways to explore different avenues for your Bond Grrl self is to read and experience what other folks have done before you. Your public library is one of the greatest resources that you have in this arena. At the library, if you are a reader, you can check out everything from the original Ian Fleming/James Bond novels, to books, novels, videos or DVDs about Paris. If you're not so much of a reader or don't "have the time," you can check out books on tape (or on CD, or, at one local library, on iPod), which are a wonderful way to experience books while you do things like clean, cook dinner, or commute. Listening to novels, books, and adventures can feed your mind, and fuel your dreams. Whether you borrow magazines to help you build your financial literacy (for example, *Money* is a great, accessible magazine that can help in this area), self-help books (like Stephen Covey or Suze Orman), or novels set in foreign countries, you will be expanding your horizons and filling your mind with dreams during a time (*e.g.*, washing dishes) that you might currently fill with less-than-charitable thoughts.

If you have an iPod® and iTunes, you can also download podcasts every day to expand your horizons — from the comfort of your own computer. Podcasts are basically the Internet's version of the TiVo® machine for television: you can listen to broadcasts on all sorts of subjects, for free, at any time that you so desire. If you have an iPod and iTunes and haven't tried out podcasts, just click over to the Podcast tab on the iTunes Store. There, you can search by subject. If you like travel, maybe you should be downloading the National Geographic travel podcast every week. If you like National Public Radio, maybe you want to download This American Life, or Car Talk, and listen to these broadcasts when you want to — without commercial breaks! If you want to hear the news from a different angle, click on the BBC link, and download the news from Britain. If you want a fabulous, motivating podcast that you can download every week to motivate you to exercise and eat right, try MotivationToMove.com with Scott Smith or Fitness Rocks! with Dr. Monte. There are podcasts to teach you French, podcasts where you can download new music to exercise by every week (like Podrunner by DJSteveboy.com), podcasts about yoga, motivation, cooking, wine, mixing cocktails (BehindTheBarShow.com is a favorite)... just about anything you can think of, free for the offering. If you're a Bond fan, check out CommanderBond.net or BeingJamesBond.com, for some great Bond-related podcasting.

If you download your podcasts in the morning, you can bring them with you, and listen to them as you commute, or clean the house, or walking your 30 minutes every day, or whenever else you have a little time. I am absolutely addicted to podcasts, and change what I'm downloading monthly to match what's taken my fancy. Give it a try — I think you'll wonder how you got along without it.

 Invest in Yourself

My friend Brian once told me a story that stuck with me. One day, he was standing on a corner in Vienna, Austria, and struck up a conversation with an older woman. He asked her what her advice would be for someone just starting out. This woman told him, "I have only one piece of advice I give young people: invest in yourself, because you never know when you'll have to flee." Though we can only imagine what might have been in this woman's past, her words remind us that our education and our learning will always come with us, no matter where we must go and what we must face.

Preparing for Paris

If you've done the cleaning out from Chapter 1, you're ready to be whisked off (or whisk yourself off) to Paris at the drop of a hat. You've got your bag of necessities, and a plan to get the kids, plants, and pets looked after. You've divided your clothes, shoes and jewelry for easy packing, and organized your closet. So, let's go!

You're on your way to that romantic weekend, or taking yourself on a long-awaited trip. What are you going to do when you get there?

One of the best chapters in Paul Kyriazi's book *The Complete James Bond Lifestyle Seminar* has to do with how to handle swanky hotels, tipping, and such. I cannot recommend his book enough, and in particular, the "Hotels" chapter. Though this book caters to would-be Bonds, a Bond Grrl needs to pack light, know how to use a valet, know how to tip the housekeeper, and the like. If you're traveling on your own, knowing the ropes will help you feel comfortable. And if you're traveling with your James, you can surreptitiously be sure that things go right (such as leaving money for housekeeping if your James doesn't). Just be sure that he doesn't see you and take it as somehow insulting to him! You can do it — you're a Bond Grrl! Here are just a few things that you should know:

1. *Use the Valet Car Service.* If you valet your car, there's no stressing out over trying to find a space, carrying all your luggage from the car, and such. Be sure to tip everyone involved: A couple of bucks to the guy who signals the valet, then to the guy who takes your car away; when you pick it back up, a couple to the guy you hand the ticket to, and then another couple to the guy who drives it out. Sure, seems like a lot of money, but it's well worth the effort for the decrease in your stress level. By tipping everyone, too, you show that you appreciate that they all have a part in keeping your car safe.

2. *Use the Bell Desk.* Nothing looks or makes you feel less like a Bond Grrl than schlepping your stuff to your room. Also, if you get to your room and the card-key doesn't work, the bellhop will go down and get you a new one. (This has now happened to me not one, not two, but three times — well worth the few bucks not to tramp all the way back down to Reception and wait in line again!) You can also ask the bellhop to fill your ice bucket if you like. I tip $10.00 each time, though I never have more than two bags. I also call for a bellhop to collect my bags early on the day I check out, and usually store them at the bell desk. This leaves me free to go about my business on that day (unless I have an early-morning flight), without having to worry about my belongings.

3. *Tip Anyone that Does Something for You.* If they call a cab for you, open the door of your taxi, or the like, have lots of $1.00 bills ready.

4. *Tip the Housekeeping Staff Every Day.* Leave $2.00 a day on your pillow for the housekeeper — and pretend she's your mom: don't be a pig! Leave the room tidy, with the towels you'd like replaced on the floor and (duh) trash in the basket. If you tip every day, sometimes you get "treats," like manicure kits from Suite Floors (this often happens in Vegas). Housekeeping makes next to nothing, and they have to deal with all sorts of slovenly pigs on their rounds. Make them relieved to be of service to you! Their grateful energy directed at you will buoy your day.

The Truth about Etiquette

Of course, an etiquette class can go far towards helping you to feel confident in more upscale situations as well. Speaking of, do you know what "etiquette" actually means?

My James and I were returning from our honeymoon (yeah, that's me, Mrs. Bond...) and a gal in front of us had one of those head/neck pillows around her head, and the tag was sticking up. Since we were in Canada, the label was in French and in English.

I was bored (and she was right in front of me), so I read the pillow label, first the English, then the French.

You know that part that says "Don't Remove this Label"? In French, "label" is... "étiquette."

I think that is beyond perfect.

Your "etiquette" labels you to others. The French word is a derivative of "estiquer," a verb that means to attach, or "stick." Your "etiquette" — your behaviors, proprieties of conduct, and how you deal with others — "sticks" to you. They "label" you.

I remember a Bond Grrl student once asked me one of those "If a tree falls in the forest and no one is around, does it make a sound?" questions. She asked "If no one is around that 'knows you,' does it matter if you put on a professional appearance?"

Well, seeing that pillow and where the word "etiquette" comes from answers that question. Are you "labeled" because of etiquette? Yes, you are. It sticks to you like a tag. I know, you didn't make the rules. Maybe it IS easier to push the peas on your fork with your finger, or to wipe your hand on your pants. But this etiquette is labeling you — not just to others, but also to yourself. Unlike the pillow tag, you can't just remove it when you want to; you need to be conscious, or at crucial moments, you'll slip.

So remember, though "etiquette" sounds like a pretty word and makes people roll their eyes and say they are "someone else's antiquated rules," in reality, your etiquette is your Label. And you want your actions to brand you as Gucci, Manolo, Neiman's — not McDonald's, Target, or Goodwill. It makes no difference what brand you're putting on; it does matter what brand you're giving off.

 **Language**

If you use curse words in your vocabulary as exclamations, there is no question that if you get excited, angry, or the like, even if the words would be totally inappropriate, you will use them. Example? Yours truly. I used to use swear words to punctuate my speech, like many of my friends. I thought I could stop myself. And then I wound up winning a contest at work. When they announced it, I was completely and totally shocked, and as my hands flew to my mouth in surprise, I breathed, "Shut the f*** up!" Right in my boss's boss's boss's face. Yes, I did. Scared me sober. No more sweary words for this Grrl. What to use instead? How's about "Holy Cow!" Or "No Way!" Or (my new favorite) "Shut the Front Door!" I know — sounds stupid, huh? But you gotta curb the (*&@#$ words now, to keep them from slipping out, later.

Making Impressions

So perhaps you've been invited to a posh party, either alone, or with your James. You've been watching your etiquette, and maybe taken a class or two on what fork to use. But as you step in that door, what else is there to think about?

Lots.

Remember back when we did the Smiling in the Mall exercise? Well, it's time to graduate. Because the aura that you gave off and inspired in others during that exercise is where we start. At a party or gathering of any kind, you need to step it up, Bond Grrl. We will talk about Listening as a separate subject, but there are some easy things that you can do, that go far towards making a great impression on others.

When you meet someone, whether you know them or not, speak first. Introduce yourself, giving your first and last name clearly. And, especially if you recognize someone you don't see every day, realize that they might be blanking on your name and the connection. If they are standing with other people, introduce yourself to someone you do not know first, then indicate the colleague and say, "Steve and I were on the bowling league together, must be like four years ago, right Steve?" Then you have "saved" that colleague from having to remember you, your name, and how you are connected. If there are name tags, always wear yours on the upper right side of your shirt or jacket. As you shake hands, your label will be facing the reader. (If you wear in on the left, they will need to obviously "look at it" when they are shaking your right hand; it's less obvious if you wear it on the right side.) If it's a gathering with a purpose (say, a parents' gathering at your daughter's pre-school), you could put "Suzy Q, Jesse Q's mom" on your tag. This will help spark people's memories when they see you.

If it's a soccer regional party, you could even go so far as to put "Suzy Q, Mom of Jesse, the Eagles' goalie." Just keep your writing legible!

When you are listening (always listen more than you talk!), be sure to make direct eye contact, smile with your eyes, and laugh at jokes, no matter how bad (unless they are insulting or prejudicial; then smile, but excuse yourself as soon as you can). And if you're talking to someone, be sure to use their name at least once; that indicates to them that you are really interested in who they are personally, they are not just an audience for you. Throughout, make sure that you give off a happy and radiant energy. Even if it was a Bad Day that day, the next person you meet at that party might be the key to unlocking your Life! Remember, you are in control of your Life, it doesn't control you. Be brave, be optimistic, and be sure that everything that comes out of your mouth has some sort of positive attribute. If you can't be positive, don't moan and whine — keep your mouth shut, but keep smiling! Watch yourself and be sure that you're not giving off a Victim Vibe, trying to get someone to ask you "What's *wrong?*" That's manipulative: Stop it. If anything, you want folks to come up to you and say "Wow, what's *right?*"

Finally, you want to speak with people at the same physical level. There was a Cornell study where it was shown that waitresses that "bend their knees" when handing over the check (to get down to the level of the table) had much higher tips than those that didn't. (Heck, they will study anything won't they?) For me, as I'm quite tall (6'2" in my stocking feet), I usually wind up sitting on a chair arm, or finding another way not to tower over people I'm around. This makes us both feel more comfortable.

 ### *Aura of Mystery*

> Recently, I was interviewed by the Chicago magazine *Echo*. One of the questions the interviewer asked was how Bond Grrls should flirt. I stated, "Bond girls don't 'flirt' — they 'are.' Their lives are congruent. They're chic, they don't have negative thoughts, they are willing, they aren't Eek girls. They walk the walk and talk the talk. They listen and aren't know-it-alls. Why flirt? Just magnetize."

Secrets of the Divas

Both Susan Baker (SusanBaker.com) and Mikki Williams (MikkiWilliams.com) are speakers I admire.

A while ago, I saw them together at a National Speakers Association seminar entitled "Day of the Divas." A lot of what they shared was applicable to a Bond Grrl settling into her fEmpowered lifestyle.

Each woman suggested a book called *Don't Let The Funny Stuff Get Away* by Jeanne Robertson. This book suggests keeping a humor/story journal, categorized into various subjects. Susan Baker also spoke about keeping a "speaking journal." For you, this might be a "party journal." Susan, a professional speaker, keeps in this journal what she wore, what stories she told (or didn't have time to tell), what handouts she used, and the like. She makes sure she has at least half an hour after every speech to complete this journal, to immediately record what worked/didn't work, what questions she got, etc. She says that she doesn't like doing it, but it has made her a much better speaker, and when she comes back, she doesn't have the embarrassing situation of telling the same story twice to illustrate a point (or wearing the same suit).

Perhaps as part of your ƒEmpowered lifestyle, you will be attending get-togethers, or perhaps even speaking and teaching is part of your Passion. Though it might seem like a lot of effort, keeping track of items like this can help you to see what is "working" for you in bringing your Inner Bond Grrl out. Not only that, but if you keep track, you can study up on some of the party attendees beforehand in your black book, and Wow them when you recall what you two discussed, last time!

 ### *The Quirk-O-Dex*

I have a great cookbook called *The Surreal Gourmet: Real Food for Pretend Chefs* by Bob Blumer. My James and I love to entertain, and the back of this book has a portion called the Quirk-O-Dex. In this section, you can write what foods your guests are allergic to, don't like, or even things that they love to eat. It's a fantastic idea, and one that I utilize. By just taking a bit of extra effort and keeping track every day of what "worked" for you that day, what folks commented on, and the rest, you can hone your outer Bond Grrl to really be congruent with your Inner Bond Grrl. And when it comes to things like the Quirk-O-Dex, guests will be amazed at how you "remembered" things about them, and how incredibly thoughtful you are on account of it.

David McCullough, in his book *John Adams*, wrote that President Adams was such a student of people that every time he met someone, he would go home and write down their names and what made them special, then alphabetize those names so that he kept that information handy in case he met them again. Apparently he did it for everyone he met.

John Adams... Bond Grrl?

Be Who You Are: WYSIWYG

Mikki Williams, one of the speakers I mentioned above, is very unique-looking. She looks a bit like a cross between Barbra Streisand and Bette Midler: last time I saw her she had HUGE hair, a bright blue miniskirt dress and serious (5-inch?) blue and rhinestone platform heels.

ƒEmpowerment®

At the Day of the Divas, Mikki recounted how she first decided to become a public speaker. She had been a gym owner (and formerly an aerobic instructor), and had done motivational talks for the other instructors. One of the "ditziest" instructors brought her husband to hear Mikki's talk, because she had been so inspired by it. He turned out to be a Big Wig, and asked her to speak for *Inc. Magazine*'s 500 Top Entrepreneurs for her first "paid gig." She said she "almost fell over" when he proposed the fee he would pay her, a gym owner, to talk to them, some of the world's most cutting-edge CEOs.

In talking to him about her speaking engagement, she asked what she should "look like" and "talk about." He wisely said, "Be who you are — just like this — and talk about what you're talking about — just like this." Apparently the year before they had had one of the top CEO/motivational speakers on the circuit, but were "bored."

When she gave this speech and stepped out on that stage, she faced the 500 biggest entrepreneurs of that year — the CEOs of Subway Sandwiches, of Federal Express — waiting to hear what she had to say. She was who she was, she did what she did best, and the CEOs in that audience were so taken by her that nearly all of them hired her to speak to and motivate their companies. So the moral of that story, for you as a Bond Grrl, is really to be who you are, and let your Inner Bond Grrl out. And don't forget that the unlikeliest ("ditziest") person you meet could be the link to your loftiest goals.

Also, as Mikki said, "Play up" what people will notice about you when you introduce yourself, if possible. Mention it first. That defuses the potential negatives of them "talking about" you. She said you want to be comfortable about whatever "it" is (whether it's the fact that you're pregnant, or heavy, or very tall, or have big hair, or are in a wheelchair, or whatever). Self-effacing humor is how we diffuse the comments about us and stop people from judging us — which is what stops them from listening to what we have to say. If you seem different from someone, but then address that difference, what you're basically saying is, "I'm in your head and know what you're thinking." That translates to, "See, I'm just like you!" — which helps them bridge the gap, instead of staying on their side of the gap where you are "different." If you're different, often you will not be considered an expert or listened to as closely — even if the "difference" is something seemingly silly or that should not be meaningful. A Jersey accent. Big hair! If you're the only white woman in a room (which has happened to me), address it right off, and make a little fun of it. Then everyone laughs, and we're all on the same side of the "gap." Help make people comfortable, and they will appreciate you.

One of the phrases Mikki used that I also use with my students is to remember the phrase WYSIWYG (What You See Is What You Get). Be authentic; don't change who you are for your "audience." Find that Inner Bond Grrl, and be congruent with her throughout all aspects of your life. Be comfortable with yourself, which will help others be comfortable around you. Remember, my issue and why I chose the name Solitaire was that I had the *Runaway Bride* syndrome: I was constantly trying to adapt who I was to the people I was around. It's hard to keep track of all your personalities that way, and you're going to seem (and be!) inauthentic. Find your Inner Bond Grrl, love her, and then make sure you are congruent with her, inside and out. If some folks don't get along with her — maybe some of them friends you have had — make sure that she is authentically you, and be brave. Keep her, lose the folks who are trying to push you back down into an old Self just so that they can feel more comfortable, perhaps, with their own lives. For example, if you decide that your Bond Grrl does not want to go out and get wasted on Friday nights, be brave and realize that's you; when your grrls try to get you to go out for 10 Cosmos with them, go along, be fun and bright, but drink tonic water. If they try to "change you back," they're just trying to make themselves feel comfortable with how they are ruining their own lives. Stay yourself; stay Bond Grrl.

 ## *The Gibson*

If you drink cocktails, you may know that a Gibson is a Martini, garnished with onions instead of olives. Rumor (and Mr. Martini on BehindTheBarShow.com!) has it that this drink was concocted by a popular Mr. Gibson in the 1940s, who did a lot of social drinking as part of his business. So that he wouldn't get sloshed by going from three-martini lunches to three-martini dinners, he asked on the sly for his martinis to be made with water — and then to have onions garnish it instead of olives, so he could see it on a cocktail tray. As martinis were then made with gin (not vodka), I imagine that his onion breath would disguise that he was not imbibing the gin!

Whatever the true story of how the Gibson got its name, I also often have cocktails with clients, in my law business. To save myself from having to match them — and to allow them to feel free to have a cocktail themselves, if faced with my ginger ale order — I usually hit the bar about 15 minutes early. I slip the bartender ten dollars, and explain that regardless of what I order, I want the vodka replaced with water. Pomegranate martini? Pomegranate juice and water. Vodka martini, extra olives? Water, shaken hard, brandishing a staff of olives. You get the picture. I sip slowly, and no one's ever the wiser. I also alert the bartender (and the cocktail waitress, if there was one) that if at the end I wind up paying, please charge me for water, not vodka, though I will tip as if I have been drinking "real" cocktails. If the client winds up picking up the tab of course, hey, charge away!

If you find yourself in a situation where you would rather not drink, just a little forethought and making the bartender and wait staff your allies can go a long way. All they really care about is that they receive a full tip. And, of course, you can share a sly wink when your client says, "I'll have what she's having!"

Listening

Remember not only to say the right thing in the right place, but far more difficult still, to leave unsaid the wrong thing at the tempting moment.

— Benjamin Franklin

Some of the most influential women that I can think of really know how to listen. Think about Oprah Winfrey or Barbara Walters. Their incredible appeal is their ability to project that they are interested; that they are "with" the person that they're interviewing. This is because they really listen, and go with the flow. When you watch Oprah, you know that she might have some question she wants to ask, but if it isn't part of the flow, it goes unasked. She isn't like some interviewers, who don't even seem to care what the answer is to their question, they just have a set of things that they want to get out and say. If Oprah is interviewing an author, you know that she has read the book, not just a question sheet put out by the author's publisher. And, you feel that she and Barbara Walters care about the answer, even if they are interviewing someone they don't understand. This is a trait that you can cultivate. Believe me, being "listened to" is absolutely one of the biggest turn-ons that there is in Life! How's about treating any social situation as if you were Oprah or Barbara, and had to come up with three facts about everyone, that no one else knows? You'd need to make them feel comfortable. You'd need to coax them out. You'd need to — well, kinda act like a Bond Grrl, huh?

It seems that being a good listener has gone out of fashion. People don't understand how powerful it is. Instead, everyone seems to listen just long enough to get a hook upon which to hang their own experience. It's as if people listen-listen-listen but don't really HEAR anything. They're waiting, waiting, waiting... until EUREKA! The speaker says something that jibes (even tangentially) with their life, which lets them vomit back their own experience onto the speaker.

I think that in its nicest form, this is just a version of trying to be empathetic; to indicate to the speaker that the listener is "with them" in their story. But in reality, a lot of it is the listener trying to be "seen" by the speaker; it's a "me, too" response. At its worst, it's one-ups(wo)manship. And please, if you learn one thing from this book, banish the words "I know just how you feel" from your vocabulary. Because, truthfully, you do not know how that speaker feels, even if you've had a similar experience.

Economy of Dialog

Bond Grrls are women of economy. This particularly goes for dialog. Bond women don't try to get Bond to listen to how their day was; to banter back and forth; to, in short, have him be their grrlfriend. That is not what a Bond grrl's relationship with her James is about.

I mentioned this in a previous Chapter, but emotionally, I believe women often act this way to psych themselves up. They blather on about themselves, to try to prove that they are interesting — that they count.

However, there is also a physical component to this. By downloading a tough day verbally and talk-talk-talking, women increase their serotonin. This chemical lowers a woman's feeling of powerlessness and overwhelm. And the thing to know is that men already have much, much more serotonin than women do, so if you try to get your serotonin up by blathering on to your James, it's likely to do what an overdose of turkey does to him — make him comatose! (As I mentioned in Chapter 2, if you're interested in the whole serotonin thing, check out John Gray's book, *The Mars and Venus Diet and Exercise Solution*. There are other great books on this subject, but his is definitely the most accessible.)

When a man has had a tough day, he needs to change a different chemical in his body to get relaxed, which he does through going to his Cave and doing things with goals — like playing video games. Talking doesn't fix it. So I'm not saying you should "be a guy" — far from it. What I am saying is you need to realize that some things are best left for your Grrlfriends, and you need to be sure that you understand that you must treat your James like the chemically-different entity that he is.

 The Sounds of Silence

We live in a culture that supports the tennis-volley approach to conversation: "You say something, and quickly, I say something next." This happens almost without pause or without us taking a breath. We are all guilty of formulating what we are going to say next, even before the person speaking stops sharing their thoughts. What if the words you did not speak were more powerful than the words you did speak?

— CoachingCompass.com

The only way to learn something new — really — is to listen. Not to talk. I personally am guilty guilty guilty of talking like an auctioneer, especially when I am trying to impart five hours' worth of training into one three-hour seminar! But in a social setting, the more you get the other person to talk, the more information you're going to have, and the more you will learn. Also, the more attractive you will seem.

One of my trainees, Gold Rush, was talking the other day about dating again after losing her James to cancer. She was one of my very first "Baby Bond Grrls." She has found her new dating life somewhat uncomfortable, as she has a big, big house, and this makes guys she invites "over for a drink" nervous. She also has some food allergies, and when she goes out for a dinner date, these invariably somehow come up. Finally, she has a very high-powered job, and owns her own company.

I told her, "You're giving Too Much Information, Grrl!" Once you have won over your James (or your boss, or whomever), then whatever you need to do that's out of the ordinary — take care of your kids, have a special diet, or whatnot — will be "no big deal." Because they already appreciate You. But in the beginning, don't give anyone too much information on yourself. Just listen. Be free and easy. Be yourself, of course (don't lie) but don't get too deep into You; instead, get into that boss/James/etc. You want to see what makes them tick. Once they see that you're interested in them, you can let little bits of your "stuff" out — because by then, they "like you." But more importantly, you will know enough about them to see whether you even *want* them in your life or to know your intimate details! How many times have we given out a ton of information about ourselves, to find that the person we're talking to is a colossal bore, who now wants to glom onto us because we have something he desires? By listening to that person first, you get to choose whether or not they should have any information about you. Listen, Listen, Listen, Decide, then Share (a little, at first). Then Listen some more, and see how they handled what you Shared. Then Decide again.

The more "things" or "titles" that you have, the more that someone else is going to have preconceptions about you. For example, if you have a food allergy, right away you become a "picky person" — even if you really aren't. I have food allergies too, but I never, ever mention them. I just order stuff I am SURE won't have what I'm allergic to as an ingredient, or I call the restaurant in advance to be sure that I can get a meal I can eat.

Slim Down Your Résumé

Let me give you another example. For a while, I reviewed résumés for a living, and matched those folks to jobs. I would often counsel the recruits who came to see me that they needed to cut back the information in their résumés; otherwise, they would seem overqualified for the jobs that were out there. That we needed, frankly, to "dumb them down" a bit.

There would often be a lot of pushback on this. Because to the folks who fought me, their résumé was *them*; it was a list of everything they had accomplished; it was their Life (on paper). It was Pride on a Page. In truth, a résumé is a tool to get that person into an interview, and must be tailored accordingly. Once in the job, their boss might find out that they were over-qualified — that their new janitor had a Masters in Psychology. But once they have met the candidate, they can balance that "overqualification" against the recruit who is there, doing a good job, and radiating positive, can-do energy, in living color. Someone they would have cut on paper because of their own preconceptions might in actuality be the Godsend they had been praying for.

If you're a high-powered executive or wealthy, and a date finds that out before really knowing you, he might label you as snooty or expect you to think you're "above" him. You know that you aren't (well, hopefully), but your labels tie back in the listener's mind to their own pre-conceptions; to the traits they have attached to the titles that you hold.

So, like the recruit with the overqualifications, you want to be sure that you are in the door, on the second date at least, before you start telling war stories (if you tell them that soon). Listen, be yourself, enjoy, and let your date have that spotlight. Don't lie or be cagey, don't dumb yourself down, but do watch how you're being perceived. This all presumes, of course, that you *want* the job, or the date!

Once someone decides they like you, it doesn't matter as much if you're allergic to cats or peanuts, afraid of flying or spiders... if you're a magician or a mathematician (oh wait, those are the same!). Any generalizations that the other person might have attached to these titles will not apply. But do remember, not everyone deserves You and your attention in the end, anyway. Be friendly, happy, and a listener; only give information about yourself to those that you truly feel you want in your life, not just as a reflex/tennis-volley.

The Worst. Date. Ever.

In writing about what to do and not do on dates, I am reminded of my Worst Date Ever. It's funny now — well, actually, it got pretty funny, even then. It was something you'd see in a movie and say "That could never happen in real life."

I was fixed up on a blind date by a friend. My friend said that he thought we would have a lot in common, so I gave the guy a call. He was very engaging on the phone, and I thought it might be fun. I mentioned that another friend of mine had a dance recital I wanted to attend, and he said that sounded good; what if we were to make a picnic and have that beforehand, then go to the recital? Great!

On the afternoon of the dance recital, the guy came and picked me up at work. He was nice looking, and had a great car. He even opened the door for me.

We drove to a park that was near the dance hall, and he was very happy to chat about himself. In fact, exceedingly happy; he didn't ask me a thing. The drive to the park took about 20 minutes, and by the time we got there, I really knew a lot about this guy; he didn't shut up much. He didn't know a thing about me. I actually started to find it amusing right about then. Good thing, too.

As we got out of the car, he unloaded a super-amazing picnic basket — you know, one of those ones you see for a couple bills in magazines like *Forbes Life*. As he swung it up on the picnic table, he got a very smug look on his face. I knew right then that he had packed this picnic before, and it was one that must have Made The Women Swoon. I couldn't wait to see.

He had a white tablecloth for the picnic table, little cushions, china, silverware, glass glasses, the whole bit. The first thing he pulled out was a bottle of chilled champagne — a very expensive brand in fact. Which I don't like. And caviar. I'm allergic to fish.

(Stop giggling, it got worse.) I was speechless. He, of course, took this for a loss of words, because I was taking in how spectacular he was.

So I took a few sips of the champagne, and when he looked away, I would pour it bit by bit under the table. I couldn't do much about the caviar, but he didn't really notice as he shoveled it into his mouth; I ate crackers.

With great pomp and circumstance, he took out our next "course," with a bottle of Pinot Noir. Now, the reason I don't care so much for champagne is that my taste buds revolt at the taste of Pinot Noir grapes. It tastes like smelly feet to me, so when I have champagne, I try to get a chardonnay-based one (because most champagne is Pinot-based), and I certainly don't drink Pinot wine. He then pulled two containers out of the basket that were marked from a very expensive deli, and expounded on how He Had Discovered that the taste of these little delicacies was truly brought out by the Pinot. He took the china plates, and onto each, he ceremoniously placed lamb kebabs, and a Chinese chicken salad. OK, the two other foods I'm allergic to? Lamb, and peanuts.

I am not making this up.

I knew it would be a lot harder to dump the food under the table (especially as I had a little puddle of champagne and Pinot going at my feet already). So I kinda left it, and pushed it around with my fork. When he looked puzzled that I wasn't enjoying his feast, he accusingly said, "I thought you said you were starving!" So, I truthfully said, "Well, yeah, but I'm afraid I'm allergic." I kept nibbling the crackers. He, of course, was very huffy that I wasn't appreciating All He'd Done for Me. Hmmmm. With just a little forethought (oh, asking whether there was anything I liked to eat perhaps, or at least what I *couldn't* eat), he could have made this a magical, romantic time. Oh well.

The end of this story is even funnier than the whole picnic thing. We did go to the dance recital to see my friend Tansy. She is a belly dancer, and had two acts, one with two corn snakes, and one with her big boa. She asked me to hold onto one of the corn snakes, in between the acts. I had no problem with that, though did ask my date how he felt. He said Oh, No Problem, so of course I took him at his word.

We were sitting in the audience watching the next dancer, and I realized that the corn snake I was holding (who was, I guess, about four feet long) was getting "smaller and smaller" on my left arm. I had the tail end; he's a very friendly snake, as snakes go, and not that fast, so I wasn't all that worried. I followed the snake with my eyes from my left arm, where his tail was wrapped, up and over my shoulders, and then across my shoulders to my date's shoulders, down his right arm... and down into the top of his button-down shirt! I laughed, and was going to make a comment about how the snake was trying to "get us closer" or something, until I saw his face. Do you remember the first *Raiders Of The Lost Ark* movie, where Harrison Ford's character has a stricken look on his face, and says "I... HATE... snakes!!!" Well, that was this guy. It was all I could do not to burst out laughing. I got the snake's head out of his belly button inside his shirt but, needless to say — no more dates from him!

True Invincibility

What makes a Bond Grrl Invincible? Guns? Some little sexy trick she "duz"? No.

What your James (and all the people around you, and you, too!) really crave is to be understood. If you can help fill this need for those special to you, you are going to be an amazingly special woman indeed.

People will seek you out because they need to be heard. I don't mean you should let them talk your ear off. You can set your boundaries. But how often are we talk-talk-talking, and suddenly realize we haven't shut UP for five minutes, and don't even know what the other person is thinking or feeling?

Once you have listened to someone, they are "emptier" and a lot more likely to want to listen to you. Just make sure that they are done talking before you throw up your fabulous wisdom on them. Hey — I use the "vomit" analogy because it's gross. It's also memorable. If you think of your words as Pearls of Wisdom, then you're going to want to share and spill these priceless wonders all over everyone, for which they should be grateful, right, Princess? Hmm. If you just change your analogy, perhaps you will be a little more parsimonious with what you say, and let others get a word in. Of course, if you are not much of a talker, then by all means, start thinking of what you have to say as Pearls, and get them out. But most of the folks I talk with need to hold back more than they need to speak out. When a speaker feels heard and understood, they will definitely be more present for you.

One of the best ways to show that you understand is just to take a bit of what the speaker says and mirror it back to them. Just say, "Wow, I heard you say X, and that really makes me feel Y." Period. If you don't agree with what they say, don't argue. Just say how it makes you feel. (This is particularly good if you're in a disagreement.) The speaker can't argue with how you *feel*, though they can argue if you try to lay something back on *them*. ("Wow, I heard you say X, *you* must be/must feel Y" or "If you think X, *you're* just wrong/stupid/uninformed/etc.")

Try to be empathetic, listen, be curious, give a tiny bit, and keep them wanting more of you (for example — get another date!) If you shoot your whole "wad," then how interesting are you gonna be? And besides, the most interesting person is the one who gets and keeps the most interesting conversation going. And what do you think that is about? The speaker, of course! Don't fake it — well, a little if you must — but practice this. You will get deeper information about someone. As often as not, you'll be talking to someone you think you dislike, and the thing you thought he did that you hate will turn out to be tied to something totally fascinating you knew nothing about. Be an archaeologist, digging for hidden treasures.

 ## *Asking Questions*

Someone once said to me that I know more about people than anyone else they know. I think it's because I ask questions, and am genuinely interested in the answers.

I am also not afraid to ask questions, even fairly personal ones. (Sometimes very personal.) I figure the questionee can just tell me to buzz off if they don't want to answer — but usually, they do want to answer.

I was recently in the Emergency Room. (Remember, I mentioned cat scratch fever in a sidebar in Chapter Two?). The nurse was a guy named Fred. I happened to ask him (as he was dressing my wounds and hanging my I.V.) what he had done before he was a nurse. Turns out Fred had owned and been the head baker for 20 years at a local bakery. This bakery is where my dad used to go every Friday, to bring treats home for our family on Saturday. When I mentioned this and described my dad, Fred said he remembered him. I thought he was shining me on, until he mentioned that Dad "always had the best matching ties/bowties and suspenders." That's my dad!

By finding that connection, I think that I was given better service. (Either that, or Fred is just the Nurse From God). I also found out some fantastic information, by being friendly and interested. It turns out Fred's mother was in the Marines, and was the one who actually received the information that the Japanese had surrendered. His eyed welled up when talking about his Mom. This came up because we were trying to figure out when I had gotten my last tetanus shot — and I said it was likely when I was in the Marines. How fantastic, to hear this story! It was like living the History Channel! Life is so great, and full of wonderful connections. Just listen a little.

Try Being Civil

One of the things that often comes up when my James and I are out together is how "nice" we are to one another. We say "Thank you" and "You're welcome" to each other. We've been together now close to a decade, and we are still very civil, and enjoy each other's company. Because Jameses are often pre-occupied, I believe it's a Bond Grrl's responsibility to keep that civility going. The more Please and Thank Yous that you say, the more you are likely to receive.

I'll give you a little example. Recently, my James and I were driving around Austin, Texas. I was driving, my James was navigating — because I'd rather be the one making the U-turn than the one missing a street, then saying, "Oh, dear, um, make a U-turn...." We got quite lost there for a while, but we stayed very cordial. "Oh, my mistake...!" "Uh-oh, I'm sorry, I thought that we needed to go left..." "My bad...." Even (and most importantly!) when it was blatantly obvious to one (or the other) of us that the other person had made the mistake.

 ### *Shaken or Stirred?*

On a recent visit to the Ahwahnee hotel in Yosemite, we saw someone get really irrational at the check-in desk because their reservation had gone missing. We stopped to listen, because our reservation had been mislaid as well, and these folks came in just as we were getting things squared away.

In anger (unlike James Bond's martini), one should be stirred, not shaken. When something goes wrong, sure, it's going to stir you up — but don't let it "shake you." These folks were super upset and rattled because of the mix-up. The woman was looking at her husband, and getting more and more upset at how things were panning out. She made it very clear it was His Fault, showing anyone within range what a Loser she thought he was. In *The Complete James Bond Lifestyle Seminar*, Paul Kyriazi discusses thinking about how your reactions will affect the people around you. This was a great example of that phrase in action: the wife's loosely-bottled infuriation was upsetting her husband, and vice versa.

My James was not happy that OUR reservation had been lost, either — but, at my gentle prodding, he "stirred" our receptionist into action, slowly adding and mixing and getting what he wanted. The other guy just started (metaphorically) shaking his reception gal — hard! — as if that was going to help. We wound up getting a suite. Never saw the other couple again; who knows what happened? Maybe this comes down to that old adage: "You catch more flies with honey than with vinegar."

When was the last time you thought about civility? Is it really that important to point out the other person's failings every chance you get? I think if you were to drive in a car with my James and me, you would think we had come out of some 1940s movie. We pay attention, and we keep it that way. We don't get angry and blame each other; instead, we figure out how to get out of the jam. We are gentle to one another. (The worse the other person has messed up, the gentler we try to be.) Yes, even after nearly a decade.

I think that this might be a nice little homework assignment for you. How about a little civility toward your James tonight? And I'm not saying to do it because HE is going to do it back. Remember this: You teach people how you want to be treated, in the way you treat them. Pretend that you're in a 1940s movie. Kind of sassy; very civil. Raise the bar. I dare you.

Laugh at the Villains

In the Bond films, the Bond Girl usually faces villains because Bond somehow put her in harm's way. This is where she needs to let him do what he's supposed to do: dispatch them and get on with the mission. Villains are not really her responsibility — and he'd best understand that they're his!

But usually, we're not looking down the barrel of a gun or kidnapped by a bad guy. Usually, the biggest villains or enemies in a Bond Grrl's day-to-day life are her own attitude that she can't do something, or her own complaining, gossiping and overall generation of negative energy. There just isn't enough time in life for that.

Other villains can certainly be found. When a Bond Grrl tries to move ahead or improve herself, there will always be people to talk behind her back. And there will be those who tell her "for her own good" that others are saying things about her that aren't complimentary. The fear is that a superior will hear these comments, then attribute them fallaciously to the Bond Grrl.

What to do, to nip such a villain in the bud?

When dealing with people who are "dissing" you, LAUGH. When you hear that someone is saying "bad stuff" about you, it hurts. I know. Been there. But when you hear it from a third party, just laugh or smile about it. (Don't feel like laughing? Come on now, you're a Bond Grrl... *Act*.) If someone were to say that you ate guinea pigs or that they caught you on a postcard doing the nasty with a donkey (I just heard you say, "OH, can she WRITE THAT?"), what would you do? Would you get all "huffy" and "belligerent" and "defensive"? Unlikely. You'd smile, laugh, roll your eyes, say "Man, can you BELIEVE that?" And you would be DONE giving energy to it. Because it would just be that crazy. (Remember, this only works if you don't give people things to talk about and your actions are protective of your reputation!)

When it gets back to the gossiper that you laughed, it takes their power away. And don't forget, the intermediary that brought you that news also has some sort of agenda. Even if they say they are telling you because they want to be your friend, they are really in that frenemy category. Why? They want to see what happens when they tell you what's being said. They are getting a carwreck, rubbernecker thrill. But if you don't give any juice to the gossip, if you laugh about it and then (this is the hard part!) you DON'T PUT ANY MORE ENERGY INTO IT — guess what? The gossip will die out. And perhaps next time, that intermediary will not bring the gossip to you; instead, they will diffuse it as soon as they hear it, and support you. Then, they're being your friend.

It's hard to do. But it gets easier if you practice it. The trick is to take what they are saying, and make it a lot more "untrue" in your mind (thoughts of the guinea pig or donkey variety). Hold that picture, roll your eyes, laugh at it, and treat the gossip that way. Don't start getting down, obsessing about what people think, or being defensive. This makes you a Victim, and the gossiper becomes your Master. The gossiper gets hold of your emotions, your insides, and your stomach. If the false stories were a little more outrageous, they would not grab hold of you — because you would just say, "Pfffft no WAY!" and laugh. Then you'd tell the person who passed this on to you, "Hey, thanks for letting me know, but you know what? That's just trash," and move on.

So if something is said and you think it might affect your life because people who matter will believe it, then go to those folks, and address the issue strongly and succinctly. (And, by the way why would they believe it? Haven't you been #1 at your job? Hmmm?) For example, you could call that person (if visiting them personally is out of the question). Be prepared to leave a voice mail message stating that if there are any "potential issues that need addressing," you'd like to discuss them. After, you could follow up with an e-mail asking the same thing. Short and sweet. A voice-mail (or in-person visit) is always friendlier (and harder to dismiss) than an e-mail. E-mail is not very personal, and easier to ignore. Even if someone doesn't answer a voice-mail, they hear your voice, sounding cheerful, bright and light. You're You. In an e-mail, they read your "voice" filtered through however they are feeling about you at that moment (which might be colored by gossip, by their bad lunch, etc).

Again, if you think the gossip will NOT be damaging because people will NOT believe it, or if the people who believe it don't mean ANYTHING to you — laugh it off! Stop wasting your precious time and get your attention onto something less destructive.

What happens if the damage is done; if that person that matters believes the trash, and you lose a job, or a friend, or a lover? Then it wasn't an energetic match for you. Don't try to save things by going to extraordinary lengths, or start complaining about unfairness. While it can hurt, there are always more friends, lovers and jobs out there. In fact, there are so many people who want to be your friend in this world, that there are not enough hours to spend quality time with all of them. Similarly, there are a bunch of great jobs out there. If you take the effort and the risk, they are waiting for you. The Universe is a loving and a giving place. Let it fill your cup with champagne, now that it's empty of beer!

When people laugh they relax — and when they relax, they can take in more information.

— *Mikki Williams*

The Value of Humor

[from my BondGrrl blog]

Humor can defuse a tough situation. If you can make a bad situation humorous, it gets people breathing... and it keeps them from being so dug into their positions. There is a lot to be said for laughter.

After having a bad day today, I was weak, and sent on one of those e-mail chain letters. A Prayer to St. Theresa, where you need to send it on to 12 people within the next 5 minutes or your prayer "won't come true." You know the ones. Anyway, it was a nice prayer, so I sent it on. One of the (12) gals I sent it to immediately wrote me back, chastising me that I of all people was intelligent, educated, blah blah blah enough to KNOW BETTER than to send a chain letter. Huff, huff, huff.

I replied that actually, I thought that intelligence and education and the like often got in the way — that really if one believed a bit more in prayer and was a little more in the Heart versus in the Head, it might do everyone some good. (I said it nicer than that, but that was the gist.)

She wrote back (still with a "head of steam on") that of COURSE prayer is great "if you believe in it," but what SHE objected to was the "send to 12 people part." She went on and on about that.

I thought about it, and deleted her message (first). But I knew she'd worked up quite a head of steam. So instead, I sent back an e-mail that just said, "Hey, how do you know? 12 might be St. Theresa's lucky number..."

She sent me an e-mail that just said "laughlaughlaughlaughlaughlaughlaugh." And I knew I had made her laugh, too.

She'd gone from being up in arms and snooty and such at me and "people who send these things" to — blam! — defused. It was over. I knew I shouldn't really have sent that email on, but once I did, I didn't get defensive at her response. I just made a joke of it. Humor is often your best tactic, especially if you do something you know that, maybe, you shouldn't'a done.

Have a Safe Place

At a recent speaking engagement, San Francisco District Attorney Kamala Harris was asked her views about suddenly having a very public life. She said, "You have to have a safe place in your life — a place to laugh inappropriately, a place where only friends can access you — and you must go there when you're being attacked, to get a sense of perspective. And the higher you go, the bigger a target you are. Don't get mad that you're being attacked. Don't fight it — you can't fight the nature of some things — in this case, it's always the same. You just need to know that this will happen. Keep going where you are going, and know that there will be some ugly parts. Don't fight it when it happens, but be sure you know how to deal with it. Be strong — and have your safe place for perspective. Never lash out — you can never get those words back again."

Keeping Your Promises

We have discussed your reputation here; now it's time to discuss your Word. As the old saying goes, "your word is your bond." What this means is that what you say you will do — what you promise, you must carry out. Because you are only as good as your Word.

We all know folks who say that they will do something, and then never get around to it. As a Bond Grrl, you should be very slow to make promises... because you need to keep your life and your time free. More importantly, you need to *keep* any promises you make, to others and especially to yourself.

Once you make a promise, go about completing it as soon as possible. And, if you have promised to loan something to someone, be sure to send it off the next day, but keep a record in your calendar or the back of your little black book, so when you go looking for it, you remember where it went!

A Bond Grrl's reputation and her word should always be her... Bond!

Life is either a daring adventure or nothing.
Security does not exist in nature, nor do the children of men as a whole experience it.
Avoiding danger is no safer in the long run than exposure.

—*Helen Keller*

Chapter 5

∞

*What an immense power over the life is the power of possessing distinct aims.
The voice, the dress, the look, the very motions of a Person,
define and alter when he or she begins to live for a reason.*

— *Elizabeth Stuart Phelps*

Taking Action

Now that you've survived the "Bond Grrl Boot Camp" of the first four chapters, it's time to tackle some serious subjects: money and work. We've touched on them a bit, but let's get down to it.

The first step towards taking control of your life and becoming its master (mistress?) is to Make a Plan. Hate your job? What if you had a cushion, so that you could actually say "Take this job and shove it"? What would it take? You've found your goals through your daily writings — how to really go get 'em?

The first thing to do, now that you have your Dreams and Goals, is take stock of your current Lifestyle. If you're eating out every day, buying your kids whatever they want, and living a "Have it now, pay later" life, well Grrl, you'll never, ever, get ahead. If you're brave enough though, it's time to look at where you can cut back. Get it to what you Need, not what you Want, until your debt is flat and you can start piling up some savings. For example, I bet there are things in your life that you think are "mandatory," but aren't.

This month, every day, assess your monetary outlays, then cut back just a bit. For example, pack your own lunch, and be sure to take the money you would have spent and put it in a jar. Or take the bus in, and put the money you normally spent on bridge fare/parking/tolls/etc. in the jar. Make your coffee and put it in a Thermos from K-Mart, instead of heading out to Starbuck's and, you guessed it, put that money in the jar. (If that Starbuck's Run is your break from work, walk around the building and get some fresh air, instead of standing in line at the coffee shop!) What about suspending your TV cable for 2-3 months, and using your Couch Potato time to exercise, instead? I actually suspended mine for 10 months (the cable company would rather do this, than cancel), and put the $40/month towards my debt. Whatever you do, stick to it for a month, and make sure you put the money you did not spend into that jar. Then see what it adds up to. At the end of the month, put that money in the bank and write a check immediately to your credit cards (if they have a balance) — or start a new savings account for your Dream. (Remember the Passport Account Example we mentioned in Chapter 2?) Feels good just thinking about it, doesn't it? What can you do differently the month after?

Stop drowning your sorrows in shopping and running up your credit cards, because your Victim-self feels upset. That's not your Inner Bond Grrl. You need to get out of debt, then start working on being able to retire in — oh, say 15 years. Completely impossible, you say? What were you planning on doing? Not getting old? Time to have a plan, Grrl.

You can meet a financial planner and they can work the numbers for you. We have a fabulous guy at Merrill Lynch, but any company like this worth its salt will do a "no obligation" assessment for you. You can also use many of the financial planning websites on the Internet — just be sure to use one that's recommended by an expert like Oprah or Suze Orman or is a name brand like Merrill Lynch or Charles Schwab. Be wary of anything or anyone who won't help you without you paying them or giving them vital information, like your social security number. There are lots of scams out there.

Do you remember the fable of the Ant and the Grasshopper? The Ant spends the summer putting away for the future, while the Grasshopper parties and makes fun of the Ant. When the winter comes, well, you know which one is in trouble. By constantly living in the moment and ignoring tomorrow when it comes to your finances, you'll be out in the cold, too, when your financial winter comes. You'll never have enough to get out of a dead-end job, or to go on an exotic trip, or buy a house. You become a slave to your debt and your desire to have it all Now. Time to break those chains!

Beware of Treats

You do realize that you really are a slave to your Things, right? You have to dust them, pay interest on them (if you put them on a credit card), pack and unpack them when you move, and so on. The more shoes, purses, and the like you collect, the more they become your anchors. I also think that often we treat ourselves with small stop-gap items (Frappuccinos) that make us feel good for that moment, instead of adding up all the "mini treats" and trading them in for one huge, satisfying treat (going to Paris!). That's what putting money in a jar will start to visually show you. You have goals and dreams, from the work you did in Chapter 2. Now, let's find a way to help you realize them... part of which always involves having enough money. Specifically, what are you doing today that you can stop doing (if it's money-draining), or do more of (if it brings you money), to move yourself closer to your goal?

It's All a Choice

Money coming in and going out is always a matter of choice — not chance. What you do for money should pay for the lifestyle that you've chosen; in other words, the lifestyle you live should not exceed the money you bring in. Have you read the book *Rich Dad, Poor Dad*? If you're just living to work and working to live, without any opportunities for cash flow, then you're never going to get out of the rat race. (I wish I had read this book in my early 20s instead of my late 30s. I would have led a different life.) In fact, everything that you bring into your life (and everything you complain about) is a choice.

In some circles, even health issues are considered a choice, meaning that it's your own energetic resonance that draws those issues to you. I happen to suffer from debilitating migraines. Since I have adopted this way of thinking, if I get a migraine, the second I "come to" after a headache, I look at my life and figure out where I need to slow down, or relax, or just appreciate things more. I have given up complaining. It's hard sometimes. Complaining is like crack: it's very addictive, and what good does it do? When I find myself out of true in some way, I re-correct my course and slowly, softly, move my life and my Self more towards my own inner Bond Grrl. She is migraine-free!

Financial Congruency

Can a woman on a budget live a Bond Grrl life? YES! How? First, do what she's passionate about, and have a plan to eliminate the rest within a certain amount of time. Second, live within her means. Period.

Oh, you pout, not that! Yes, that. Are you acting, dressing, and spending in a way that is well outside your range, just hoping to win the Lottery to save yourself? Time to stop. You're living an external life that is not congruent with your actual "internal" finances. I don't believe the grrls who tell me that they *must* have the cocktails, bling and things in their life, or they will *die* without them. (I've heard it all!) If I were to sit you down and ask you, are you passionate about those cocktails? That purse you just bought? What about three weeks from now? Have you moved on from it, forgotten?

Bond Grrls figure out what they're passionate about, and that's where they put their energy. Money is just a tangible representation of that energy. But when it comes to clothes, makeup, car, purse, bling and things, Bond Grrls don't waste that energy. They pare down to the minimum that will help them to be chic, savvy, confident, appealing, and above all, ready. In fact, the less a Bond Grrl has, whether it's things or debt, the better. The less you have, the less you need to worry about, were Bond to say, "Time to help me with this adventure."

I have had women attend seminars who are hair stylists, COOs, owners of their own companies, housewives, students, millionaires. Each of them has been serious about going through her life, every single bit of it. And all have ultimately (sometimes after some kicking and screaming) realized that the key to being a Bond Grrl is traveling light through life. That means having a light attitude, first and foremost, and getting rid of frenemies, debt, negativity, and the things and bling that are just life's dust-catchers. Bond Grrls choose their image, then they go for it — within their budget. A "wealthy" life used to be a life of relaxed success and leisure. These days, we worship and revere Type A workaholics, with lots of "toys" but no time. I think it's time to trade in the toys and ulcers, don't you?

Does it Cost More to Be a Bond Grrl?

Being in debt is really like being in prison, as all the Debt Diet books try to explain. Ultimately, you will get to the end of your financial rope, and the bars will slam down. While some folks try to "look a role" to make themselves feel better inside, Bond Grrls need to be Æmpowered from the inside, out. If you are in debt, don't just put a smiley-face sticker over an empty gas gauge and say "It's all JUST FINE." It's not going to work that way. You will ultimately coast to a stop — hopefully not in the fast lane on the freeway!

So don't Bond Grrls eat Godiva chocolates? Maybe so. But it's because they appreciate the quality. If you eat one amazing dark chocolate truffle, it can satisfy you more than ten Hershey's bars, and it will certainly make you feel more prosperous. Besides, the reason we often eat, eat, eat even when we're full is that our body doesn't get the chemicals it is searching for in what we feed it.

Good chocolates, for example, can sate us immediately because they contain the pure cocoa and good cocoa-related chemicals our body searches for, but can't find, in a Snickers bar. So they cost us less — in money and in calories — in the long run.

I had champagne by myself the other day in a celebratory luncheon, and it was the same price as a glass of wine, but I felt special all day because of it. I sat alone in that restaurant, enjoyed the view, was catered to, ate salad, sipped champagne, and then left a big tip. It felt great, and the energy of it made me smile all day. I could also see out of the corner of my eye that a number of tables were looking, and smiling, at me. I was obviously alone, and obviously having a grand old time. They were curious! How often do you need to eat alone, and all you exude is Poor Little Me energy as you look down at the table and shovel in your food? A little mystery buoys everyone's day!

 Frugal Fun

Shel Horowitz has a wonderful website, called FrugalFun.com. There are a lot of ideas on his website and in his books that can help you creatively realize that being a Bond Grrl does not need to cost you an arm and a leg. Some of the Tipsheets in his Archives that you might like include:

- **"Play Millionaire: A Fabulous Day of Romantic Fun" (May 1997);**
- **"How To Make Something Special Out Of Not Much More Than Air: A Romantic Evening in an Empty House" (September, 1998);**
- **"Just Off-Season Vacations/A Frugal Fun Postcard From Greece — A Week in Greece for $23.85 per day for Transportation, Lodging, and Food" (June 2000)**
- **"Abundance v. Prosperity" (February 2001)**
- **"Enjoy Evenings Out: Set Up a Child Care Co-Op" (September 2004)**
- **"Splurge Restaurants: Shel-Style — $15 to $20 per Person" (July 2005)**

His book, *The Penny-Pinching Hedonist: How to Live Like Royalty with a Peasant's Pocketbook*, is how I originally found him; it is available as an e-book from his website, or secondhand at Half.com.

Hang Out in Prosperous Locales

Just spending time (not money!) in high-class locations can be a way to upgrade your life. Remember, you can dress appropriately, visit a swanky hotel in your town, order bubbly water, then just relax, watch people, and hang — or if you are so inclined, get a glass of champagne, and slowly sip. As I mentioned, ordering champagne actually makes everyone look at you and wonder what you're celebrating. We know, of course, you're celebrating the gorgeous, sensual Inner Bond Grrl You! If you also get a cat-that-ate-the-canary look on your face, I promise you, all sorts of folks around you will start smiling every time they slyly sneak a glance at you. Think of how you have just uplifted the energy in their lives, and the ripples that will make — just like the Smile in the Mall exercise.

Your Relationship to Money

So, Bond Grrl, where do you stand financially? Do you have a huge balance on your credit cards? Do you just put your bills in a drawer? Well, time to come up with a plan to get rid of them. Are you spending money because you hate your job, or because you're stressed out, or trying to keep up with your best friend? Time to knock that off.

We don't usually get into debt trouble because of a huge crisis. We get into trouble by doing things like getting our nails done or going out for lattes and such, putting them on credit, then not paying it off. Many people don't realize that even if they pay the minimum payment on a credit card bill, that won't keep the debt from mounting, even if they put nothing more on that card. Later on in this chapter I'll give you an example of what happened to me, and how I've pulled out of it. I want to use myself as an example, rather than embarrassing anyone else. Just know that paying the minimum, if it doesn't equal or exceed the Finance Charge listed for that month, means you are leaving interest on the card, then paying interest *on* that interest until you pay it off!

Money and Passion

One of my big heroes is Suze Orman. Her website is SuzeOrman.com, but I first discovered her by going to my local library and taking out some of her books on tape. That way, when I would go out walking, or had a long drive, or was doing housework/folding laundry, I just popped the tape in my player, and could listen to her... for free. (The library is a wonderful thing.)

In one of her books, Suze talks about following your passion even if it doesn't pay that much, because if you love what you do, you're less likely to spend to "feel better." I totally agree with that. But one of the things I learned by reading the book *Ask and It Is Given* (Abraham-Hicks.com) is that you can "attract the right stuff" only if you are in a positive space about it. And you have to get into that positive space before jumping to what you think is your "passion," or else that "passion" can burn you!

Also, as Barbara Sher (another favorite author) points out, if you discover that your passion is something like painting, don't just say, "I'm quitting my job and becoming a painter." You'll starve, and it will drive you CRAZY trying to be passionate for eight hours a day, if you turn painting into your Job. Start small. Join groups, get your passion into your life, then see about expanding its place in your life. To quote Esther Hicks/Abraham, "Don't jump out of an airplane and THEN look for the parachute." You're going to hit the ground in a big resounding SMACK that way. Do a little planning.

The Life Balance Pendulum: My Example

In one of her tapes, Suze Orman talks about the idea of life balance. She basically says that if you look back on one of THE worst times in your life (at least five years previously), something equally GREAT came out of that period of time. In other words, the Universe works a balancing act: If the pendulum swings too far in one direction, it will come back the other way just as strongly if you let it and take advantage, tick... tock....

I remember listening to that book on tape and thinking about the worst period of my life, which had at that time been five years before. My goodness, it was a bad time. Basically, I had loaned a friend a big hunk of money that I had gotten because my company had been bought by another company, and we received a "stock payout" from that purchase. We're talking five figures here. The friend was WAY behind on his mortgage and second mortgage, and was getting kicked out of his house. He had told me he now had a steady job and could keep up the payments, but couldn't catch up. So, I gave him the entire amount of money I had gotten in the payout.

Before you figure that Mama raised a fool, I DID make him change the title on his house so I "owned" that house if he stopped making payments to me and/or stopped paying the mortgage. (Of course, I never thought I'd really have to call that loan, silly me...) In exchange for giving him the ability to pay down that back debt, I would get the mortgage deduction for the property on my taxes. Since he had a second mortgage at an outrageous interest rate — something like 15% — he had never been able to even touch the principal payment with his monthly payments; he was only paying interest and never getting ahead. In fact he wasn't even paying all the interest at that rate, so he was getting stuck with interest compiling *on* the interest. (That's the problem I mentioned with credit cards, and will mathematically lead you through, later in this Chapter.)

Anyway, to make a long story even longer, I wound up finding out that my then-live-in James had another gal on the side. I had been the one paying our rent and utilities, etc., but he refused to move! He also had about 20 tons of stuff behind the house and on the property (he was a contractor), and I realized that if I were to leave, I could leave all that behind. So I did the math, and realized that I should buy a house, since the mortgage payment (after the deduction I would get for it in my taxes) would be about what I'd paid in rent. I thought that life was Swell.

Then, the following happened:

- I found a fixer-upper house I could afford, got into contract, and in trying to qualify for the loan, found out the "friend" I'd loaned the money to had been lying to me. (Talk about frenemies!) He hadn't made any payments on his mortgage, which was now in MY name. When I questioned him about it, he said Gee, he was very sorry. So I had to make all the "catch up" payments and beg the mortgage company not to put it on my credit report. I lost the house I was trying to buy before the dust settled, and it was not pretty.

- The landlord for the house I had been in with my then-boyfriend found out I was moving, came to visit, saw all the junk on the back acreage, and sued us both. Since the boyfriend had no assets, I was the one stuck with it, and the landlord ate my entire security deposit and then went for more blood, in court.

- The company that I was working for at the time was spinning out subsidiaries to take advantage of the dot.com boom. One subsidiary wanted me to go with them and asked me to work on the legal paperwork necessary to form the new entity. The "mother ship" found out, and said they would fire me if I did — so I was faced with potentially losing my livelihood.

- My then-James took my horses, "stashed" them with a friend because I wasn't paying attention with all this whirling down on my ears, then wouldn't give them back until I promised to give him two of them. I had been willing to give him one, but the other one I had found an AWESOME home for, at an eventing stable. He's a nice enough guy, but he doesn't actually ever really ride the horses, he just likes to say he has them. So this was a huge blow because in giving up that horse, a foal my lead mare had birthed on my property, I was basically consigning this little, beautiful, intelligent, sassy being to becoming Lawn Art instead of the brave little eventing champ I knew she could be.

- I wound up having to — get this — EVICT the guy who owed me that 5-figure sum (after making his mortgage current, of course). Then I had to sell his house.

- I sold the house, and the "profit" didn't cover the amount of money that he owed me. Worse, since I sold the house without owning it for two years, I had to pay income tax on the "profit" I made. *Plus, I had to pay income tax on that stock payout, that I'd loaned him!* I wound up losing a HUGE chunk of dough and THEN having to pay taxes on it — which I couldn't afford. Oh, and I also had to pay out on that landlord thing.

I'm sure there was other stuff going on, but that gives you some idea. In the end, I was over $30,000 in debt. This does not include the "stock payout" money I had lost, after loaning it to the guy; that was just gone. The $30k was true debt that I owed, over and above that. So in reality, if you factor the money I'd loaned the guy, I was "out" double that amount. And, of course, I lost the contract on the house I was in escrow on, and they were really wicked about it.

I remember listening to that Suze Orman book in my car, pounding the dashboard, and saying, "No *way* is there anything good that came out of *that* awful period!" And then I started thinking... after all that:

- My real estate agent stumbled upon, and then we were able to purchase, a WAY better house, in move-in condition, that I still love though I now rent it out. That has its own story — the house was in a probate sale, and the rains were so bad on the day of the court hearing, they closed the county line so no one could come down to the courthouse to bid... I had spent the night near the courthouse, and was therefore the only bidder. I got it for 20% undervalue (all I could afford!), in a scorchingly hot market where houses were going for upwards of 20-30% over asking. And we locked in a mortgage rate that now, nearly a decade later, I haven't been able to beat in a re-fi.

- I did go with the new company — and met my current James (now my husband) there. He is without a doubt the love of my life, and a perfect "match" for me.

These may not seem to be enough "balance," but they are.

So what happened with the $30,000 debt and taxes I had to pay? I actually got a financial program (Quicken) and started logging in every PENNY I spent. Yes, every cent. For a month, I just logged everything, without changing my habits. Then I ran a report on where the money went. When I saw what was going where, I started making changes. I needed that whole month's worth of records to examine before I could make intelligent changes.

What did I get rid of? Lots. I got rid of subscriptions to magazines I could read at the library. Those magazines would pile up without being read on my coffee table, and I needed that $20 a year. These are the sorts of things you forget to consider, but that add up. The nails. The lattes. Bottles of wine. Cable TV. The gym. Eating out. Gave up some friends, too — when I realized that all we did together was go to the Mall.

Amazingly, I did pay that $30k off. I remember when I made the last payment — woo-hoo!!! It took YEARS. But it taught me something. You CAN "do without" all that stuff that you think you "must have." For example for Christmas, I became the biggest "re-gifter" that there is. I looked around my house, and found stuff that people had commented on that they really liked, or that I knew they would like — hardcover books in perfect shape, jewelry I wasn't wearing, knick-knacks, sometimes even clothes — and wrapped them up, then gave them away. This got stuff out of my life I didn't really NEED, and allowed me to do birthdays, Christmas, etc. without going further into debt.

Making Improvements

Wherever you are financially, you can do better. If your cards are paid off, it's time to put away as much as you can towards retirement, AND to have a little "stash" savings account for a Bond Grrl trip. If you take the money you spend on habits (like lattes and manicures) and save it instead toward a trip, you will really GO — without running up credit cards to do it.

It's time to eliminate worry from your life as much as possible, and one of the biggest darned worries is money. So, take a deep breath, and start logging where every dollar goes for a whole month. I don't care if you do it on paper with a pencil. Just do it. Don't change a thing: just log, log, log. Then look at that log at the end of the month. Where is your money really going? Are you surprised?

The next month, start to change. Pay off your highest-interest-rate debts first, if you are in debt. Get them gone, then move to the next, and the next. It took me YEARS to get out of that $30k hole. But I did get out. And now, I'm putting away money towards retirement, etc. In the interim, I was also Downsized a few years ago. This means I'm making about 1/3 of what I made then — maybe even a little less. But because I pay a lot more attention, I keep debt to a minimum and I continue to save for my retirement (and also a Bond Grrl trip or two).

What sorts of tricks can you use to keep yourself out of debt? How can credit cards help you? Now, I put everything I purchase (even $4.00 at the grocery store) on a WorldPoints MasterCard that costs me no annual fee. My James and I recently went to Hawaii for two weeks, and I paid for the plane tickets through WorldPoints. But the key is that I keep receipts for every dollar that goes on that card, and total them up each week. I write a check at the end of the week for that amount, so that when the credit card bill comes, I can pay it with the four checks I have saved each week for that month. I am never blindsided by the bill. Moreover, this account doesn't accrue interest the day that I charge on it (some do — make sure to check yours!). It actually only accrues interest on a balance that remains unpaid after the payment due date (this is called the Grace Period). So my groceries, gas, and other daily expenses are now buying plane tickets, and I've paid NO finance charges/interest, because I pay it every month. How great is THAT?? By having one card and putting everything on it, I funnel those benefits back to myself. I cancelled my gas card, and all my store cards, when I figured out I could rack up travel benefits by just using that one card. Of course, again, the key is to add everything up spent on that card at the end of each week, and write a check to cover that amount, each week. Can't quite do it one week? You'd better not spend ANYTHING more, and find a way to pay off that amount before the bill comes in! No surprises.

Turn Your Cast-Offs into Cash

My cousin Robin, who got downsized herself in a job shift, recently started going around her house and putting things on eBay. It's been amazing. She had a signed copy of *Harry Potter* that just "paid" her over $900! Selling that book will pay her expenses for a long time. Why is she so successful? She writes really funny descriptions for each item she sells. These descriptions have helped her sell items like two-thirds of a tube of hair color — for more than a new tube costs! Sure, she has to package everything up and mail it out, but the point is, she's actually downsizing and "streamlining" her life... while living off it. Could this fatten up your bank account, while whittling down your dust-catchers?

A Double-Oh Bank Account

With every paycheck that comes in, you must pay yourself First. I don't mean buy yourself treats! I mean that first, you need to pay your debts; once they are gone, save for retirement. (It's coming sooner than you think!) After getting those taken care of each month, it's important for every Bond Grrl to have a special fund for positive contingencies — like going to Paris. (People that put money away "for a rainy day" are saving for *negative* contingencies, and you know by now that you don't want to resonate those thoughts.) Aim to take 10% of the money that's left after you pay your debts, mortgage, retirement fund and the like, and sock it away towards something positive. (Did you just say, "What money that's left?" If you did, time to really take a look at your Life!) I also personally try to save 10% to give to charity, too. I think that having a wider world view is a wonderful thing, and charitable pursuits help me with that perspective.

A Place to Call Your Own

It's all well and good to have a little savings account/nest egg, but I truly believe that what every Bond Grrl needs is to have a down payment on a home. And not a home where she pays No Money Down, where in reality the debt is being stacked against her at the end of the loan. No, I mean saving up 20% of the purchase price, and then getting a fixed-rate loan so that the payment each month is set, until the mortgage is paid.

You might not live in that home for the rest of your life. In fact, what you're really looking to do is buy a place that you can rent out a few years later, and at least pay the mortgage with the rent. Then you'll buy a bit better place by "leveraging" your first home as an asset, live there for a few years, then move on and rent *it*. A house is an asset that will force savings on you: with each mortgage payment you make, you are building up an asset that you can ultimately use to finance another asset and then another.

If you're a Bond Grrl without a James, don't wait 'til you get married to get a house as an asset, honey. That was me. I had this feeling that by buying a house (which I did a lot later in life), I was going to be a spinster forever. As I mentioned, I finally did buy my Dream Home — which proved difficult to rent when it came time to move on. It is exactly what I wanted: a tiny farm house with a hot tub, a huge lavender field, rose garden and orchards, set away from the road so my dog/cats can run free, sunlight in every room, etc. But it's not in a great school district, it's small for two people, it's not that close to town, it's on a well and septic, etc.

If I had read *Rich Dad, Poor Dad* before I bought that house, I would have bought something totally different. I would have gotten my emotions out of the way. I could have made just as nice a home out of a suburban house with bigger bedrooms, in a better school district. Instead, I opted for land, which is hard to maintain. So think strategically when you buy — remember, your Dreams may change as time goes on, so always be a good Bond Grrl and know your exit strategy!

Avoid Artifacts of Wealth

The book called *The Millionaire Next Door* was recommended to me by a number of people, and so I recently borrowed the unabridged version of it on CDs from the library (love the library) and loaded it into my MP3 player, so I could listen to it in the car, at the gym, doing housework, etc.

The book talks about the differences between what the authors call UAWs (Under Achievers of Wealth) and PAWs (Prodigious Achievers of Wealth). One of the biggest differences between UAWs and PAWs is that PAWs do not collect "artifacts of wealth." The authors surveyed millionaires — all folks that have socked away $1-10 million in their own lifetime, not inherited it. (This amount did not include the worth of their homes.) What the authors discovered was that the millionaires do not have fancy cars, do not shop for fun, do not have fancy clothes, etc. The #1 car in the group is a Jeep Grand Cherokee (or a Ford F-150). The suits PAWs wear are generally from JC Penney (which apparently *Forbes* recently noted has suits that hold up in cut and fabric "blind tests" against much more expensive brands). All millionaires have budgets, and stick to them. They know where their money is going. They know where their spouse's money is going, and where their kids' money is going. Everyone in the house understands that Frugality is the way to live, because whoever "dies with the most toys" does NOT win; he who dies with fully-funded college programs for his kids and grandkids, and passes on a way of living that will help these kids succeed, plus perhaps a large endowment for charitable purposes, DOES win. That person leaves a "legacy."

So who buys those artifacts of wealth? People that want to *service* millionaires (such as stockbrokers, attorneys, etc.), and people who want people to *think* they are millionaires. This reminds me of folks I met when I was doing martial arts. The lower-level belts would brag about the fact that they did karate, or could "Kick your *ss." The actual black belts were very quiet about it. Remember that, when you see someone carrying a Gucci bag; is she just carrying credit card bills around in it??

The lessons from *The Millionaire Next Door* are perfect for the nascent Bond Grrl. Don't buy for the sake of buying. Trim down. Travel light. And whatever you have — LOVE it and USE it. We covered etiquette before, and one should of course know how to act when faced with caviar, escargots, or champagne. But that is not what you'll eat every day, even if you can "afford it." The authors of *The Millionaire Next Door* suggested that everyone should take 15% of every paycheck, and put it away in a Wealth Account. (Assuming all credit cards are paid of course.) Plan, plan, plan. PAWs all live in middle class neighborhoods, not palaces — and their mortgages don't kill them. Most of them have actually paid off their houses. How's about you?

*f*Empowerment®

 ## *Who Goes First?*

Why do you pay your credit cards, before you pay yourself? And why do you pay the highest interest rate first, not the highest balance?

Though this is not a financial treatise, it's important to understand how interest rates work. Here's a little homework for you: Pick up the newspaper, or just browse the ads in the windows of your local banks, and see what sort of interest rates are being offered. What amount of money will you need to give them, and how long will you have no access to that money, to get that rate? For example, a 3-month certificate of deposit (CD) means that you can't touch that money for three months; if you get a one-year CD, you can't touch your money for a year. The interest rate on the one-year will be higher than the 3-month, but that's because they are paying you a bit more to lock your money down for an extra 9 months. What do they do with your money? They lend it out to other people, as mortgages, lines of credit, and the like. They need to pay you less than the amount they are receiving to lend it back out, of course, or they don't make a profit.

I am confident that you will not find a bank that will offer you an interest rate on a CD or savings account that will be higher than the rate on your credit card. (Unless you're locking your money down for years and years — and who wants to do that? You want it accessible to you!) This is why you need to pay your credit cards before you put money into savings. Let's look at an example: by putting $100 into savings at (let's say) 3% interest, you get a big $3.00 in interest. And you will need to pay taxes on that interest income — so it's actually even less. But if you have that $100 on a credit card at 5% (or 12%, or 24%!), you are going into debt to the tune of $5.00 (or $12.00, or $24.00!) by keeping the balance outstanding. Since your $100 savings account earned $3 (less taxes), you wind up in the hole by $2 (or $9, or $21) because you didn't put the $100 towards your credit card! Worse, we have talked about this a few times, but let's say that you have a 24% card with $10,000 on it, and, to choose easy numbers, let's say the minimum payment is $150/month. You have a $10,000 balance, which means $2,400 in interest ($10,000 x .24) accrues by the end of that year if you don't pay down the principal balance. If you only pay the monthly minimum ($150 x 12 = $1,800), your principal balance by the end of the year will be $10,600 ($10,000 (principal) + $2,400 (annual interest) - $1,800 (total minimum payments)). See where you are now? Your balance is actually higher than before (because your minimum payment was less than the interest accruing each month). And in reality, even if you have no new purchases on the card, you will have paid more interest than the amount outlined here, because each month, you will pay interest on the interest balance from the month before, and the month before, and...

Stop putting things on cards. Then, each month, pay the minimum on them all, of course, but the extra money you are squeezing out of your life, put towards the one with the highest interest rate. Pay that off. There are also ways to get credit card companies to decrease your rate. (Believe me, they want your balance on there, even if they need to decrease your rate by a few interest points; they hate folks like me who pay it all off every month, because they don't make any money!) You can learn more about all this by going to Oprah.com, and reading her Debt Diet recommendations from her finance experts.

How Much Do You Need?

According to *The Millionaire Next Door*, the way to figure out how much wealth you are "supposed to" have accumulated by your age is to take your age, divide it by 10, and multiply it by your gross annual income from all sources. So if you're 40, and you make $50,000 a year, that means 40/10 x 50,000 or $200,000. To be in line, you should have $200,000 in actual investments (stocks/bonds/401(k)/IRA/whatever), *excluding* your house (if you live in it), vehicles, furniture, "bling," etc. These are not "investments": A house is only an "investment" if it's a rental and you're the landlord.

When I read the book, I was only at about half of where I am "supposed" to be, so I was an Underachiever of Wealth. But I recently rented my house, so it became an asset/investment, and now I'm in line.

The point of having this much money set aside is to ultimately have enough wealth that it generates income you can actually live on without working. That's what retirement really means: that you have assets that are kicking enough money out to you, without your labor involvement and without decreasing the principal. Compare having a rental property to having a job. Any rent you receive over the amount you pay for mortgage and upkeep is income to you, without you "doing" much of anything (*e.g.*, slaving away 40 hours/week). It's taxable — but only Federal and State tax, not the social security tax, Medicare, disability, self-employment tax, and other taxes that you see coming out of the money you trade for your labor each month. Making enough money to live your life through investments is a better way to make money than by "earning" it through a paycheck.

Frugal Generosity

Santa Claus Is Coming To Town... or is it the Grinch?

As a Bond Grrl, you are Resourceful. Right? That's your middle name! And you haven't even been trained to be Resourceful, you just ARE. Think about Bond. He went through tons of training, and Q even gives him all sorts of gadgets to help him out. I bet that Moneypenny, if asked, would even go out and do his Christmas shopping for him.

But, you see, YOU are a Bond Grrl! You don't get all this extra help — but we all know that you can do it, even so.

As I mentioned before, I often "re-gift" things I already have. Beautiful coffee table books, for example. Or, somehow, I wound up with a boatload of wine glasses, so I recently got rid of them and made room in my closet by tying two to a bottle of wine (usually Pinot someone had brought to my house as a gift). I gave these as presents, with a note that explained the "scene" to the recipient: drop off your kid with Auntie Solitaire for a few hours, then go and enjoy the wine — and each other. They get some free babysitting, some wine, and it's fun. Costs me the price of the ribbon. If you decide to do something like this, ham it up in the cards you give people, to "set a scene." If you have some extra unopened olive oil, or spices (which go bad after 6 months, so get rid of any that are close to their expiration date), then go onto a website like epicurious.com and pick a recipe that uses those ingredients, write up a cute recipe card (copying the recipe from the website), and then give a gift pack to a friend who loves to cook. Heck, make up a holiday. Call it Miss Chef America Day, and explain solemnly in your card that your friend has been picked to represent your State. Get outrageous. Be fun.

People really don't care about gifts per se. What they want is your effort of thoughtfulness. If you show that you made an effort related to them, then they are going to remember that far longer than if you were to give them a $100 Pamper Day at the spa.

So start looking around your house again. What do you have that you can part with? Can you make up a story to go with it, so that the story can make the person really excited to have that re-gifted thing? It will show that you were thinking about them specifically, when you came up with the gift. How's about that candle holder you got at an import store, that could somehow have a story that ties it back to the Kasbah? How about some lotion that you haven't used, that with a little effort and a story can transport your friend to a fantasy where her James is rubbin' it all over her?

I have gifts that I was given a long time — even decades — ago. Gifts that were fun, but didn't cost that much. I will give you an example, because it's sitting right here in my office. It's a kid's toy hammer. It has, pasted to the side, a label that says "The Hammer Of Knowledge." I bet the whole thing cost $2.95.

I got this a long, long time ago, when I was a first year lawyer, and went about something "the hard way." My boss gave it to me when I successfully got out the other end. I also have the other part of this gift, which is a sorcerer's hat with stars on it. Again, this probably cost about $5.00 at a Toys-R-Us. By going about the project "the hard way," I had come up with a unique idea that even my boss hadn't contemplated — which wound up saving the day. So I was given the "Hammer of Knowledge," but also the Sorcerer's Hat, for having "magically" solved the problem.

And look — I still have it all. I have had gifts worth ten or a hundred times as much, that are no longer with me... but The Hammer of Knowledge still resides on my desk.

I also have a papier mâché chicken that a study buddy and I got for each other after we passed the Bar Examination to become lawyers a million years ago. That has a big long story attached to it, and he's a big bad executive now, making TONS of money. (Definitely the "James" type, in his Lotus Elise sports car!) But in an e-mail I got from him a while ago, my hot shot friend wrote, "P.S., I still have my chicken, do you?"

These are the best gifts, because they tie to your time and effort, and don't cost a ton of dough. They somehow show, in a little typed label and a Toys-R-Us hammer, that you care, more than even a pearl necklace. Not quite sure why that is, but it's true.

So as you contemplate birthdays and Christmas, don't reach deep in your pocket. You're a Bond Grrl: you're resourceful, smart, and full of bright life. Reach instead into your mind, and make up some stories, tied to lower value gifts. I can almost promise you that these will be the gifts that wind up on someone's desk or dresser, still giving them a smile ten years from now, when a $100 Spa Day would be a long-forgotten memory.

Aim for Abundance

In unleashing your Inner Bond Grrl, you are aiming to expand your life in many ways. When I tell students they need to concentrate on Abundance, and especially being able to save to care for themselves as they age, they often hum that old Beatles song, "Money Can't Buy Me Love," espousing that "people" are "supposed to" aim for joy, happiness, and the like, instead of money. But then they obsess about it, anyway. I feel it's just laziness — "joy and happiness" are supposedly "free," but money, prosperity and abundance take some actual planning and effort. If you can live happy nekkid in a tent, eating fish you catch, and drinking from the stream, hey, go for the happiness, forget money. But if not, get your mind around prosperity — and not dwelling on lack.

Remember, you must avoid "scarcity thinking" because, in accordance with the Law of Magnetic Attraction, you will get what you are putting your energy into (scarcity). The best way to slow down the good things coming to you is to dwell on the lack of them. The problem? We all have a little voice inside. Some of us call it the voice of Reality, but I like to think of it instead as the voice of a little Goblin who wants power over me. By putting it like that, I kind of straighten my backbone and think, "HEY, I am not giving my power away to It!!" Because, you see, you ARE giving it away when you listen to that voice's negative and scarcity-based trash.

So what does it take to make that voice go away? The best way is to shoot rays of bright light at it; rays of optimism and abundance. If that voice keeps harping on a job you "hate" where "they don't deserve you," it's time to concentrate instead on what you "intend to do" or "where you're going." If that little voice proclaims that something is "too scary" to change, how about considering it a "challenge" and "exciting" instead? Tell that voice that you are *choosing* not to buy something, when it fires back that you can't have it because you "can't afford it." Envision. See the opportunities. Keep the power!

 ### Whoa Is Me

Yeah, yeah, you spellers out there. I know, it's W-O-E.

But not really.

To use a horse analogy, you are the rider of your own Life — and just like a good horse, your Life is responsive to your every move. It trusts that you know best! So are you giving it an exhilarating run, or plodding along in the weeds, or steering (or not steering) in a way that's going to ultimately scrape you off on the overhanging trees? And then, are you going to blame Life for your fall?

When you spend time and mental energy on your "woes," it's just like yelling "whoa" to that horse called Life.

Sometimes, it seems that Life dishes out some doozies. I certainly have been known to wind up on my backside after being scraped off by the tree branches, cursing either the tree, or Life! Maybe I was steering... or maybe I was just lollygagging, with my reins slack and my feet hanging loosely, completely oblivious. But wherever I wound up, *I* put me there. So it's *my* responsibility to get me out.

Sometimes it's hard to get out of what you steered (or floated obliviously) into. Sometimes it will take time, effort, and money to get back on course — or get back on the ride at all.

You are not alone if you find yourself steering Life onto your Path to Passion™, then backsliding out of fear and/or putting to the side the things you love — usually to "make some money" or make someone else happy. Been there, done that. It's all a process; just do your best not to get in your own way *too* often. Find your Path to Passion, and let your horse called Life go. Even if you wind up in the weeds, just keep your eye on the Path, and as you get better at steering, you'll stay on the Path that much more often. But whatever happens, bite back the Woes. All they will do is grind that horse called Life to a Stop, until you start urging it forward again.

Goblin Exercise

Starting today, LISTEN to the little goblin in your head. Really hear what s/he has to say to you. A LOT of it is not so nice! Every time that it starts up, I want you to take a big breath in through your nose on a count of 5, hold it for 2, then breathe out firmly through your mouth for a count of 5. Close your eyes. (If you work in a cubicle, go do this in the bathroom. If you have an office, close the door.) When breathing in, see that breath gathering up all those negative things that the goblin is saying. When you hold your breath for those 2 seconds, you're tying a knot and trapping those phrases inside your breath. Then when you breathe back out, breathe them into an imaginary bag that you envision right in front of your face. Pick a color that is powerful and meaningful to you (mine are usually orange). Once that wind and all those words and gunk get out and in that bag (maybe a dozen or so breaths), in your mind's eye, tie up that bag, and blow it to smithereens! Yes, real fireworks! Blow it up, and see all the parts fall to the center of the Earth, to be burned up.

It doesn't take that long from when you realize that your "goblin is on" until you have blown up the bag, but it gathers and focuses you. For me, it helps the goblin voice to quiet down for a while, too. Goblins must not like to be oxygenated by my deep breathing — I think they live in the dark, musty, unoxygenated part of my brain that yawning comes from!

 Happychondria

Dr. Robert Holden, the founder of the Happiness Project, believes that people who are chronic complainers have "Happychondria." They believe that if things get too good, that they need to start complaining, otherwise they will take a fall from this height of happiness and get hurt. Holden suggests daring to let life be great, and trusting that happiness can happen and, most importantly, can last. He also said that if you are not living your Passion each and every day, you die a little more each day, "dying before you die." One thing he said which truly made me laugh is, "Anyone who has made it to the age of 30 has enough reasons to be miserable for the rest of their lives" — so you need to let go, and "give up all hopes of having a perfect past."

His book, *Happiness Now!*, is a wonderful addition to your library. It espouses that everyone should focus not on having a job, but on having a purpose. If you have a purpose, you feel like you're making a difference and that you're significant: that you're making a contribution. Start, not by focusing on success and the trappings of success, but instead focus on significance. First, be significant to yourself. Then, become significant to your family and community. Last, become significant to the world. Yes — it must build in this manner. If you focus on becoming significant in this order, then success and abundance can do nothing but come to you.

Bond Grrls in Business

I've talked a lot about "being Number 1 at being Number 2," and I'll talk about it more when we get to Chapter 6. But in your professional life, you're Number 1. That doesn't mean you have a license to act like a spoiled brat. A Bond Grrl in business is passionate about what she does, and an expert at it. She doesn't complain, she doesn't play into office politics (there is NOT ENOUGH TIME).

fEmpowerment®

She is quietly efficient. She takes action — she doesn't brag. She listens. She gives credit where it's due, and she doesn't take credit where it's not. A Bond Grrl in business is leading, even if what she "leads at" is being a secretary. In this example, she is #1 at being a secretary (though she might be "#2" to her boss, who in this example is sort of her "James"). Bond Grrls are not "sexy" at work. They are smart, efficient, and at the top of their game. They do their job. They also know how to be #2 — and when they should fall immediately into that role.

Be a specialist. A Bond Grrl knows her territory. That's part of her responsibility. Bond is a generalist; she's the specialist. Maybe not in what wine to order, but certainly on which side streets to take in her own city. Figure out where your James/Boss will be relying on you, then let him. Gently. Don't make a big deal out of it. And figure out where he wants you to rely on him (especially if it makes him feel like an expert in some area) — and shut up even if you know a lot about that subject. Don't outshine him in his chosen area of expertise.

Be passionate about what you're a specialist in, but keep tabs on reactions to your passion. You should not be bragging about it, you should just be doing it. The work itself is the reward — not what you get to say about yourself to others. When it comes to passion, fewer words are mo' bettah. Unless, of course, you find your passion and then decide to share it with others to help them find theirs — then crow to the rooftops! Helping others realize their own passions is the greatest high there is. But again — only if they ask, and only if you're sure they are looking for you to help them!

If your passion can't be your business/job right now, don't lose track of your intention to ultimately transform your passion into your vocation. You can, if you believe you can. Just keep your eyes open. The first time I helped a friend with her walk, talk, voice, and social skills, her reaction was, "You should make a business out of this." It made me smile, but I didn't think much of it. I was a lawyer, working crazy hours, and I enjoyed helping folks. She was getting back on the dating scene after a decade or so of an awful, soul-dimming marriage. But two weeks later, when she called and said that those little things I had taught her had "completely changed her life," well, that's when I started paying attention. I started taking classes in coaching, making the time. I also had a passionate interest in helping women with sex-related issues (more on that in the next chapter!) — especially women who had gone through cancer. When those seminars started building to 10, 20, 50 people coming to friends' houses to hear and see my talks, I decided to go back to school, and get my certificate in Sexology.

Every time I would come back from leading a seminar, I would be so excited I couldn't sleep. I felt so helpful and useful. After a while, I started charging...

and the rest is history. It didn't happen overnight, and I didn't quit my day job. I expanded slowly, to see whether the passionate feelings would wear thin after a while. Nope! So take it from me — you can do it. Just start paying attention to what excites you in your life now, or meditate on what excited you as a little girl. Then bring those things into your life, and expand from there. You will be so glad you did!

Do What You Love

*There's no scarcity of opportunity to make a living at what you love.
There is only a scarcity of resolve to make it happen.*

Last night, I had my quarterly telephone chat with my college roommate. She is one of my close/safe circle of friends, and I can bounce ideas off her. Because it was on my mind, last night we talked about "pursuing your passion." My ex-roomie does a job that has its ups and downs, but mostly ups, and she's done it now for over 20 years. (Wow, how can that be, if we only feel 25?) She also has some hobbies that she enjoys, like photography, and she is now good enough that she gets paid for that work. Today when she got into her job, her boss's "inspirational e-mail" for the day was the quote above. Pretty appropriate, huh?

Don't Wait

Don't Wait, Don't Wait, Don't Wait to enjoy friends, live your Passion, and experience Joy. I recently had a "stop short and smell the coffee" moment that I'd like to share as an example. I used to see a very good but "new" girlfriend (we've known one another for a year or so) every other week at a social meeting. I stopped going because I moved, but we vowed to stay in touch. We did, off and on. You know how it goes. She telephoned me a while ago, and left a message to give her a call. I had a lot going on... and it was ten days before I called her back "for the chat."

Well, she told me that the day she had left the message, she had found out she had breast cancer. She was going in for surgery the next day. She hadn't wanted to leave the news on my voicemail... it could be bad... they couldn't tell until they were "in." (NOTE: As this book goes to press, she is through her cancer therapy, and cancer-free.)

As soon as I spoke with her, I of course dropped everything and drove on over to see her (about 1.5 hours, give or take, each way). She wanted to go to the wine country. The rain, wind and hail were so bad, I was driving about 25 MPH on the highway with my wipers on full blast — but off we went. We surprised the tasting room staff when we stumbled in from the weather, we tasted some wine, giggled a lot, cried a lot — talked a lot. Talking in the car was "easier" than if we were just sitting there on the couch holding hands and staring at each other.

The one thing that she kept thanking me for was pushing her to get back to an activity she had loved as a child, but had let fall by the wayside — horseback riding. She had brought this subject up during one of our fortnightly group meetings, as one of her only regrets in life. I remember this so clearly; at the time, we were friendly, but not true friends. I went up to her after the meeting, and said, "Look, if you're serious, I have two horses, and don't ride them often enough. If you want to compare calendars, I can get you out riding again, as soon as tomorrow." She completely re-arranged her schedule to match mine, and the rest, as they say, is history. We became best buddies, she started riding again, and now, she has progressed so far that she is riding pre-Olympic-level horses for their owners! Riding is likely what she was put on this Earth for, and is going to drive her to get through the cancer, the therapy, and all the rest.

Don't put off your passion, and don't be coy — grab any offers that come your way. And — learn from me — be sure to respond promptly when true friends call. One goal in my life is to die without Regrets. I nearly didn't make it, that time!

Don't Complain — Act!

Everything is a choice.

Yeah, yeah; easy for me to say. You "have to" go to that job you hate, or you "have to" attend that PTA meeting, or you "have to" do (whatever). Um, no, you don't. My James has been pushing me on this one, and (kicking and screaming) I am coming to the realization that he's right. Everything in your life is a choice. EV-ERY-THING. If you're stuck in a job you hate but can't get another (no other jobs in your town for example), then start consolidating and saving for a move. If your James works, why is it that both of you are working? What if you "traded" your job for concentrating on making amazing home-cooked meals, doing all the laundry, bill-paying and chores, and making a wonderful home environment? Does your dead-end job really just fund restaurant meals, daycare, triple lattes, or other "disposable" items? Could you find a way that your James will also support, that will "release" you? Not to stay home and lie on the couch and watch TV. It has to be a trade-off where your James will benefit, if he becomes the sole breadwinner. His life has to get a *lot* better, in exchange for "releasing" you from that job. Talk about it together — how can you make this work? Get a smaller house? Trade in some "toys"? What's more important to you — toys, a dead-ended job and suffering, or a more streamlined life, and concentrating eight hours a day on making your home a haven? Can you downsize your life and possessions, to "upsize" both of your happiness/contentment quotients?

If you don't have a James, or don't have a James with a job that might be able to support both of you, then at least look at your job from an optimistic standpoint, and raise your energy so that the good parts of your job start to rise to the surface. All jobs have them; you might just have to look hard. Externalize your core Bond Grrl self in small bits, keep going, keep a good attitude, and every day, make another step that sheds more of Life's little "lint balls." Most importantly, be Aware: Something better is out there. By going day in/day out to your job like a zombie, complaining, dragging home, complaining, and watching TV until your eyes glaze over, you're not keeping your eye out for a new chance. Get present. Be eagle-eyed. Be ready. Prepare to take advantage of what the Universe might have been presenting you for a long time — you've just not paid enough attention to notice.

Competition vs. Creativity

The world is a big, big place, and getting bigger every second with the advent of the Internet and the like. It is an infinite source. But one of my students mentioned the other day that she couldn't move forward in her job, because there was "too much competition" for the next level of assignments. She was looking at life like a pie: if someone else gets a bigger piece, then she's destined to get a smaller one. But Life is like a pool of water under a roaring waterfall. If someone dips some water out, there's still infinitely enough for everyone.

If you feel that you will face competition as you move forward on your Path to Passion, then you will. We usually get the Reality we envision. However, instead of being *competitive*, I dare you to be *creative*.

Can you envision creative ways to increase and leverage other people's time or other people's money? Is there a way that you can creatively approach your current job, so that you can move forward *without* facing competition? You only have competition if the higher-ups don't view you as unique; if they think that "anyone" could do the job. Through planning, foresight, and creativity you can help them see that you are the only person who would be "perfect for" that job.

Be creative. The first person to come up with the safety pin was acting creatively. The safety pin was invented while Walter Hunt was twisting a piece of wire, trying to think of something that would help him pay off a fifteen dollar debt. There were dozens of different ways to hold things together, and fierce competition between the competing methods. By thinking creatively, Mr. Hunt created a completely new market, where there was no competition at all — he had the job (and the money) to himself, until (of course) people started to copy him!

ƒEmpowerment®

Transforming Passion into Vocation

Back in Chapter 2, you started writing in your little black book, and you even thought about what you loved to do when you were a little girl. How might that translate into your vocation?

When you were a girl, did you do things like "play school" with the other kids, and help them with homework? Did that give you pleasure? (The true pleasure derived from being helpful, not the power-pleasure of being "better than" or "smarter than" them.) If so, perhaps teaching or coaching is for you. Again, what did you actually LOVE when you were little? Keep away from things you "thought you might like." Because what you loved might be something completely off the wall, that you have suppressed until now. (You can tell me.) You might say, "My Goodness, when I was a little girl, you could not GET me inside. I was outdoors all the time, from morning until night. I loved it outside, I loved the smell of the grass...." Or you might have been like me, Ms. Bookworm, reading for hours in my corner bed, without even knowing anything outside those book worlds existed.

Whatever you remember, it's time to start looking at things that will incorporate that passion. If you're an accountant and you were an outdoor kid, maybe you need to explore being the playground monitor at your daughter's school once a week, instead of doing the books for the PTA. You don't need to immediately quit accounting to become a Forest Ranger, but you do need to start to unearth, then incorporate, your Passion into all facets of your life.

Bond Grrls don't dog it out in dead end jobs! Are you active or passive when it comes to your passion? Do you believe that your life will be exciting and fulfilling — and spend time visualizing how great it will/can be — or are you waiting for life to happen to you? You know by now what I'm going to say — only the former really works. So be committed to it; and let's talk about how to get on that Path To Passion™! This should summarize what we've learned so far:

1. *Dream in Color.* You must visualize what you want sensually: smell it, taste it, see it, hear it. Details! Details! If there were no speed bumps on your Path To Passion, what would you do? Where would you be? DREAM! Better yet, dialog with a coach, who will be excited and supportive about where you're going on your path.

2. *Smoosh Your Dream Into Reality.* How does this dream match with your current reality? And how can you "smoosh" them together? If you feel dead-ended in your job, try to do that same thing, but closer to your passion. If you're a lawyer, and you want to be a rock star, become a lawyer in the music industry. Don't throw everything up in the air and start over, unless you have a back-up plan and the finances to cover you.

Remember what Barbara Sher said about the hobby-artist suddenly faced with eight hours a day of being a painter, after quitting everything else... have a plan and incorporate your passion slowly, to be sure that it's real and you're not just imagining something that looks good, but is going to take more work than you're really ready to give.

3. *Remember to think about what you want, and why you want it — not how you are going to get it.* "How" is going to present itself to you, as you move towards your goals. Your Path To Passion™ will open up. You need to dream about the details of the "What" and feel the emotion behind the "Why." Then, every night before you go to bed (I do this, no joke), spend a few moments really concentrating on why your life is fantastic. Then say to God/Jesus/The Universe/The Virgin Mary/The Great "Is"/Your Grandmother In Heaven: "My life is Great! I am so thankful! And thank you for letting me deliver up this dream to you. I am excited to see what Path you show me tomorrow, to move me along. I am committed to you and love you, and I am committed to and passionate about my dream." Note that this doesn't end with "...no matter how many obstacles are in my way." That makes your prayer and your subconscious dwell on those obstacles, which are the last thing you mentioned! Stay Positive!

4. *Let Go.* You can't have more without letting go — as I've said before, how is the Universe going to fill your cup with champagne, if it's full of beer? If you're holding onto anger related to a bad relationship in the past, or any story from your past, you are a Victim to it. You will never get a new story, because your hands are full of your old ones. Yeah, I know, I don't know *your* story. Sorry — I don't *want* to know it. I don't mean I don't care, I don't mean they were right in what they "did" to you, I don't mean it wasn't awful, but I *do* mean that it's time to dump it out of your cup. I love, honor, and believe in you. Let it go.

5. *Plan Your New Reality.* Often, this is where a coach can really help. You need to change the way you see things, because nothing really "Is." Your reality is always changing. You need to have steps (baby steps are good!) towards reaching your goal, and a timeframe. What are you going to do today? Tomorrow? Next week? Next month? If I am reporting to a coach (and paying her!) I do the things I said I would, because I want to "get my money's worth"! And always, always remember to be thankful. As hypnotherapist Susan Bird says, one should always have an Attitude of Gratitude, because "Energy flows where your attention goes."

6. *Plan Your Work — and Work Your Plan.* Keep moving forward. If you keep putting off a goal that you're juiced about, you need to re-evaluate, and see whether you need to take time from other areas of your life, to get on your Path To Passion. Use the desk calendar that you set up in Chapter 2. Also, continually keep tabs on whether you stay emotionally fired up about your goal as it approaches.

   Let me give you an example. I need to lose 10 pounds. Am I taking action on it? Yeah... kind of. But right now, finishing my book is #1 hot hot hot. However, when I was trying to fit into my mother's wedding dress for my wedding day, *you bet* I was in the gym, making room for it out of *all* other time in my week. (And the book stalled.) Keep your goals and priorities — and what you're aiming for — in front of your eyes, and also keep your emotions committed to that goal.

   If one of your goals is hotter than another, then don't try to spread your time and effort across them all. Pick the one that's hottest, and go for that. Keep an eye on the others, but don't try to do too much at once. Me? Since finishing the book is Goal A, I needed to cut back on work, cut myself some slack on working out and the like, to get this book in your hands. There are just so many hours in the day. When it's done, I'll attack those 10 pounds with renewed vigor since, of course, it'd be nice to have it gone when I'm on *Oprah*, right? But, though the 10 pounds is Goal B now, I end my day by thanking my body for my health — and reminding myself that I love my body just how it is now! I stay focused on being healthy, and will continue this when it's time to focus on the 10. I am grateful for those pounds, since they packed on as part of my comforting mechanism (mac and cheese, anyone?). Once it's Goal A, I will concentrate, not on "getting rid of" them (they are part of me!), but instead on having a healthy and whole life and body, thank those pounds for comforting me through long nights of editing, and then set them free.

7. *Keep Reaching, Stay Passionate!* Try not to dilute your focus on your primary goal by thinking about another and another. Focus on the first one, get it, but then don't rest on your laurels (or your couch, eating bon-bons). Move on to Dream #2. Make sure you keep your Dream Pipeline full; you don't want to reach your goal, hold up your hands, and sigh, "OH, my life is so EMPTY." If you only have one Dream, as it approaches you may start to procrastinate and stall out, because it means you need to admit (a) success and (b) that you need another Goal. Always have Dream 2 and 3 and 4, but just give them enough energy to keep them from drooping. Get Dream #1 first, then move the rest up the line. Dream big, and as best you can, try to always concentrate on how your dream will be of service to others.

The Firing Line

Ready... Fire... Aim!!

Yeah, I meant that. How many of us live our lives like this?

You get prepared to do something. Ready.

Then you Fire — and your shot goes way off target.

And so then you Aim, and get a little closer, Fire! Still off. You Aim again... Fire!

Why do we work this way, instead of Ready, Aim, Fire?

Because getting Ready is action. And Firing is action. And Aiming involves thinking, meditating, planning, being calm, breathing (read: inaction). But it's the crucial step.

So when you're looking at your Dreams, get yourself ready. BUT before you Fire (quitting your job, for example) — Aim.

Take a look at where you want to be, get a bead on it, think about it, plan, breathe, be calm, check the wind, check the weather. Be a sniper. Knock down that Dream the first time. You do not want to take an unaimed pot-shot at it, which is going to make it jump up and run farther away like a little bunny, and alert everyone else around you who might want to do a little sabotage!

Valuing the Goal

Many of our friends think of us as a strong mentor. We are sought out to give advice. And we do it, because we know exactly the right remedy. We can "fix" any situation, right? We're so brilliant!

The thing is, once we give that advice, it gets heard, but they might not get on it to reach the desired end. It doesn't get "embodied." Why?

We have all had a teacher that PAINFULLY made us go about finding out the answer to a question by ourselves instead of "showing" us, right? One who made us push through our Duh-ness and Stuck-ness to come to that flash of insight ourselves?

Anything that's worth having takes a bit of doing to get. It doesn't just fall in our lap. And if it does, it's devalued or spent or discarded. (Think about folks who win the lottery, and spend it all in a few years.) For example, if you plan, earn the money for, then hand over a pile of one dollar bills to buy those Gucci sunglasses you think you "need," you are going to think once, twice, or maybe more times about the exchange. It's a lot of bills! If they're just given to you, or you put them on a credit card that you don't pay off immediately and don't mentally connect with a pile of dollars, it's too easy. You're a lot more likely to need a new pair in a few months, or to leave them on a restaurant table. We all think we want things the easy way, but for items of value, the more you actively strive and keep your eye on the ball, the more you will value reaching that goal.

Test-Drive Your Dream

Remember the story by Barbara Sher, about people who "give up their life" for their "dream"? To paraphrase her, she said that people often will say, "I'm going to give up my life as a business executive, because I have always wanted to — " (big dramatic pause) " — be an ARTIST."

I actually had a friend who did this. He was supposed to be in the World Trade Center on September 11th; his law firm was there. His boyfriend, who never saw him because he worked such long hours, MADE him stay at home for breakfast that day. And they watched the planes come in.

My friend gave up his job, and did what he had "always wanted to do" — become a photographer. "Life is too short," he said. He even started a company, to try to get more money to photographers and digital artists for their works. Very awesome and noble.

So what's he doing now?

He went through all his savings — and he's back working as a lawyer. I have lost contact with him, but my guess is he's more than a little bitter.

Life isn't a Cinderella story. To me, that was Barbara Sher's moral. If you are going to make a big life change, make it in little stages. In her story, Sher said that if the executive really wants to be an artist as his vocation, he should rent the garret studio, spend a portion of his day there, and paint. Take a sabbatical to do it, but don't quit the day job! In other words, don't jump out of the plane without a parachute.

If the painting thing "works" — if people buy your stuff, and you wind up being able to support yourself, then hey! Quit the other job. But don't go Cold Turkey.

You need to try your Dreams on, because you need to really see what is a Passion — and what in fact is just a pipe dream.

You might Dream about a family, a white picket fenced house, and 2.5 kids. Maybe it's time to go work at the daycare in a gym for a little while, to be sure that you're REEEEALLY ready. Or you dream about having an awesome garden and don't realize what kind of time and effort watering systems/weeds/pruning/etc. can take. (This was my dream. Love gardens. Love them. Hate gardening! Did not realize that, until after my acre of land was planted beautifully, to my specifications. Oops. What a mistake!)

Let's say you have a daydream in which you are a concert pianist. Is it that you want to live the life of a concert pianist, traveling, wowing audiences, making music, and in your dream it's as if a genie just BLAM gave that to you? Or are you excited about putting the time in each and every day to get there, playing for yourself, just feeling enraptured by it, because piano music is your passion — and maybe some day, you could even go on tour? See the difference? A passion is all about enjoying the process. A pipedream is about the end result — without the desire to back the path.

Try on your Dream, and when you realize "YES YES YES that's for me!" go a little further... and a little further. That's your Path To Passion™!

"How" Is Not up to You

Remember, the "How" is not up to you. Your responsibility is to get your Dream as tasty as possible — and to have real emotion behind it. Sure, we all wish we were rollin' in cash and driving the Mercedes to our mansion... or do we? I can't get a lot of emotion around that. I CAN get a lot of emotion around the idea of doing a Bond Grrl Makeover on Oprah's audience. I just dream and dream and dream on that one! Or being strong and fit enough to walk so long my dog gets tired before I do (he is always a little disappointed with me).

Once you get the juicy Dream goin', and it's attached to your emotions, so you can FEEL it in your heart, in your STOMACH, then Deliver It "Up." To whatever higher power, even if it's just your own subconscious self, is going to help you with How that dream will burst into your Reality.

In fact, let me tell you a secret. If you think the How is up to you — listen here now, serious, listen — if you think that, You Are Going To Miss It. If you think that the How is up to you, you will decide it goes down a certain path, the path you believe is the correct one, and you will ignore all the little (or big!) hints along the way that are off that path you yourself chose. This means you will totally miss the path that your Grandmother/Jesus/God/Buddha/The Universe throws in front of your feet. If you're only looking for the path YOU decide is "The Way," you'll avoid any other one. Oh sure, your path will get you there — it just won't contain any shortcuts.

If you're open, you will look for any little thread of path in front of you, not be focused on Your path. You'll see other paths, and be willing to step from one to another, if you're not dead set that Yours is the Right One.

And guess what? By going about things this way, your goals will come to you so much quicker! Keep your Dream juicy, and your eyes wide open, and do the steps you know that you must (like paying down your debt, or getting into college if your dream is to be a doctor). Then, be infinitely curious how the eternal and loving Universe/God/Big Is will present shortcuts to you.

Every Single Day

The great become great because they have talent, yes — but more because they practice their passion every single day. Take someone like Tiger Woods. He had talent as a youngster clockin' that golf ball, but he still goes out every single day, and practices.

In finding your Inner Bond Grrl and your Path To Passion™, you are not going to be a pro the day after you make your decision! And though you might be letting the Universe deliver up how your dream will manifest instead of locking down the path it Must Take, you also can't just be sitting on your couch eating potato chips. (Remember the joke about God saying, "Buy A Ticket!!")

Let's put it in perspective here. You decide that you are passionate about playing the piano. So, the next day, can you sit down and jam out Mozart? Um... no. It's going to take some action and effort on your part. Just time put into it, doing scales, doing what it takes, and enjoying that. It might not be a ton of time, if that really is your gift to this world. You might breeze through it. But I can guarantee that it won't all happen in one day.

That's why it's so important that in fleshing out your dreams, and figuring out which one is Dream A at the top of your heap, you also cogitate a bit on what you can practice to help get yourself there — even if it's just practicing Patience, by paying debt instead of buying shoes!

Passion or Pipe Dream?

Desire is the starting point of all achievement, not a hope, not a wish, but a keen pulsating desire which transcends everything.

— *Napoleon Hill*

Often our daydreams are the Bling and the Merc' and the House and the Stuff. But doesn't this dream have a "Blam, the genie gave it to me" quality to it? I also smell some serious debt. Or is there some Passion behind it, where all this is just a byproduct?

Let's say that you decide that you want to be a successful real estate agent. Are you willing to check out Open Houses, entice clients, understand mortgages, get interested in the market? Would you be going to Open Houses on Sundays, just to look, anyway? Does it thrill you to think about helping someone get into their first home, no matter how small, with payments they can afford? Or are you just imagining the truck backing up to your door with the cash from all your commissions, 'cause "folks can make a killing in real estate"? One's a passion — one smells like a greed- and laziness-backed pipedream. You decide.

How Long's It Gonna Take?

Think of some steps to get where you're going — but also remember each night to "give the Dream up" to Grandma/The Universe/Jesus/etc. Do those daily things that you know are going to work you towards your success, but keep your eyes open for little miracles and shortcuts along the way.

Many believe that how long something takes to accomplish is based upon how long we *think* it is going to take. If you think it's going to take 10 years for you to get to your goal, it will. Because you will parse your effort out over those 10 years. It's a self-fulfilling prophecy. But, if you think it's going to take 10 months, if you have that urgency, you would smoosh together all those actions and steps you know to take, you will be praying every night, you will be fiercely watching for the miracles along the way and — though you might be panting at the end! — it WILL take 10 months. Remember what we learned about perception: Your perception gathers evidence, to make your beliefs right. In other words, perception gathers evidence to tell us we are correct in what we are believing. So, not only will something take as long to accomplish as you think it will, but you will actually only perceive things along the way that match your beliefs. See why it's important not to have too many strongly-held preconceptions about the path? Because that's exactly what they are: pre-conceptions. And as we have learned, whatever you believe, you conceive.

Don't forget that the difference between a success and a failure is that the successful person gets up one more time from being knocked down than the failure does. In other words: you're going to make mistakes. There will be some setbacks. But if you're afraid of mistakes, you're not going to move forward. Mistakes are part of the learning process. (Don't you hate it when people say that? But it's true.) If you experience no mistakes, you're staying on some well-worn, tried and true path, and there is no risk. If there is no risk, there is no urgency. If there is no urgency, there is no change.

Remember, also, that by hearing or reading something, you might learn it, but to actually understand it, you must embody it. (The "new parishioner" story from Chapter 2.) This means that saying that you're going to do something, or to be something, is all well and good, but if you don't do that thing and get in some practice, you'll never get it into your body: you will never "em-body" your dream into reality.

Think of the golf example. You could read all about the perfect curve of the magic swing, and all the rules of the game, but if you don't pick up a club, what then? And if you don't think you're going to shank a few balls on your way, you must be joking — heck, Tiger shanks them all the time! But each slice means a learning that you embody. Each mistake means a course correction. Dreaming about golf but not getting out on the course doesn't make you a golfer. It makes you a talker.

Whose Goals?

This is an email discussion that I had with my Baby Bond Grrl, Mica. I use it as an example of how a coach can help you realize your Inner Bond Grrl. This is only a portion of our e-coaching session, but we both feel it is instructive:

Mica said...

[When it comes to things not coming to you all at once,] this is something that I have to tell my daughter all the time: "You have to work on it." She gets very discouraged when she tries new things and she doesn't get it right the first time. I am working hard on her self-esteem.

That leads me to my "dreams" in life.... I've been really thinking hard on what I'm passionate about. The only thing I can come up with is seeing my daughter succeed in life. I know that's what every parent wants for their child but... it's what I'm really "passionate" about!

I want her to do so many things. For instance I'm always telling her that I want her to run track, play the piano or guitar, become a spelling bee champ, a dancer, be a doctor. So you see I want her doing so many things at once and being successful at it.

I have goals in my own life that I want to accomplish of course (make more money, get married, big home, fancy car...), but they aren't things that I feel "passionate" or "dream" about.

Is there something wrong with me??

I see you with all your dreams: The New York Times Bestseller book *The Bond Grrl Life*, teaching and coaching millions of women worldwide on the Bond Grrl Lifestyle, and I hope that one day I can come up with at least one non-materialistic 'dream' ;-)

~Mica~

To which I replied...

Now... I'm going to say one thing about your daughter. And remember — it's important to weigh everything that I say and see how it feels to you.

I appreciate all the things that you say to your daughter, about what you want for her and want for her to do. But you MUST have passions that are just yours. Often, women wind up "living through" their children — giving and giving to them, having their children do things that they "want them to do" — and often not letting the child develop their own passions. They hear their parent talking about how much they dream and aspire "for" them — and the kids (a) do not learn to dream and aspire for themselves (and embody it) and (b) they often do these things to please their parent — when they should be doing them through their own feeling and passion, to please themselves.

A friend of mine was in this situation, and wound up with a very rebellious teenager. Because the teenager had been the "outpouring of passion" for her mother, the girl felt sort of "responsible" for her mom, but then rebelled against it. They went to a family therapist, and the therapist asked the daughter what she truly loved; what made her heart sing. She loved to sing in the church choir. That didn't have anything to do with what the mother had "sacrificed" and "wanted" for her, or all the guitar lessons, soccer games, extra tutoring, and the like the girl was getting (which was running her mother ragged, both in time and money). Instead of talking down this rebellious teenager and getting her to "appreciate" her mother (which is what my friend thought the therapist would do), he helped my friend detach, and see she had to stop pushing the guitar lessons, soccer, extra mathematics, and the like on her daughter. The hardest part, of course, was that she had to explore her life and find something besides her daughter's success that she was passionate about. Living for herself, instead of "through" her daughter.

I think it's often hard to find our passion, because somewhere in our lives, we start doing things to please others — not please ourselves. Now, I don't mean you should be "a selfish b*tch" (that's one end of the scale), but often we will do something — sleep with someone, go to a party we're not into, drive with someone who has been drinking too much, or even just hang with someone that doesn't turn us on — because we are looking for "approval" from somewhere else or are afraid of "disapproval."

Sooooo, and remember you have to take this with a big ole grain of the sea's finest, but one thing that is so important is to truly realize what your passion is. Often, we have to go back to when WE were little girls. What would we do for hours and hours back then, if left alone?

For me, I was a reader. This is still me: if given a whole day on my own, I like nothing better than to be stretched out in bed, reading! Now, this is important, because let's just say that I was dreaming of being an Olympic track star. If I remember back to when I was a little 'un, was I outside racing people and tearing around? Um... Noooooo. So looking at that, track is PROBABLY not a passion. It's probably just a daydream, and I want something that the track star has (Applause? Team mates? Representing my Country?), not to be a track star per se. I need to *find* those qualities and bring them into my life, through an action I *am* Passionate about.

A passion can of course develop when you're older. But it is nearly always rooted in a passion that you had as a kid. And having a parent that will listen to, and help develop that passion as a kid is so important. But it has to be her passion — not your wish for her.

So that said — here's an exercise.

1. Think back to when you were a little girl. What totally floated your boat? We're talking little — like 8. What was your passion? Get your arms around it. Really FEEL it. Remember what that felt like? And no "Oh, I was a CHILD, I didn't know anything" stuff — that's not what this is about. We're connecting back to your most primal feelings of passion, and you are hard wired with some of these! Go for it.

2. Talk with your daughter, get her to dream during Mom Time. What is HER passion about? Is it music? Does she dream of being a singer? Dancer? Horseback rider? Doctor? Fashion designer? What floats her boat? What excites her? What does she do when she finds a free hour or two? Is she romping outside? Drawing pictures of new and colorful fashions? Pay attention, listen, and then instead of having lots of dreams you put "on" her, concentrate on what goes on in her mind and what she does when "no one is looking." If it's really a passion, then she's going to want to do it, even if there's no "end result." Even if she has to put time into it to succeed. Because with our Passions, we put the time in, but it's like no time has passed at all. If singing is our passion, we could be singing and boppin' and suddenly we look at the clock and four hours has slipped away! But if something's just a daydream, she will be dreaming of the end result, but with no desire to do what it takes to get there. Make sure that you separate these in your mind, and help her to, too. Not every daydream is going to turn into a Passion and Goal.

I think about piano. That was my mom's dream for me. As I understand it, she always wanted to be musical, tried various instruments, but she wasn't. I was (and am, I guess) musical. So my mom bought a piano, paid for piano lessons, the works. Was I good at this? Yup. Was it my passion? Not so much. My mom STILL talks about how great a piano player I am — but I couldn't actually even play Chopsticks these days, and I'm not too fussed about it. NOW, if it had been DRUM lessons…

Chapter 6

∞

*Does it really matter what these affectionate people do —
so long as they don't do it in the streets and frighten the horses?*

— *Mrs. Patrick Campbell
(1865–1940)*

James

Whether she's a teen on her first date or about to celebrate her 50th wedding anniversary, it's in dealing with her James that the Bond Grrl shines. Everything we've done so far in this book builds up to this important relationship.

R-E-S-P-E-C-T

Respect. That's what it's all about. Bond counts on the Bond Girls to do what they do, and doesn't make a big deal about it. That's because he respects them and their expertise. Why? Because they respect themselves. Since Bond Girls are in a supporting role (to James), they are singularly irreplaceable to him. Bond

Girls (the real ones, not the "Oh James!" ones) are secure and self-reliant when they need to be, and secure enough to understand their role as #2, too. To be respected, you must know who you are, and respect yourself. That respect will (you know what I'm going to say!) *magnetize* others' respect. And, as noted by Liz Kelly in her book *Smart Man Hunting*, "independence is a huge turn-on." By having your own life and plans — and not being jealous of his — Kelly states, "He'll respect you."

Who Needs Whom?

Many women are all excited by the idea that a Bond Grrl is passionate about what she does with most of her life, but when it comes to the equally important passion she should throw into her supporting role, they balk. Why the defenses?

First of all, Bond Grrls are 100% complete without a guy. Good thing, too, as Bond never sticks around. They "support" him, but when he moves on, they remain complete. Though some view Bond Grrls from a "women are disposable" standpoint, I think that Bond, if his job would allow it, wouldn't discard any of these women. Think about it — they're awesome. When Bond is gone, Pussy will still be running her air show, Octopussy her circus, Honey Rider searching for shells, all perfectly content and congruent in their lives though it was "nice he came on through." Can you see them moping around? No. Now Bond — he has no life of his own. He goes where he's sent, does what he's sent to do — and for what, ultimately? A government pension?

All Bond has, he has because he has an expense account. All Bond Girls have, they earned. And to reiterate, they're not broken or unfulfilled without Bond; they're not pining away waiting for him to give meaning to their lives. Far from it: they have completely complete lives without him. When Bond leaves, a Bond Girl isn't devastated — she has her own, whole, wonderful life; a life built by her, around her own specific skills and interests. Bond? There are 8 others out there just like him: generalists, fungible.

So, that is a Bond woman. She has her own fabulous life that doesn't depend on any man — but when one comes, what an enjoyment! She enjoys her interface with men to the fullest: she pampers and supports them, because she gets pleasure from it, too. Moreover, it's the best way to keep a man interested! I remember once hearing Dr. Laura on the radio; to paraphrase, she said that if women would just get over themselves and support their men for even 1/10th of the time they spend complaining about them or complaining how hard their day is, and how he should appreciate that (as a reason they aren't supportive), they'd find that he will fall all over himself to lay down his coat on the mud for her to walk over, so to speak.

Traveling Incognito

Bond knows who the Bond Girl is. No secrets. So, a Bond Grrl is transparent to her James, but mysterious to the rest of the world. He knows specifically what she does best when he's going about his Mission, though this might be a mystery to others. In the movies, the villains have figured out through satellite data link who Bond is in the first 10 minutes. The Bond Girls, however, are usually either unknown to the bad guys, or at least not suspected of being on Bond's side. That's why they can be so effective. This also ties back to being "#2." If you're not the one in front, you can usually get a heck of a lot more done to further the mission for the team.

Etiquette: Take Two

We talked a bit about etiquette in Chapter 4. (Remember, Etiquette is your Label). Perhaps Bond Grrl Book Two will tackle this subject more in depth! For now, this section includes some high points my seminar students thought should go into Book One, as etiquette relates to dating and social occasions.

Cocktails

You're out with your James for the first time. He asks if you'd like a cocktail before dinner. Assuming that you drink — if you don't, no lecture to him, right? — what should a Bond Grrl's signature drink be?

Whatever she pleases. Remember, each Bond girl is unique! (Bond? Vodka Martini, Shaken, Not Stirred. Ho Hum.) The most important thing is that a Bond Grrl knows what she likes.

A signature drink is fairly fun to design. In our Mixology seminar, we help women learn about drinks, so they don't just order "A glass of chardonnay, please" unless that is their signature drink. It's exciting to have a signature cocktail, especially if it's a 1940s-black-and-white-movies-type drink like a Manhattan, a Sidecar, a Gimlet, a Sazerac, or an Old Fashioned.

But, let's say that your drink is a Vesper Martini with Tanqueray/Stoli. I have been drinking this cocktail since reading it in Ian Fleming's original 007 books, but it's more popular now, since it made its debut on the movie screen in *Casino Royale* with Daniel Craig as James Bond. If you were to request this drink at a bar and the bartender doesn't know how to make it, however, you can either (a) explain it to him without making a big deal, or (b) you can just "fall back" to a regular "wet" (not dry) martini with a lemon twist. NEVER MAKE A FUSS. Remember, a Bond Grrl is not an Eek Girl, and she's not a complainer. She would, of course, prefer her signature cocktail, but at the same time, she knows that life is just too short to argue about such things. Besides, arguing or rolling your eyes makes you plummet from "different" to "difficult."

If you are intrigued by the subject of Cocktails, there are a number of fantastic books out there; my favorite is Gary Regan's *The Joy Of Mixology* because I think it's very accessible. However, if you'd rather listen to learn, you could download podcasts on the subject. I personally love BehindTheBarShow.com (available on iTunes). The host, Tim "Mr. Martini" Morrison, picks a base spirit (*e.g.*, whisky, tequila, gin) or a mixer (*e.g*, bitters) each episode, and covers the history, some cocktails you can make with it, and the like. The podcasts are very enjoyable, and short enough to listen to when you're cleaning the house or commuting. Listen, then expand your repertoire! One note: Bond Girls from the movies generally don't order sweet drinks — perhaps because sweet drinks are too easy to pound down without noticing. Martinis, "a double Bloody Mary with plenty of Worcestershire sauce" (Kim Basinger's drink as Bond Girl Domino in *Never Say Never Again*), and even champagne all must be sipped. If you'd like to try a quick change next time you're out, order a Campari and soda — very European, very bitter, very Bond Grrl, and not that alcoholic. And always remember, when you toast your James, to look in his *eyes*. It's considered incredibly gauche to toast by looking at your *glass*.

Wine for Women

Speaking of "A glass of chardonnay, please," I recently received a copy of *Wine for Women: A Guide to Buying, Pairing, and Sharing Wine*, by Leslie Sbrocco. What a great book! It talks about wine types, styles, food pairing, gift giving, party wine serving, and so on, in a very accessible fashion. Sbrocco doesn't go into vintages, which to me is a relief. I feel that vintages are sort of like baseball scores: more of a male bastion, where Statistics are King. She likens wine to clothing and fashion, which I personally can relate to and remember more easily!

When a Bond Grrl is running her circus, her aerodrome, or her business, a book like Sbrocco's is invaluable. It helps make wine effortless — and effortlessness is definitely part of the ƒEmpowered lifestyle. However, it's important to watch it when you're out with your James.

You should, of course, know what you like — I, for example, hate oaky/buttery Chardonnay and so if I want a white wine, I ask for an "unoaked" Chard, or am always safe with Sauvignon Blanc, which is generally aged in steel. If your James is choosing a bottle of wine and asks what you might enjoy, just be careful not to carry on (or grab the wine list!), and run the risk of being labeled (etiquette!) a Know-It-All. If you know there is a wine (or food) you don't care for (Pinot Noir, for me), then just say "Any red but Pinot sounds fab to me." He gets to choose for you, and show by his deliberations that he is thinking of how best to take care of you; you might get to try something new and fabulous, depending on what he orders!

If you're having your James over for a romantic dinner, Sbrocco's book gives you some suggestions to help you be a more effortless hostess. Part of being a Bond Grrl is that effortless preparation and nonchalant excellence. As you actually become more accomplished in various areas, you will lose the need to toot your own horn or brag about what you do. Of course, the first time you serve the perfect wine with a gorgeous plate of cheese and some artistically arranged dark chocolate, you're going to act completely nonchalant, but then excuse yourself as your James or your guests are Oooh-ing and Aaaaah-ing to call your best Grrl on your celly from the bathroom! I know — been there. Just stay cool in public, Bond Grrl.

One little trick: As you'll learn in a few pages, your James is a voyeur, so using your hands suggestively can ensure he only has eyes for you. We've all heard the "play with your hair" trick — but what about using your wine glass? Slowly ("absently") trace your finger around the top of your wine glass, as you hold it by the stem of your opposite hand. Or, if the glass is on the table, again "absently" move your fingers up... and down... and up... and down the stem. You want to do this as if you are not paying attention to it, so that your James thinks that he's seeing into your subconscious. If you do these tricks and look him in the eyes, raise an eyebrow, or wink, he's going to think you're flirting on purpose, which is much less of a turn-on.

b & d

(No... that isn't an S&M reference. Sex — later!)

I was at a networking luncheon recently. (Beware: anything that advertises itself as a "luncheon" instead of a "lunch" means you're forking over Bank to attend.) The gal sitting next to me — who pulls down big 6 figures and takes clients out to eat all over the world — didn't know which plate was hers at the round table at which we were sitting.

I thought everyone knew the "b" and "d" thing, which I shared with her. Certainly, my Baby Bond Grrls know! This apparently was also news to the other 6-figure gals at the table. Three of them leaned over, and said "Show me that again?" So here we go:

If you're sitting at your place at a table and are surrounded by bread, salad, water, etc., often it's hard to keep straight which bread plate/salad/wine/water is yours and which belongs to your neighbor. How to do it?

Turn your hands thumbs up (wrists in towards one another). Now, touch the finger next to your thumb to the top of your thumb. You're basically making an "OK" sign with both hands, keeping the rest of your fingers together and straight and your wrists facing each other.

If you look down, your left hand looks like a small letter "b." And your right hand looks like a small letter "d." The "b" stands for "bread" (and any other food substance). So your bread and salad are on your left. The "d" stands for "drink." So your water and wine are to your right. Then, if you turn your fingers upside down (clue: Turn your wrists TOWARDS you) and put the thumb-and-forefinger ring up to your eyes, you will have the "Up in the Air, Junior Birdman" goggles position. Or, alternatively, you'll look like me, trying to show the "b" and "d" to a terminally perplexed woman across the table, who was desperate to learn...

Men Are Dogs

(Finally, something you can agree with, right?) I remember one of my Baby Bond Grrls laughingly told me in a seminar that "All men are dawgs." She said this is the way that she had been brought up, and this is what she and her grrls incessantly discussed. You can imagine how I felt about that.

But, in some ways, men *are* dogs. Men don't have anyone in their lives they can go to when they have a "hurt paw" from a curve ball Life throws them — except their woman. Women, on the other hand, always have their grrlfriends to go to. If a man goes to his guys, they're like a dog pack. He will be one down from then on. If a grrl goes to her grrlpack, she's sharing, everyone throws in their two cents, and usually sort of forgets about it later. (Unless of course she complains over and over again — not cool.)

If you treat your James like #1, really listening, with some things thrown in like rubbing his stomach, flattering him (not lying, just some Atta Boys), giving him treats — he's going to be there for you. And you're the only one in his life who can really do this for him.

Yeah, now you're going to say, "So why can't he do that for ME?" Because you have other outlets — he does not. Men are just dying for someone to really See and Listen to them. You will hold them in the palm of your hand if you just give them that attention 20 minutes out of the day.

And... if your James were to give you that attention, would you accept it, anyway? If you tell your James "You are SO hot," he purrs. If he says "Baby, you are so sexy" out of the blue, do you say back, "Oh, but doesn't my butt look fat?" Hello: This is the way to train someone to NOT compliment you. So if you get a few compliments out of him, say thank you, smile, and give him one back. No more "Buts" (butts?), and definitely no more coy little "Oh... you think so?" That's just you fishin' for more. Knock that off.

If You Believe It, It's True

What are your beliefs? They're your Reality and your Truth. That is all you will actually see as you walk through Life. Men Are Dogs? That's all you will see. Because our senses gather evidence to make our beliefs right, and block out anything that isn't congruent with that. We also energetic draw to us what we are Vibing on. We have all gone through the experience of deciding we will research or explore something (buying a new car, for example), and then suddenly, every third car on the road is the car we're researching. This is because our mind can't take in all the information bombarding our eyes every second we're awake, and selectively blocks out some information over others. So to make sure that your mind is not blocking out your way to success, you need to assess your beliefs, and be ready to understand that some of the things that you think are True just are not. In the quantum physics realm, the physical world doesn't really exist as a static Truth — we project ourselves, and what we think we deserve onto that world, and that's what we see and receive. In other words, the world is not set and True. The world outside mirrors the world inside of you. Think of a friend who seems to have all the Luck: Why is that so? Because she actually doesn't believe it can be any other way. That's how her world works. What you say, and what you believe, is your Truth and your Reality. And yours is different than mine, or your James', or your parents'.

Twenty Minutes

So, it's time for another little homework assignment. Each and every day for at least a week, give your unabashed, full and devoted attention to your James for twenty minutes.

WHAT, says you? HE has to go FIRST!

Twenty minutes is probably about the time you take out of your day to go get coffee. And what I'm suggesting is that you devote it to the man you (supposedly) love unconditionally: You know what that means, right? "Without condition": without requiring something back or something first.

Excuses, excuses, I can hear them now. I've heard 'em all, by the way. Women tell me that:

- He will require more and more, and then they will be doormats.
- He has to go first, she gives enough already.
- Why should she always be the one to give all the time?

However, if you're like 99% of my students, I bet if you looked at your life truthfully, you'd find you don't particularly give any time *specifically* to your James at all. And then you wonder why he doesn't fall all over you.

Do you sit down, make him comfortable, really listen to him, make light conversation? Or do you yell at him to take out the garbage, and have him fend for himself for dinner?

Could you just give him a break and some directed lovin' for 20 minutes?

As I mentioned above, you're the only one in his life that will take the time and effort to make him comfortable, and give him space to let his feelings out. Your true Grrlfriends have your back emotionally. He likely has no one in the Dog Pack.

What I'm suggesting is unconditional giving; giving for giving's sake. Giving because it increases the happiness in the world, by one guy. Your James. And when you see the light (and surprise) in his eyes, it is going to increase the world's happiness by one grrl too — you.

How's about just greeting him at the door with a true and unabashed hug, or, once he sits down, going behind his chair, slowly tilting his head back, and looking into his eyes? My James has the most beautiful eyes. I tell him all the time. They're sort of a tan-brown, with little flecks of blue and green near the edges. I bet your James has gorgeous, liquid-brown, or bright blue, or cat-green eyes. Start looking. Start complimenting. Yes — you go First. And Often. How's about truly listening? I heard Alissa Kriteman (MeetTheDreamer.com) speak on her podcast; she stated that men respond in layers. If we are talking with a man, we need to wait 30 or 60 seconds longer than we would with a woman, before we jump in. They share the most general thought, wait to see if the listener is still interested, go a bit deeper, then a bit deeper. This is how men share — like peeling an onion. You don't get to the good stuff if you jump in and stop the process. It takes practice, but you can develop the gift of being silent, and help your James' dreams unfold and ignite. The Law of Attraction works for him, too!

If you'd like a little exercise to try, sit down next to your James, and ask him to recount a dream to you, for two minutes. Ask him to let his senses run free — to pepper his dream with what he sees, tastes, hears, and feels as he experiences it. Just listen, with your eyes smiling. Slow your mind down, and really pay attention to what's being said. Don't cut him off if he's flyin' at two minutes — go ahead, and stay present, and give him 5! When the time is up, take 30 seconds to a minute just to repeat what he said to you. Start by saying "I heard you say..." and then repeat what you heard. Not what you thought, but what you heard him actually say. There is nothing more soul-fulfilling than being well-and-truly heard. Then, after that time, tell him how you feel, using this equation: "When you say ____, I feel ____." Not "Wow, that's GREAT!" Or "Gee, you dream big!" Or "We don't have that kind of money!" Instead, relate your feelings. "When you say that you want to go to Costa Rica, I feel excited at the possibility of adventure for you." (And if he didn't mention taking you, don't bust him about this — don't pout and say "Hey... do I get to come, too?" Don't dampen his sharing with you, by corralling his dream.)

I don't believe that your chosen James (unless you are one awful chooser) is going to wring you dry and walk all over you if you start giving him your undivided attention daily. Why? Because the vast majority of the people I see doormatted are *men*. These guys do so much for their Princesses and get so, so little. And the Princess is constantly sitting there with her arms crossed, saying, "Give him an inch and he'll take a yard." B.S. The Princess just doesn't want to make the effort.

And tell me why, again, he has to go first? Don't you know that if you are happy and giving, that this will bring more happiness back to you? You say you give and give and give and no one supports you? Yeah, yeah. You and my other grrlfriends and students. Your James doesn't "treat himself" to a mani/pedi, dish on you with his Dog Pack, buy a purse here, a lipstick there. If he spends money on himself, it's usually something like golf, which winds up blowing his ego even more. Stop right now, and think. You have your grrlfriends supporting you, and your "giving" is to them, your kids, your community — but I'll bet it's seldom directly to your James. Really — put this book down and run over it in your mind. And I'm not talking chores. That is traded off in your life — for example, you do the laundry and get the dry cleaning, he pays the bills. Even if that's lopsided now in your life, that is not giving time/paying attention to your James. You can't count that time. So — got any time in your week you're clean, happy, sultry, and supportive with all eyes just on him? That's what I'm talking about. Remember why you picked him, and show him you're glad you did. Give him those 20 minutes, and you know what? You will get more than that back.

Don't think you will? Do it anyway; practice for your next James. Because if this one really is an ungrateful lump, plan to leave, and get out. But I'll bet you this attention to him and intention to show him you love him will do wonders. Don't sass that "it won't" and not try. Put 100% effort into it, because, Sister, your life is what you've made of it. If he's disrespecting you, you showed him how. If you want him to love and appreciate you, show him that, instead.

I think that women get married to men, and then do as little as possible to keep them. It's that chase/catch mentality. If you were to honestly look at things from your James' eyes, would you want to stay with you? Would you REALLY? Why?

What do you specifically do each day, to make your James' life great? Again, not the things you're doing because you want to, like pick up the clothes off the floor. He doesn't care about that, YOU do. That's not "for him." Get him a martini when he comes home? A little glass of wine? Ask him for his advice on something and then listen to it? Smile? With your eyes? Leave him a little love note on his pillow? Pack him a lunch? Buy him sexy undies and leave a note to match, in his drawers drawer?

No? So why should he stay with you? You say you "Give him a clean house and wonderful kids." Does he really care? Does this have to do with him, specifically? Likely, no. These are likely things that you wanted. (If you hadn't wanted them, you wouldn't have them, face it. It's an exceedingly rare man that would "make" you have kids or keep the house clean. Isn't it your own self that wanted that?) In fact, he's probably "given you" a lot of things he didn't particularly want, that you wanted. Maybe a big house, when he'd rather have a smaller place and save for retirement. New furniture, when the previous stuff was fine by him. So, you put dinner on the table every night and he doesn't appreciate it? Aren't you eating, too? It's not done for him, specifically.

I don't believe that women are taken for granted as much as their Princessly Selves think that they are. I think that women believe they should be waited on hand and foot, and not have to do a thing for it. I think this is a tragic epidemic. Hey, I'm glad I'm a woman "this time around." Being a man would suck. Especially with the way most of them are treated at home.

Again, be brave, assess yourself. Get out your little black book, and list what you do (ever) that is specifically for him, to make him feel great. That you do because it's something you know that he'll love. Not the laundry, not the chores, not the vacuuming, not buying the groceries, not the dinners — unless it's a candlelight dinner with you in lingerie, if that's *his* bag (not if it's *yours*). If you're packing an awesome tailgate picnic for him to take to the game — especially if you hate football and are not going — then that's what I'm talking about. Especially if you leave it for him on the counter with a little love note, not hand it to him with a Make A Big Deal Of Me look. How's about it?

Reliance = Respect

When I was in the Marines, there was a big physical wash-out rate for lawyers (including me: I blew my knees out). Why? Because the Marine Corps believes that everyone who is a Marine is basically a grunt/rifleman first. The other services send lawyers and doctors through a process that's somewhat uncharitably referred to as Knife and Fork School, where you are taught how to salute, and which knife and fork to use at a fancy dinner, but soft-soaped through the combat stuff. As a Marine, though you might be a big bad *ss JAG lawyer or an officer that everyone salutes, you went through Boot Camp like every single other Marine. You can field strip an M-16. You ate the same chow. You slogged through the swamp in 110 degree heat, running in file while carrying a telephone pole by your belt with members of your platoon. (Yep. Been there.)

Let's say I hadn't gotten hurt. A Marine needs me to defend him in my role as JAG (Judge Advocate General — a military attorney). I didn't just go to Knife and Fork School. I had to go through the wringer too, just like him. I have done something that he respects. I understand a bit about where he's coming from. So he can relax and let me Do My Stuff for him, even though he may not understand what that Stuff is. He can rely on me.

Know What James Relies on You For

As you know, in the Bond movies, the Bond Girl generally has an expertise, for which Bond relies on her. It could be flying a plane, or diffusing a bomb, or driving a car — when she's called on, she does it. It's complete trust on Bond's part.

What does your James rely on you for? It could be something small. My James relies on me, for example, to pour him a glass of wine or shake him a Negroni (if he calls to tell me it was a really bad day) when he gets home. Does this make me a "doormat"? Nope. Are some of you saying "Hey, HE should pour YOU a glass of wine when YOU get home." Whyzat?

I can do something fairly simple like this and know that he's completely relying on me for this area of our lives together, and it's a blessed relief for him. It helps him leave his stress on the doormat. Okay, he also relies on me to do the laundry, stuff like that. I don't mind doing these things, and he hates doing them. So here, he knows he can rely on me. I don't make a big deal of it, either.

Don't cut down these activities, lessening them by labeling them as "demeaning." Why are these more "demeaning" than, oh, paying the utilities, or cleaning the gutters, for which I rely on him? I hear women constantly stating that they are

ÆEmpowerment®

"so sick of doing the laundry all the time" and that their James should "pitch in," or "at least say thank you." Why? I'm sure he's doing something that they would rather not do. Is it really so bad that you do these things for the Team? But don't elevate these chores either, and count them towards your "only for him" time.

Have your lips let loose the pout that your James doesn't "appreciate" what you do? How do you know? Just his relaxation when he gets home and it's done is appreciation, even if he's not falling all over himself praising you to the Heavens. Besides, are you doing it for the appreciation (outward motivation/desire for kudos), or for the inner satisfaction of knowing that things are getting done right? You need to look at your true motivation for doing what you do — and find your pride within, from a job well done. Satisfaction, from doing the laundry? Yes, because, in my case, I know that it's done right, and I know that my James is immensely relieved that he doesn't have to do that chore any more. Same with unloading the dishwasher. For some reason I hate this chore, but I know he hates it more — and won't do it, he'd rather the dishes mount in the sink. Besides, we're more likely to cook together when it's neat and clean in the kitchen with everything in its place, which is fun and romantic for both of us.

So, what does your James rely on you for? Even if he doesn't cry "Oh, thank you, Babe!" every time you do whatever it is that you do, he relies on you. He trusts you. He appreciates it, but you should be getting inner satisfaction from it, not require a calligraphed thank you note every time you raise a finger. When a Bond Girl drives the car while Bond is shooting the bad guys, or defuses the bomb that Bond brought her along for, he doesn't stop to gush "Oh, thank you." It's implied.

Oh — and do you want the big kudos for doing the laundry, or picking up the kids, or getting dinner on the table, but don't mention the things that your James does, like taking out the garbage, or keeping whiskers out of the sink, or getting the leaves out of the gutters, or bringing home the bacon, or taking you to the movies?

Just wondering.

Stop complaining. Start changing. If you're really in the wrong relationship, then start planning for change. But do take a good look before you act on your thoughts. (Ready, *Aim*, Fire.) Maybe your James is so "awful" to you, because you haven't been appreciating him. Remember, you get what you draw to you. How's about acting from your Inner Bond Grrl without asking anything in return, and see how it might change your relationship. Remember, you drew this to yourself! Are you enjoying complaining and playing Victim? Shame on you...

 *Wake Up*

Imagine you're in a plane. The engines start to sputter a little. What do you do next? Complain? Start considering your options? Jump out?

How does this analogy work in your life? Are you conscious of what's going on around you, particularly in your relationship? What's sputtering? What's starting to smoke? Don't let it all burst into flames before it gets your attention. If you are a Bond Grrl, you are paying attention to your life, in every dimension. You didn't "suddenly" get into a huge amount of credit card debt, or an awful relationship, or a dead-end job. Your James doesn't "suddenly" leave you. Fess up. You were unconscious, weren't you? Bond Grrls stay present. So take a look around your life, and see what's what. Maybe even write it down in your little black book, and what steps you're going to take to put out the fires, get the sputtering engines tuned back up, and especially get more of — and take time to enjoy! — what's going well.

If things are going well, they take less of your time. You know that, right? You will have so much more time if you take care of the stuff that's going off course, before it *really* hits the skids. Complaining and gossiping about it takes time. In the hour that you were on the phone with your grrlfriend complaining, perhaps you could have done something that would actually have been productive. If you'd given 1/4 of that time to your James, do you think perhaps the stuff you have to complain about that involves him would start to disappear?

I dare you. Take a day, and be present all day. Be present to what you say and what you do. How much of a downer are you, really? How much time are you whining, in your head or to other people? I bet you'll find that you are "spinning your wheels" a lot more than you thought. I once told a friend that she had the clutch in on her life. She was always putting a lot of energy (gas) into talking about things, but she never seemed to move forward! Vroom! Vroom! Going nowhere? Be present, engage the clutch, and move forward, so you can coast a little, later!

Bond and Marriage

What? Bond got married? Yes, he did — in both the film and book versions of *On Her Majesty's Secret Service*. I find it very instructive to look at Tracy, who became Mrs. James Bond. Though not brought out in the movie, Bond's reasons for marrying her in the book are quite specific: "She's adventurous, brave, resourceful. She's exciting always. She seems to love me. She'd let me go on with my life. She's... not cluttered up with friends, relations, belongings. Above all, she needs me. It'll be someone for me to look after. I'm fed up with all these untidy, casual affairs that leave me with a bad conscience."

Take note of that quick description! She "seems to love" Bond, meaning, she's not fawning all over him, catering to his every whim, but, "above all," she "needs" him. And he knows it. She stays a little mysterious. She keeps him on his toes. But she isn't going to curtail his life: she trusts Bond and their bond.

When was the last time your James really felt needed — wanted? Is he just a taxi service for the kids, or an extra set of hands for you? If he goes out with his Pack, do you do the passive aggressive jealous "huff" on him? (Or, worse, take up poker so you can do it *with* him and the Pack?) All men, at their core, really are Bond. Regardless of how unlikely it might seem for your chosen James to get into some of the exciting and adventurous situations found in the Bond films, that does not mean that he doesn't dream of being that way. In our homes, it's our job to bring that part of our James out. Or look out — perhaps he will find some other woman that will!

Note, however, that Tracy (Mrs. Bond) is also "adventurous, brave, resourceful." As stated in the book *Smart Man Hunting*, men "value confidence... it's a sign that a woman loves her life, which is important to men. They don't want the burden of fixing it — or giving it meaning — for her." What happened to Tracy, you ask? Oh dear — better rent the movie!

Reclaim Your Sensual Spark

When was the last time you felt really, truly feminine? My students often say that they feel they have lost touch with their sensual spark. It's my firm belief that a large part of this is all the time spent trying to "one-up" the men in their lives, and therefore winding up on the short end of the stick with respect to gender identification. Believe me, I know it's tough. Women are now expected to earn their own way, be powerful, take charge, and all these yang attributes. They are almost never taught how to be empowered by their femininity. If raised by women who felt disempowered in their own lives, they are often doubly pressed into that "kick-*ss and take names, don't let anyone walk on you, you will be the woman I was never able to be" role.

If you look at the Bond women overall, they are not only all-powerful in their own way, but they know how to shut it off and Be All Woman. They are mysterious without keeping secrets from Bond. They take pride in themselves, for themselves. They do not "let it all hang out," taking the lazy, easy way. Can you imagine a Bond Grrl with no makeup, in a frumpy smock when James sees her after his Mission that day? Um, no.

And all those Bond women look so at ease when they fall into bed with James! That's because they leave their other stories at the bedroom door. What can you do, as soon as you get home, to get into that mood? A bath? Not enough time? How's about a sensual shower, with a sexy-smelling soap? Have you trained your kids that there are areas of your life that are just for you and your James, or do you cater to their every whim? Spoiling a child like that is doing him/her no good, when it comes to dealing with the real world. As soon as they are able to understand, make sure that they know from the time your James calls to say he's on his way home, to about 1/2 hour after he's there, it's time just for the two of you. (Believe me, he'll call if he knows what it will lead to!) No homework help. No fights. No "Oh Daddy, me, me, me!" And no solace in your bed either — sorry — if nightmares come, they should call and know you'll come, not dive between you and your James in your bed. If that's your household, then it's time to break the cycle. It will be well worth it, believe me. You'll feel more like a sexy woman and less like a motherslave; your James will feel cared for and nurtured. Even if you decide to do this only on Tuesdays and Thursdays to start, the only way to reclaim your sensuality is to take action.

Traits of Sex Goddesses

I was reading *Cosmo* the other day in the auto body shop waiting room. There was an article on what Sex Goddesses have that us Mere Mortals do not. There were a ton of "tricks," but three things were mentioned that MY James has told me really work with him. I thought I would share them, because they are very Bond Grrl.

1. *Use His Name.* OK, we all know this from the Bond movies. The Bond Grrl who has just had a Nice Time of It always sighs, "Oh, James." My James is all about this. When I say his name — not "Honey," but his actual given name — he loves it. Now, when he uses my name, I find it jarring. I like "pet names" better, especially in Sensual Situations. Perhaps this is because I am being Ms. Solitaire and when I hear "Sandy," that jars me back into my real world self, worries, and the like.

   Interestingly, what the article said was that when you use his name, it reminds him he "beat out the competition" on you. Honest! I would not have listed this, if it wasn't one thing that totally rocks my James. As the article said though, you can't use it all the time; the deal is to sort of drop it in during sensual situations, here and there. Men dig it.

2. *Tell him less: he'll want you more.* Very Bond Grrl. You don't want to Tell It All to your James. They just don't care about the specifics. They don't care about stories, either (unless of course you're telling your James about how hot you told your Grrls he was). Men don't care about the details. Details are a grrl thing not a guy thing. They are not wired this way. Grrls want to know what the waitress in your story was wearing

ƒEmpowerment®

— right? Your James doesn't even want to know there was a waitress, or you were in a restaurant, or that you were with your Grrl Gang, or — you get the picture. *Reader's Digest* Version. At Most.

Cosmo was saying that the deal here is that if he asks what you were up to, you want to say "Oh, out with my Grrls," then stop. If he asks, don't be all coy or seem like you're trying to get something by him, just be brief, but not snotty. When he has enough info, he will stop asking, and then (duh, Grrl) stop talking. Don't be all bent out of shape when he doesn't ask for details that are on the tip of your lips to spew forth. It's not that he doesn't care. It's that men get full-up on details much quicker than women do. Listen to his stories to you. They are all about the Verbs. Women talk all about the Adjectives. In other words, Grrls love the Atmosphere. Your story? It goes: "This tall white woman was wearing this ugly yellow dress kinda right above her porky little knees and talking on her celly so loud you could barely hear yourself think, when she walked into the corner restaurant — you know, the one we had that great lasagna at on my sister's birthday, I think she got the recipe, in fact — and she tripped over this piece of linoleum that has been sticking up forever, right there in front of the front door, you know, I think I mentioned it to you even once, and...". Your James' version? "This gal tripped." See? This is all hardwiring. Back when men had to go out and hunt, they had to be quiet, sit side-by-side in trees or behind bushes for hours with their rocks or bows and arrows, waiting for game to kill for dinner, shhhhh. We women were back in the village, taking care of the kids, picking berries, and being loud and talking and laughing to scare *away* the game, so that we didn't *become* dinner. Get it? So save the details for your Grrls. Think Action, not Atmosphere!

And how you address your James may be hardwired, too. As pointed out by Helen Fisher in *Why We Love: The Nature and Chemistry of Romantic Love*, "Men and women tend to get intimacy differently. Women get intimacy from face-to-face contact. We do what we call the anchoring gaze. It comes from millions of years of holding your baby in front of your face. Men tend to get intimacy by doing things side by side, because for millions of years they faced their enemy but sat side by side with their friends." So while you might think that looking your James deep in his eyes and complimenting him would be the best strategy, instead, saying the same thing to him as you're sitting on the couch or cruising on the highway might actually have a more lasting effect. (Strange, huh?)

3. *Compliment him at least once a day.* And DO NOT EXPECT IT BACK, SISTAH. Remember, you're about the Adjectives. He's not. It takes a Big Change (like, you shave your hair off) to get a notice from your James. Wait for your Grrls to tell you DANG that DRESS IS GOOD ON YOU! Get it from them. As *Cosmo* said, which totally cracked me up, your James is not EVER saying to you, "Hon, does this shirt make my pecs look flat?" We do it all the time to our Jameses ("Does this dress make my butt look big?"), and they're so screwed, whatever answer they choose. If it's "Yes," you're going to be pissed he said it, even though that outfit shouldn't be in your closet, and you know it in the back of your mind anyway. If he says "No" and you think it's "Yes," you think that he's an idiot. Just remember, a James will not fish for compliments. That's why it's up to you to give them; his Dog Pack will not! They might mention a nice jump shot, but then they're going to try to beat him out on it next time. They certainly aren't saying "James, dang man, your biceps look so awesome in that shirt!" or, "Dude, that color totally washes you out." Uh, no. So that's your job. And don't let some other woman sneak under your radar because you're not doing it!

Sex

Flipped here first, did you? Or perhaps you're a James, seeing if you should buy this book for your Bond Grrl? Caught you! (And, Yes, buy it.)

Even though Bond Girls can play as rough as the boys in action films, they are NOT sexy-but-gender-neutral like many women in films (*e.g*, Sarah Connor/ Terminator 2, Lara Croft). They are feminine, sensual, and sexual. In fact, part of their attractiveness is their understanding of sex and its power. Bond never just "takes" a Bond Girl. He has to earn it. Bond must be "good enough" for her — not vice versa.

 **Book Report**

Have you read Gail Sheehy's book *Sex and the Seasoned Woman: Pursuing The Passionate Life*? Another Grrlfriend recently read parts of it to me. It's a book about women and sex — and taking control of your life in that area, Grrls, especially if you're "between forty and death," as the flyleaf quotes from the play *Mame*. Check it out!

Screaming for Information

I am constantly amazed at how much people don't know about sex. "Happily married" people. Young people. Bar none, my most requested seminars revolve around Sensual Secrets. Maybe I should have subtitled this chapter "Things you wish your mother had taught you (but maybe she herself didn't know)."

I love learning, exploring, and teaching about sex and sensuality. I am depressed at how Puritanical the typical American household remains. From my experience, women are screaming inside for information about sex and sensuality. And it's one of my missions in life to help them uncover it, without any sort of judgment.

Since it's *part* of my business, I *make* it my business to know about things that I perhaps might not "do" myself. I think it's important to remember that anything between two consenting adults is A-OK. Don't let society dampen your spirits. Don't do anything you don't want to, but try something new each month that you might enjoy, with someone whom you trust. The worst thing that could happen is you wind up dissolved in laughter. The best? It might really excite you both! So in this section, I will discuss a few of the baseline issues that I cover in my classes, though you'll need to wait for the next book for the advanced techniques!

The Big O

(Um, no, I don't mean Oprah.) Our bodies' capacity for Orgasm is seemingly infinite; we can come over and over again, and still be ready for more! We even have a body part, the clitoris, whose only purpose is to give us sexual pleasure (and did you know that the whole clitoral structure is actually as large as a man's penis? Yup — we just see the tip!). This may all seem a bit unfair to men, who typically reach a precipice, fall over the edge, roll over and go to sleep! So why is it that so many women are frustrated (or faking) rather than fulfilled?

It's time for women to take responsibility for their own orgasms. And the first place to start is that most important of sexual organs... the Brain. Unless you can shut off Thinking, Thinking, Thinking every moment and concentrate on the pleasures of your own body, you won't have orgasms. Worrying about how you look. How you smell. How you taste! If you think about your tummy fat quivering and that your daughter might walk in the bedroom door any second, you're out of the Present and in your Head, not experiencing the input of your senses. Plan, then relax. I will help you learn how.

It's Up To You

Let's talk just a bit about human sensual response. Imagine a Bond movie: here is this sexy Bond Girl, lying, all seductive, on the bed. Mmmmm. James approaches, slowly. And the next words out of her mouth are...

"Look — it was a hard day — I'm just not into it."

or how's about

"I'm not ready yet."

or how's about

"I need more time."

or how's about (put your hands in front of your eyes, I'm going to get nasty)

"No, wait, you didn't take long enough, get your mouth back down there."

Can you imagine? Come on, Grrls. I am shocked and stunned, when I take informal polls at my classes, at how many women still believe that it's "the man's job" to get her to her "O."

What's your usual scenario?

You rush home from work, are a little tired and grouchy, or have been trying to put the kids to bed and just don't feel in The Mood. Does this sound familiar? I want to pose a more ƒEmpowering strategy to you.

You know that you're going to have an Evening with your James. You come home earlier than he does: you plan it. I don't care if your boss wants something at the last second — tell him/her you have a "female appointment." (S/he won't dare keep you — especially if your boss is a man.) Remember, your Life must come first. Get home so you have plenty of time.

Set the stage. I don't care if you and your James have been together for 30 years! Why should that make romance a thing of the past? Just drawing the blinds and lighting a candle on the dresser somehow magically changes things. Women have a problem: We are multitaskers. We can be doing one thing (Oh, kiss me James, kiss me!), while thinking of another (Did I put a saucer under that candle, in case it drips? And shoot will the cat grab the blinds now that they're down... I wonder if he can see the dust in the corner from here?). It's time for you to get your brain and your body congruent, like your James, who is hardwired to do one thing at a time, succeed at that Goal, then move onto the next. Just try to talk to him when he's on the phone, if you don't know what I'm talking about. You're watching TV, clipping coupons, chatting with your kid, stirring

ƒEmpowerment®

the saucepan, keeping the dog out of the trash, and also listening to him on the phone, with enough presence of mind to comment on his conversation; he can't talk on the phone and hear what you are saying, too, much less do all the rest. By setting the stage romantically, you'll help your brain stop flitting around, and concentrate on one thing only — Bonding.

Now, I know this will come as no surprise, but on average, it takes women a lot longer to get ready to Be Ready, so to say, than a man. I recently heard that it takes an average of 23 minutes for a woman to Be Ready, and only about 4 for a man. (Four minutes, not four seconds, but remember, that's all men on average, all ages!) As a Bond Grrl, if you learn and adopt nothing else in this book, the most life-changing thing to adopt will be to take full responsibility for decreasing those 23 minutes to Readiness!

Some of us are faster than that — some are slower. You are you. You are perfect, however you are. So how to take matters into your own hands, as it were? (Oh, bad. I know.)

Men are voyeurs: of our five senses, their main responsiveness is from Sight. That's why men like sex pictures or X-rated videos: these appeal to their Visual sense.

A woman's main sense, however, is Touch. And one of the best ways to help start those 23 minutes ticking is to take a bit of time and to really touch and feel your skin, and luxuriate in a nice bath or shower before your James comes home. (Of course, if you allow your partner to see you preparing, you will be heightening his #1 sense, too!)

When you are getting ready to go out (or stay in) with your James, do you currently leap in the shower, because you're running late? Scrub, scrub, scrub-a-dub, and you're back out in 5 minutes, slap on some lotion or cologne, then... Where are my pantyhose? Where is my bra? Rush rush rush.

How about being luxurious in the bathroom, instead? Planning is everything.

Take a nice shower or bath. Really LOVE your body in there. Run your hands all over your body first, with no soap. Slowly. Second time, with soap. Even more slowly, as you feel that slippery goodness that is you. (Are you embarrassed just reading this? Why? I'm getting you back to the bathroom now, but think about this, if it's so.) Now, as you rub that soap on your body, close your eyes. Imagine your hands are your lover's hands. To put your brain further in the Mood, it's nice to have a special soap that you only use before meeting your James. I love using a gorgeous, organic lavender-rosewood soap — in fact, I love it so much, I now distribute it on one of my websites! (Mooncrafting.com)

 ## Kegels and Ben Wa Balls

While we're in the bathroom (is nothing sacred?), we need to talk for a second about Kegel exercises. Kegels strengthen your pelvic floor muscles. These muscles, basically, hold your insides in. As we age or have babies, they loosen. If you have any sort of bladder control problem, you should be doing Kegels.

Where to start? Well here, in the bathroom! When you sit on the toilet to pee (ok, "urinate," fine, have it your way), practice stopping the flow two or three times. The muscle that you contract to stop the flow is the pelvic diaphragm muscle we're looking to strengthen.

If you can't stop the flow, then you really need these exercises! Do it each and every time you pee. Once you get your strength up, you will be able to stop the flow, no problem. Once you can accomplish this, spread your knees wide, so that you're really straddling the seat. This will make stopping the flow more difficult.

Finally, once you've mastered that, time for Ben Wa Balls. I know, I know, everyone thinks these are some sort of Japanese sex-toy number, designed to give women constant orgasms while they walk. Not really. They're basically barbells for Kegels. You could strengthen your bicep by just bringing your hand in and out to your shoulder, but it will go faster if you put a weight in your hand. That's the theory here. Ben Wa Balls add weights to your Kegels. Start with one Ben Wa Ball, and hold it inside of you (squeezing your pelvic floor muscles) while you kneel on the floor. If you can, keep holding it, and stand up. Still there? Walk around. Still fine? You Goddess! Do two. Of course, if at any point it/they fall out, that just means you need a little practice at that level.

The tighter you make this muscle, of course, the stronger you can hold your James' Love Muscle. This will give him more pleasure. More importantly, this will give *you* more pleasure. As you control this muscle and contract the walls of your Vuh-jay-jay (as Oprah would say — close your eyes here Oprah... grrls, that's "vagina" to ya'll) to tighten around him, the internal skin will tighten your outer labia, which will tighten around your clitoris, which — ta da! — is our little Love Button. Kegels = More Sensation. More Sensation = Ooh, La La!

Interestingly, our local hospital is now passing out Ben Wa Balls to all pregnant women, to help them strengthen this muscle, in anticipation of labor.

So start those exercises today; once you get them down on the potty, you can do them at red lights, in a boring lecture, in the movies, *reading*... you get the picture.

Make sure you don't miss the "bits" that turn you on! (Get out, did she *say* that? Yes, I did!) I don't care what it is: inside your elbow, back of your neck, or of course the "usual" bits. If you're squeamish about your body, breathe slowly and deeply, and realize it's Time to discover her, in all her glory. Keep your eyes closed, keep that water warm, and imagine that you're under a warm Hawaiian waterfall and your James (or a fantasy lover!) is caressing you! Touch every part of your body and say 'thank you' for it being there. Roll your neck. I'm not talking about being in the shower for an hour; it could just be an extra 5 minutes. But the 5 you were taking before in a rush plus this 5 equals 10 minutes, and you have nearly Touched Your Way halfway to 23! And we're not even to the lotion yet!

After you shower or bathe, step out and slowly dry off with a fluffy towel. Really take time to wipe the water off every bit of your body, and caress yourself doing it. Luxuriate. Don't hurry. This is part of the seduction — the seduction of you, by you. Fill your brain with sensual buzzing, wash out other thoughts, and magnetize the same to you by setting the mood, before your James is even there!

Next, apply lotion. Sense-u-a-lly and Slo-o-owly! As a final touch, apply a little lubricant "inside." You should always use a lubricant, and you might as well get a little head start. Don't use a ton, just get a little in there. (Stop wiggling when you read this!)

Touch yourself luxuriously. Tell yourself, "Wow, you are SO HOT!" Smile. Get your mind around how smooth your skin is, and how sexy you are. You will feel your eyes get soft — that's when you're there!

Dress for Sex-cess

So you're lotioned and relaxed — it's time to step out of the bathroom, and into your closet. Maybe you set a glass of wine, champagne, or a cocktail near your closet, to keep your mood unhurried and sensual. Slowly put on your sexy undies/bra/etc. You got rid of your granny panties and such during your closet purge, right? And remember, the outfits that you have for your evenings don't have to be cross-your-heart-pull-it-all-in-comfy-to-wear-all-day undie/bra combos. They can be a cute little thang you barely stay in, because it is just for this purpose, this Ritual. In fact, putting on one of those little handkerchief numbers, putting the lights down low, lighting your candles and sipping your cocktail or glass of champagne (if you drink) or bubbly water in a gorgeous crystal glass (if you don't) will make you smile just doing it! And please — if your James has bought you something, *wear* it. I don't want to hear how "whatever" *you* think it makes you look. He bought it because he thinks you are sexy and he wants to see you in it. Now — throw the Dog a Bone!

Here is a radical concept. You might be, at the end of all this, Ready To Go!! (Yes, could happen, and your James is not even home yet!) So why do you have to go through dinner, etc. before you have sex? If you're feeling ready, call your James on his cell phone and tell him that dinner comes "last" tonight. Oh dear — you'll hear on the Morning News about some guy breaking all speed records comin' home! If you know he's going to want to shower and change, then get it all ready for him. Is your wet towel lying around, mirror steamed up, etc.? Come on Grrl! Maybe have a scented soap for him to use, that turns *you* on. You certainly want that fluffy towel ready for him, and how about being there to rub him down with a yummy massage oil? Did you lay out your favorite sexy pair of his undies on the bed? Start the music playing? Draw the shades? Light the candle?

Slip Slidin' Away

Most women need extra lubrication, and gynecologists recommend that all women keep a lubricant handy. But the most typical reason is one you might not think of. Dehydration.

Nearly 75% of women are chronically dehydrated, which means our bodies are forced to make tough choices. Vaginal lubrication is the least necessary fluid we have, so it is the first one to be sacrificed. Our bodies would rather have lubrication in our eyes and in our mouths than Down There. As if that's not bad enough, we further deplete our vaginal juices by:

- Drinking Alcohol
- Chemotherapy and other Cancer-related Therapies
- Caffeine
- Too Much Fat, Salt and Sugar
- Taking Drugs: Birth Control Pills, Antidepressants and Antibiotics
- Hysterectomy
- Pregnancy and Childbirth
- Breastfeeding
- PMS, Depression, Anxiety, Fear, Anger (Emotions with a drug-like effect)
- Menopause
- Inadequate Foreplay
- Ceiling Fans
- Sex in Water

Bedroom toys, some sexual positions, condoms, marathon sex, and the like also require lots and lots of lubrication.

But in all honesty, the most important reason to always use a lubricant is that it will help decrease performance anxiety. Think about it: Men often believe that if women aren't Wet Down There (did I say that? Yeah...), they're not doing it for their Bond Grrl. ("Hey baby, don't I turn you on any more?") I think men believe it's supposed to be an instantaneous gusher as soon as we see them, like the girls in those X-rated movies. But if you have any of the issues above (or even if you're lying down, where that little bit of lubrication you make has to work its way down inside of you sideways, against gravity!), just having to worry about your lubrication is enough to turn you Off! Using a lubricant every time can help you have fun and enjoy without worrying about Producing, so to say. It becomes a habit.

Lubricants are also a great way to cut down on infection, because having sex without enough lubrication can cause chafing, which can open up your sensitive parts to bacteria. And if you get chafed inside, you can heal with a scar, becoming that much less sensitive. Finally, any time you use a lubricant, you feel more. By being more sensitive, you can get to the Big O faster!

Pushback

Why do I continue to be amazed at the initial pushback I get from women when I advise the above? I just am. They cross their arms, give me the side-to-side "snakeheaded mama" shake, and state that their James should be in charge of their Big O. And besides, Why should they "cater to him like that?"

Hello.

First off, you are actually catering to You. Then, you are *sharing* with him. How much time, in true reality, are we talking about here? Probably half an hour extra for you (by you) if you go in real slo-mo, and 10-15 minutes for him. And you know what? He will feel like a King. Yeah yeah, you want him to make you feel like a Queen (first). But Grrlfriend, to be ƒEmpowered is to be in charge of your Own Life. And in this private part of your life, it's time to take that empowering control; to be in charge of your own happiness and know without a doubt that you can affect his happiness. And yours.

Do this a few times, and your James is going to be grinnin' when he sees you. His eyes are going to light up when you enter the room. That light in his eyes, that's worth it all. You can even have fun, and leave him a note in his pocket, saying that Today starts "10 Days in 10 Ways," and then detail what you're going to do with him, when he gets home, as Day One! Plan out those 10 days, and feel the empowerment that it will bring you. At the end, your James is going to be one happy, big, smiling panther! And guess who is going to feel more relaxed, invigorated, and youthful? That would be you, Bond Grrl...

And, since you've learned how to take control and decrease your time to the "Big O," you can not only relax and "have it" (smile), but you are going to make him feel like the hottest thing around when you're Writhing to his Music. And when our Jameses are feeling hot and "expansive," it's all to our benefit. Promise me now that you will take care of and work on decreasing your time to "liftoff" every time, from now on. (Don't sass me, I mean it.) You want to take on this responsibility, because it's going to make your sex life light years better. By taking that control, you're not stuck lying there, thinking, "Oh, please keep doing that a little longer, please keep doing it," while he's getting a cramp in his hand/neck/whatever, lamenting to himself, "I am not doing a good job, I am a bad lover, I can't please her, oh PLEASE get off, Grrl." I would like you to consider making this promise: to take AT LEAST this area of your life into your own power, starting today. When you do, your James isn't going to know what happened, and he doesn't need to know. Even if you come home 5 minutes early and "work out the kinks" with a vibe a little, it's going to decrease your time — and we ALL know that there is no relaxer like the Big O anyway, right?

I'm Pickin' Up GOOD Vi-bra-tions...

What ABOUT vibrators?

Vibrators are intended to enhance — not replace — our men! Many people think that using vibrators is a "solo" activity. It doesn't need to be.

One of the top five male fantasies is either watching a woman use a vibrator or using one on her. Remember, men are voyeurs: they get turned on by what they see. They like to watch our facial expressions and how our bodies move. Besides that, there are definitely spots to which you can apply a vibrator on your James, to help *him* have a headboard-bangin' good time!

But the most important reason to purchase a vibrator is to help *you* achieve better orgasms. By experimenting on yourself, you can explore without "performance anxiety," and discover what really works for your body.

If you have gone through cancer therapies, it's *particularly* important to use a vibrator. This subject is tough for doctors — they can read the studies that state that a "vaginal dialator" (a dildo or vibrator) can help the lining of the vagina from becoming thickened and scarred during radiation therapy. Then if they talk to a female patient with cancer about how a vibrator or "sensual touch" can help her heal, suddenly her father or husband is bringing them up on charges. Many women experience sexual dysfunction after cancer therapies: 64% have decreased desire; 42% have arousal disorder; 44% have orgasm disorder; and 38% have pain disorder. This is not surprising, since 43% of women without cancer report low sexual desire. It's time to talk about it!

Some women believe that they will become addicted to a vibrator, and won't be able to have an orgasm without one. It's simply not true! A really good vibrator will help teach your body how to orgasm better, more completely and faster. Moreover, by using a vibrator, you can experience stimulation from three different areas at once: the clitoris, the vaginal opening and deep inside where your G-spot is located. With that much stimulation, controlled by you, you don't have to think so hard about reaching orgasm; you just let it happen. By practicing with a vibrator, you'll learn how to move on top and under your James, to achieve those same sensations. If he uses it with you, watching your reactions will teach him just how important stimulation is to you in certain areas, so he can learn how better to move inside you.

There are many different types of vibrators; it's important to find one that's going to work for you. As I mentioned, I do Sensual Secrets seminars, where I bring along vibrators and have women handle them, test them on the tip of their nose (sensitive as the tip of their clitoris), and decide what appeals to them. As a general overview, I would say that a first vibrator should be soft (not a hard plastic one); if you get a silicone one, be very careful not to put it next to other sex toys or metal, because the silicone can melt.

Happy exploring!

'Home' is where I plug in my vibrator.

— *SARK, Succulent Wild Woman*

Keeping Your Sex Life Off Life Support

A few "To Dos" — and some "Not To Dos" for you to consider!

1. Plan. Yeah, I know, how prosaic. But sex should be a priority, like eating and sleeping. On *Oprah*, Dr. Oz mentioned that everyone should be having about 200 orgasms a year. 200! (Yes, women too.) And in a recent interview about his book in *Esquire* magazine, Dr. Oz explained that the part of our brain that feels sated can often be sated by either food or sex. So if you want to lose a few pounds, instead of reaching for the potato chips, reach for your James instead!

    As part of planning, it's your responsibility to set the mood. Though Jameses, I believe, appreciate candles, scents, and the like, we all know that they could have sex on concrete if it's offered there. So be sure to take responsibility for a setting that is going to help you get in the mood.

2. Most important: Talk. The key to an interesting, active sex life in a relationship is continually communicating what works, what doesn't (be gentle!), and what might be fun to try.

3. On that note, don't be afraid. You need to Share your desires, in a trusting environment. If you make your James share first because you're embarrassed, shy, or scared, then whatever he says, don't laugh, and don't put him down. If he wants to have a three-some and that's not for you, how about coming back with a big, sexy smile, saying, "Wow, you're enough for me!" Or even, perhaps, suggest that you make love with something like that on the TV? He's opened up to you — help him realize his fantasies, in a way that will work for you, too. Then believe me, he will help you with yours, even if yours involve him putting a ladder over the bed and showering you with rose petals!

4. Discuss what you expect. This is usually best before you get into bed with a guy the first time! Knowing that your expectations are roughly parallel will go a long way towards a fulfilling relationship. We are all different in the sex department — having someone who's at least close in their expectations is key!

5. Be Adventurous. Being adventurous with the one you love is the best way to keep the spark alive. Look at your James with new eyes, every time you're being sensual. See his attractiveness. Discover something new about him every week — believe me, you can do this for years! Talking and being willing to explore are what makes good sex great

and is the glue to long-lasting relationships. Part of being Adventurous could even involve setting a two-week period where you will touch, tease, but *not* have sex. This can stoke up your lust fire even after 20 years! Everyone wants what they can't have!

6. And finally, if you want to have great sex that night, your plan should start that morning. Maybe give your James a deep kiss as he's leaving for work, let your hand work its way Down There, then act surprised and say, "Oh! Dang, that's for tonight!" You could also leave him notes in his jacket pocket, or send him short, sexy texts or emails during the day. Doing this is going to get you in the mood, and of course keep him wanting you all day long! NOTE: Only do this if you've really set a date for that evening and your James isn't hip deep with work. It can be very annoying to your James if he's in a business meeting, and receives some X-text from you. Make sure you are cognizant of what his day is like, and make your little love-notes short, sweet, and non-interruptive.

What Not to Do

1. *Be a b*tch.* Do you ignore your James, act grouchy, complain, whine and moan (to him or to your Grrls), and then expect to have a fabulous sensual evening with him? Come on. If you're complaining to your Grrls, you're telling your subconscious that your man is a Dog, so how is your subconscious going to bring sexy on that evening with this Dog? Similarly, if you ignore your James all day and then want some that night, how's he going to feel? Like something that's just scratching your Itch, that's what.

2. *Lose Your Sense of Humor.* Your sex life is not going to match what you see in the movies. Oh, maybe sometimes it will — but sometimes, some squishy sound, or cramp, or what-have-you that never happens on the big screen is going to take you down. Remember to laugh. And please don't compare yourself to anyone else. The *ss is always greener on the other side of the fence, my Sister. (OK, shut up, I thought it was funny...)

Having A Game Plan(ned)

My Advanced Sensual Secrets classes include many tricks and flicks for my Advanced Bond Grrls. There is never so much fun as when a dozen or so Bond Grrls are learning tricks and planning to take them home to their Jameses! The first trick that I teach women in the class is to plan a Game with their James, especially if it's an older relationship where they're looking for something new.

Remember, a woman's #1 sense is Touch, but a man's is Sight. Moreover, men love to have Goals! So, what easy Game can you play, that will take advantage of this and be sense-ational for you, too?

Take any sensual, tasty flavoring that will melt into your skin without a trace (*e.g.*, Passion Powder, put out by Passion Parties), and secretly apply it to 4 places on your body when you're getting prepared. Then — tell your James it's in 5, and it's his Goal to find them all! (We all know how men love Goals!) Tell him he can only use his tongue (oh!) and he has to find All Five of those places. And of course, put it in spots he doesn't normally go for: maybe the inside of your ankle, or the back of your knee, or the nape of your neck. What then?

Blindfold your gorgeous Bond Grrl self, lie down and get comfy, then tell your James to Go Slow, Baby.

What? Blindfold?

Yes, blindfold — because if you are blindfolded, he gets permission to just STARE at your luscious body — which he adores! And you know when we are stared at, even if we are feeling hot, we start thinking, "Whoa... wonder if he can see my back fat?" (I see you, nodding and laughing...) So if you are blindfolded, you get to let him stare (exercising his #1 Sense), and he has a Goal, too, to find those spots! When he finds one, of course, moan and groan and let him know what a good job he is doing! What a good way to get him to think, "Hmmmm, wow, she sure likes that spot," a spot that perhaps he's never tried before or tends to forget. He won't forget next time!

He will be touching you all over (your #1 sense), so your 23 minutes will be zooming down to zero! And, remember, you put it in 4 places and told your James it was in 5... so he keeps searching and searching... and when you are ready, you can just whisper to him in your Bond Grrl voice, "You know [say his name], let's find that last one next time."

Good game, huh? And it works for both sexes, playing on each of your Strengths.

 *Surprising Sex Facts*

I have gathered a number of quotes from various areas, in my Sexology studies and online. A great place to start is RealAge.com; put "Orgasm" in the Search Box, then follow the links. Many more great snippets are located there, and in the articles listed.

1. Gynecologist Dr. Dudley Chapman states that *orgasms boost infection-fighting cells up to 20% in women.* Psychologists at Wilkes University in Pennsylvania found that students who had regular sexual activity had a third higher levels of immunoglobulin A, an antibody that boosts the immune system and can help fight colds and flu.

2. The Kinsey Institute's reports stated that *sex reduces stress, and people who have fulfilling sex lives are less anxious, less violent, and less hostile.* A '70s Duke University study and a British Medical Journal article entitled "Sex and Death: Are They Related?" found that the frequency of sexual intercourse for men was associated with lower death rates, and that *the enjoyment of sexual intercourse by women was associated with a longer life.*

3. Dr Winnifred Cutler, a specialist in behavioral endocrinology, reports that *women who enjoy regular weekly sex have* significantly higher levels of estrogen in their blood than women experiencing either infrequent sex or no sex at all. The benefits of estrogen include *a healthy cardiovascular system, lower bad cholesterol, higher good cholesterol, more bone density, and supple skin.* There is also growing evidence that estrogen is beneficial to brain functioning.

4. Another important hormone that seems to be affected by sexual activity is DHEA. Right before orgasm, the level of the hormone DHEA in the body spikes several times higher than normal. DHEA is believed to *improve brain function, balance the immune system, help maintain and repair tissue, promote healthy skin, and possibly improve cardiovascular health.*

5. Both testosterone and estrogen levels increase through regular sexual activity. Testosterone can help *strengthen bones and muscles,* and is also beneficial to a healthy heart. For women, the health benefits of estrogen include keeping vaginal tissues suppler and *protecting against osteoporosis and heart disease.*

6. A study from the South Illinois School of Medicine found that *having orgasms can help with migraines.* Working with 52 migraine sufferers, 16 reported considerable relief after an orgasm and another 8 reported that their migraines were completely gone.

7. Orgasm can help treat other types of pain. In research by Beverly Whipple and Barry Komisaruk at Rutgers University, women found that they had a higher pain threshold through regular *orgasms, which helped with conditions ranging from whiplash to arthritis.*

8. According to research done by David Weeks, a clinical neuropsychologist at the Royal Edinburgh Hospital, *making love three times a week* in a stress-free relationship *can make you look 10 years younger.*

9. *Increasing sex frequency from once a month to at least once a week provides as much happiness as a $50,000-a-year raise,* according to a paper entitled "Money, Sex and Happiness: An Empirical Study," submitted to the National Bureau of Economic Research, one of the leading organizations in its field.

10. A study headed by Gordon Gallup, a psychologist at the State University of New York, found that *semen might reduce depression in women.* According to this study, mood-altering hormones in semen are absorbed through the vagina, and are beneficial to women as anti-depressants.

11. *Sex burns calories.* As noted on Oprah's interview with Kerry McCloskey (*The Ultimate Sex Diet*), a good session can burn 200 calories, or about equal to 15 minutes of running at maximum effort. And HOW much more fun!

ÆEmpowerment®

What Men Really Want

I've saved my best story for last.

A couple of years ago, my friend Domino and I took a trip to Las Vegas to check out the viability of a Vegas 101 long weekend for ÆEmpowerment seminar attendees; a full immersion ÆEmpowerment Finishing School and Training Academy including Baccarat training, walk/talk/laugh practice, etiquette, driving Formula One racecars, self-offense training, and the like. We also decided that we would have a professional courtesan discuss sex with the attendees, since sex is definitely a Bond Grrl Must!

The closest legal prostitution to Vegas is a small town about 90 miles away called Pahrump. (Yeah, pronounced just like it looks.) We couldn't get anyone to chat with us on the phone about it (surprise surprise), so we decided to drive on out there.

As it turns out, all the bordellos are along one dead-ended Strip. There we are, driving this Lincoln Towncar (that's all they'd had at the rental agency), realizing that all the OTHER cars driving down that road (100% filled with, guess what, men) were — well, going to do what they were going to do. And if we would pass a car, or pull up at a light, they would look at us, and WE knew what THEY thought that WE did for a living. (We found this pretty amusing.)

So, we drove up first to The Chicken Ranch. It was featured in Dolly Parton's movie *The Best Little Whorehouse in Texas*. It's kind of a sad place. It is basically a bunch of trailers with a false front that looks like a two-story Southern-style mansion. We pulled into the parking lot — then couldn't get out of the car. We couldn't figure out what we were going to ask. We'd spoken to other business owners: at the driving academy, self-defense and weapons school, casino, etc. But here, we just sat.

Well, there we were, sitting in the parking lot, and we looked up at the next (and last) place on the Pahrump Strip. It was called Sheri's Ranch. It was a nice, clean, BIG, low-profile structure. Under the Sheri's Ranch sign, it said "Tours Welcome."

Domino and I looked at one another. Tours? What the heck!

So we pulled over into their parking lot, and started cooking up this big story about how our friend was getting married, and we were checking out bordellos for his bachelor party. Then I looked at her and said, "Um, no. We came for a business reason. Let's just say what our reason is, and be businesslike about it. Why are we lying?" I mean, really.

With great resolve, we both opened our doors at once, and a sirocco whirled out from the desert and grabbed ALL of our paperwork/business cards from the dashboard, whisking them all over the parking lot and out into the desert. Off we madly dashed in our high heels, since we figured if we didn't retrieve every SCRAP, the next man to pull into that lot would be one of our "real life" clients (Domino is a real estate agent, I'm an attorney), and he'd — SLAP! — get one of our biz cards on his windshield, right before his baby blues! ("What were *you* doing this weekend, Ms. Shepard?")

So we got all the paperwork back, tidied ourselves, pushed our now slightly limp hair off of our faces, and approached the door. It didn't even have a peephole.

We had barely knocked when the door was answered by a pleasant looking woman in her late 40s, wearing a dark, feminine business suit. We were ushered into a quiet, comfy, understated anteroom with hardwood floors, a big, plush leather sofa, and a crystal chandelier. To the left was a bar with a lot of very beautiful women in it, laughing, playing pool, and, well, having fun. They were of varying ages and to some extent sizes: the only difference between them and perhaps the typical Girls' Night Out was that, OK, they were inside a bordello, but also they were all wearing short-shorts and 6" Lucite heels. Before us, across the long hardwood floor, we could see floor-to-ceiling plate glass windows looking out onto an internal courtyard and grounds.

The woman who had ushered us in (the maîtresse d'?) asked us how she could help us. I said that we had seen the sign, and would like a Tour — that I wanted to understand what Sheri's Ranch did and how perhaps I could tie it into the ƒEmpowerment business. Then (because I couldn't help myself), I said, "How did you get to the door so fast, across all this floor? Do you just stand there? There's no peephole!" She smiled, and said, "Oh, my dears, there were dozens of cameras on you from the second you drove into the parking lot."

(Can you SEE the guys in the video room laughing their *sses off at us scurrying around the desert chasing our paperwork? Oh yeah. Yeah, yeah. Yeah. FABulous.)

So, she walked us over to overlook the grounds through the plate-glass windows — a swimming pool, volleyball courts, some special cabanas, etc. On the wall, there was a listing of the Services offered with somewhat euphemistic names, but with descriptions that left nothing to the imagination. ("Fire and Ice," for example, was a courtesan performing fellatio on a man with hot tea in her mouth, and then with ice cubes.) There were also photos inside some of the cabanas, which could be rented all night, with the added extra of being able to have any food or drink you wanted. Sheri's Ranch has a chef in residence. As explained to us, you were either brought to Sheri's Ranch in a complimentary limo, or (if your "party" would be sufficiently pricey), they would send their helicopter for you. And with just a tiny bit of notice, their aim is to make their clients' wishes all come true — from limo, to lobster, to steak to... sex.

The gal in the suit buzzed one of the "free" courtesans, and we were introduced to Aspen Rain. She toured us around the open areas of the facility. It was midday, so most of the "play" rooms were free. As we peeked into the bubble room, the pole room, and the like, I tried not to grin as a statuesque blonde in Lucites and shorts passed us, giving a tour to an older guy in a plaid shirt and a matronly woman in a smock dress. They looked like they had just walked in off a field in Oklahoma!

When asked, Aspen Rain clarified that the little call button she wore worked not only to call gals out who are free, but also as a panic button if anything went wrong. As she explained, when a patron first comes in, they are interviewed by the door hostess to find out what they desire, and their general price range. If a patron wants a line up (instead of booking a specific girl, which s/he can do, since they each keep their own calendars), the patron sits on that big leather sofa, and the girls that fit the patron's preferences are called by those buzzers. The patron might want a certain color or height, and the courtesan must be willing to "party" the way the patron wants. For example, Aspen Rain said she did not do lesbian sex on patrons, nor did she do Fire and Ice. ("Makes my teeth hurt.") The patron picks the woman of his/her choice, chooses the room that s/he wants (differing prices) and then they go to the room and discuss the price of the "party" in private.

Aspen Rain explained how she had been a dancer in Kansas, and that Sheri's Ranch is the "gold standard" of bordellos. They only accept a certain number of girls; to be a Sheri's Ranch girl, you had to interview, and Aspen Rain said she was "honored" to have been chosen. The courtesans had their own cook, gym, etc., and though they are independent contractors, Aspen Rain said they are provided access to people to help them with everything from financial planning to education options. She explained that she had a couple of kids back in Kansas, and that she had already funded their college trust funds, plus she would likely be "able to retire" in about 4 years. She is flown to the Ranch about once a month, for a few days, and then flown back home. She also said that all the courtesans here were well protected, from the initial screening of the patrons, to the "hot and cold running bouncers" available 24 hours a day at the touch of a panic button.

She was articulate, poised, proud. Who knew? And OH MY GOODNESS gorgeous.

We talked to her a bit about her "job," and she was very frank about it. We asked her how she might feel about being paid for an hour or two of her time, just to talk to Empowerment Vegas 101 attendees about sex — like, for example, what men generally wanted.

Aspen Rain said that she would be overjoyed to offer this to women, as long, of course, as they would respect her. In her words, "what I do is not rocket science. In fact, often men — husbands — just pay me to massage them and tell them that they are good providers, strong, sexy, wanted. They want to cuddle. They even pay me to massage ME. Then they want a little sex, and to go to sleep in my arms. If their wives would just do what I do — and I don't do any 'nasty stuff' — I would still have too many clients to handle. And those husbands would think they had died and gone to heaven."

How eye-opening. Her clients came to her, paid her to listen to them, make them feel wanted and sexy, then just have "regular" sex or "the occasional blow job," and cuddle.

Want your James to feel like he has "died and gone to Heaven"? With small cost to you, and amazing benefits? Listen to someone whose business it is to know.

After our tour, we spoke with the manager. She was fantastic. She even took us out to another wing of the Ranch. It's a full-service hotel. The rooms are as nice if not nicer than the standard Vegas Strip room, but for far less of an outlay. By staying at the Ranch, you have access to a gym, masseuse, the pool, the bar — and of course the girls if you so desire. The manager was very proud to point out that Sheri's Ranch not only has the only corporate sponsorship in the "industry" (the Bud Light bubble room, complete with surf boards and bar), but they also are the only one to have a full hotel facility.

I loved it. I imagined taking the students from my seminar out there after a hard day driving race cars and shooting guns, to be pampered, given great food from the on-site chef, get their nails done — and then to have some frank talk with a courtesan about sex and pleasing men in a fun, respectful, and non-threatening setting.

On our drive back to Vegas, Domino and I couldn't stop talking about getting some Grrls out to Sheri's, to start busting stereotypes and introduce them to some women running their own businesses with passion, putting money away, and making men feel great.

How do YOU feel, after reading this?

The End — or a New Beginning?

So, here we are — at the end of the book. If I've done my stuff, you have a clean home, some Goals, and a Plan. You've started to take charge of your Life and all that's in it. You understand that you have drawn everything in your Life to you — the good, the bad, and the ugly — and you are set to take control.

If you have a James, you are appreciating him more, and perhaps have a few new thoughts in your mind (or tricks to try!) You are well on your way to not only realizing your Passion, but also fully developing your supportive side.

By becoming fEmpowered, you are giving the world a great gift: *You*, at your Bond Grrl best, congruent inside and out. As your energy changes, it will draw both more empowered, and more supportive, energy to you. By realizing that you alone are responsible for your Life, you take the first important step towards bringing the Life of your dreams to fruition.

Sure, you may backslide. Your closet might get messy in a few months, or you might catch yourself gossiping. But just read through this book again, and step by step, get back on the path. Life is a Journey. I'm honored that you took me on a few miles of yours.

— Solitaire

www.ingramcontent.com/pod-product-compliance
Lightning Source LLC
Chambersburg PA
CBHW081128170426
43197CB00017B/2782